THEODORE ROETHKE: THE GARDEN MASTER

Theodore Roethke: The Garden Master

BY ROSEMARY SULLIVAN

University of Washington Press
Seattle and London

PS3535
039
0
Z89

This book was published with the assistance of a grant from the Andrew W. Mellon Foundation.

Copyright © 1975 by the University of Washington Press
Printed in the United States of America

Library of Congress Cataloging in Publication Data

Sullivan, Rosemary.
    Theodore Roethke: the garden master.

    Bibliography: p.
    Includes index.
    1.   Roethke, Theodore, 1908–1963—Criticism and interpretation.
PS3535.039Z89   811'.5'4   75-15527
ISBN 0-295-95429-9

98788

For Doug

A Strut for Roethke

Westward, hit a low note, for a roarer lost
across the Sound but north from Bremerton,
hit a way down note.
And never cadenza again of flowers, or cost.
Him who could really do that cleared his throat
& staggered on.

The bluebells, pool-shallows, saluted his over-needs,
while the clouds growled, heh-heh, & snapped, & crashed.

No stunt he'll ever unflinch once more will fail
(O lucky fellow, eh Bones?)—drifted off upstairs,
downstairs, somewheres.
No more daily, trying to hit the head on the nail:
thirstless: without a think in his head:
back from wherever, with it said.

Hit a high long note, for a lover found
needing a lower into friendlier ground
to bug among worms no more
around um jungles where ah blurt "What for?"
Weeds, too, he favoured as   most men don't favour men.
The Garden Master's gone.

John Berryman, 77 Dream Songs

Preface

In one of the many introspective asides in his notebooks, Theodore Roethke wrote: "A many-sided man has many rhythms." To John Berryman he was a roarer, a poetic stuntman, a lover, a garden master. Those who knew him felt most his devouring energy, his "over-need" which, though it often shattered his life tragically, also led to a wild, even hilarious joyousness. What is extraordinary is that this gargantuan energy never spilled over into the shapeless or the prolix. Working against what one must feel were the terrible odds of himself, the precision and order he exerted in his poetry were remarkable. This came from his pure devotion to rhythm, to the song: "To produce the truly singable thing, that's a glory isn't it?"

The generic self was his theme and few have so thoroughly explored the extremes of feeling: the blind inchoate longings of the inarticulate unconscious never very far from pure terror, and the oracular, half-ecstatic moments of mystical intuition when "I" and "other" were brought into a white-hot fusion of identity. Yet what moves most was his commitment to life. His ambition was always to "dive deeper into the material, substantiate." "There is no poetry anywhere," as James Dickey wrote, "that is so valuably conscious of the human body . . . no poetry that can place the body in an *environment*—wind, seascape, greenhouse, forest, desert, mountainside, among animals or insects or stones—so vividly and evocatively, waking unheard of exchanges between the place and human responsiveness at its most creative. He more than any other is a poet of pure being." In this book, I have emphasized the sources of both the suffering (at times an almost definitive agony) and the joy of his poetry. The qualities that made him his own particular kind of visionary were the very ones which brought him so often to the edge of psychic disintegration. Few words describe his dilemma more poignantly than those of Christopher Smart, one of his favourite ancestors: "For in my nature I quested for beauty/But God, God hath sent me to sea for pearls." Yet he was able to write: "In spite of all the muck and welter, the dark, the *dreck* of these poems, I count myself among the happy poets."

This book is an extensive review of his work; it brings together the new insights afforded by Allan Seager's biography and Roethke's own letters and notebooks. The chapters follow the chronology of the published work, a form dictated by Roethke's manner of working. More than most poets, he wrote instinctively in phases or outbursts of inspiration so that his work is starkly divisible into periodic oscillations between short poems, most often lyrics (sometimes neo-Elizabethan in their formality), and longer experimental works, loose-limbed structures dependent on principles of juxtaposition and violent rhythmic shifts. He held to the belief that a book must be a unit rather than an amorphous collection of single poems. After his first book *Open House,* he wrote mainly sequences, either from the perspective of the single protagonist—the lost son, the old woman, the mature mind coursing through the American landscape—or exploring a single theme from multiple perspectives—love poems, death poems, poems on the theme of God. At the same time, his poetry provides a continual sense of development, so that in any reading the mind is driven back through the whole body of his work to those images, ideas, memories, and obsessions that constitute the core of his creative personality. I have emphasized this unity by a continuous retrospection.

My themes have been those which must preoccupy all studies of

Roethke, among them: his sensitivity to the subliminal, irrational world of nature; his relationship to his dead father, who occupies the center of his work, adding to it an urgent dimension which often impels it through a persistent pattern of guilt and expiation; his attempts to explore other modes of consciousness which carried him to the edge of psychic disaster, an experience so terrible and yet so necessary to the intensity of his art; his interest in mysticism by which he sought to order and unify a life deracinated to the extreme; his debts, so well repaid, to the poetic ancestors from whom he learned his craft; and the calm joyousness which rests at the core of his work. If I have had one overriding intention, however, it has been to celebrate the poetry. "After all," as Roethke said, "there's the song, the pure thing."

Acknowledgments

I would like to acknowledge my indebtedness to those who have assisted in the completion of this book: in particular, David P. Morse, of the University of Sussex, whose criticisms and suggestions were helpful throughout, and Angus Ross, also of the University of Sussex, who read the work in its final stages. I am especially grateful to Mrs. Beatrice Roethke Lushington for permission to quote from the published and unpublished works of Theodore Roethke. I would also like to thank Mrs. Lushington for her generosity in providing me with a perspective on my subject not always open to the critic.

I would like to thank Jo-Ellen Turner of Victoria, B.C., who assisted in compiling the index. I am obliged to Farrar, Straus, and Giroux Inc., for permission to quote John Berryman's poem "A Strut For Roethke" and to *Texas Studies in Literature and Language* for allowing me to reprint my article "The Still Center" (Winter 1975). My thanks are also due to the Canada Council for their generous financial assistance.

My deepest and most personal indebtedness is to my husband, Doug Beardsley, whose devotion as a poet to Ted Roethke first brought me to my subject. I can only respond to his judicious criticisms and patient understanding with a tribute of love and gratitude which the dedication of this book acknowledges.

Contents

THEODORE ROETHKE: THE GARDEN MASTER

❧ I ❧

The Lost Son:

POEMS 1931–41

This ancient feud
Is seldom won. The spirit starves
Until the dead have been subdued.
[C.P., p. 4]

When he published his first book *Open House* in 1941 at the age of thirty-three, Theodore Roethke had a small reputation among the good magazines as a stylized and impeccably fastidious versifier.[1] Yet despite the technical resourcefulness of the book, there were few signs of the greatness that was to come. Allan Seager was later to say: "Ted started out as a phony and became genuine, like Yeats. . . . I had no idea that he'd end up as fine a poet as he did. No one knew that in the early days, Ted least of all."[2] In later years Roethke regarded *Open House* fondly but objectively: "It took me ten years to complete one little book, and now some of the things in it seem to creak. Still, I like about ten pieces in it."[3] These were formative years in which he was evolving the habits of thought and insight that were to determine his whole poetic strategy. They mark his first attempts to come to terms poetically with the death of his father and his first experience of mental breakdown. The question confronting the critic who begins to

1. All quotations from Roethke's poems, unless otherwise indicated, are from *The Collected Poems of Theodore Roethke,* hereafter referred to in the text as *C.P.*
2. James Dickey, "The Greatest American Poet," *Atlantic,* 222 (November 1968): 54.
3. *On the Poet and His Craft: Selected Prose of Theodore Roethke,* ed. Ralph J. Mills, Jr., p. 16; hereafter referred to in the text as *S.P.*

3

study his work is why, then, the oblique, even timid confrontation of such tragedies in his early poetry.

Roethke was to find the themes of his work in the fluctuations and intensities of his own psyche: in the situations and processes of consciousness and the problems of identity in pursuit of personal fulfillment. Poetry was to become almost a purgative process by which he sought to come to terms with private agonies and frustrations, and to translate these into general human concerns: spiritual alienation, discontinuity, homelessness. Such themes depended upon a thorough self-knowledge; yet in his early poetry there seems to have been something cutting him off from himself, as it were, damming up the sources of creative energy. The pervasive feeling of his early poems is of the sheer torment of identity, what he called in a commentary on *Open House* that feeling of self-contamination: "My taste was me" (*S.P.*, p. 22). The phrase is Hopkins': "I am gall, I am heartburn. God's most deep decree/Bitter would have me taste: my taste was me," [4] lines which seemed to have echoed a personal state in which essential consciousness of guilt and self-loathing were intrinsic qualities of his being. Even though declaring open house on himself in his first book, he often despaired of penetrating to the core of his frustration:

> If I should ever seek relief
> From that monotony of grief,
> The tight nerves leading to the throat
> Would not release one riven note:
> What shakes my skull to disrepair
> Shall never touch another ear.
>
> [*C.P.*, p. 22]

His attempts to come to terms with this "monotony of grief" go largely unrecorded in *Open House,* where the poems are usually impersonal and interpret his suffering in orthodox terms: the spirit recoiling from the taint of the flesh. And such poems were often evasions which in no way confronted the real core of his agony. To

4. *The Poems of Gerard Manley Hopkins,* ed. W. H. Gardner and N. H. Mackenzie, p. 101.

understand this fully one must include in any study of the early work the large body of poems, unpublished or published individually in magazines, which record a different story: the drama of a poet slowly edging in on his own psyche, discovering himself. In these poems Roethke rejected the usual superstructure of metaphysical imagery in favor of an exploration of the terrors and frustrations of private psychic disorders. In an unpublished poem called "Difficult Grief" he began to probe tentatively to the personal source of his suffering:

> This is no surface grief, but care
> That catches at me unaware,
> A grief too difficult for tears
> That ravages my greenest years,
> Destroying innocent peace to start
> A swell of sorrow at the heart.
> Since I am young, it does not find
> Sufficient mastery in the mind.
> Since I am careless, it may be
> As treacherous as ecstasy,
> And though it leave, it will return
> To mock me with embittered scorn:
> A sorrow ponderable as clay,
> Old desolation, young dismay,
> A fear too shameful to confess,
> A terrible child-loneliness.[5]

The catastrophe which was always at the center of his life was his father's death in 1923 when Roethke was not yet fifteen. With the sensitive adolescent, the nexus of fear and guilt inflicted by the early death of a father can be profound and destructive throughout a lifetime. It seems inevitably, through a complex defense mechanism of projection and introjection, the child implicates himself in the parent's death. With Roethke this process was exacerbated by a childish sense of inadequacy. When he would later relive the impact of his father's death in the *Praise to the End!* sequence, he would describe the child he once was as feeling angered and aban-

5. *Selected Letters of Theodore Roethke,* ed. Ralph J. Mills, Jr., pp. 22–23; hereafter referred to in the text as *S.L.* Most of Roethke's uncollected poems are now available in *Selected Letters.*

doned: "Kisses come back,/I said to Papa;/He was all whitey bones/And skin like paper" (*C.P.*, p. 73). Yet this resentment is a defensive response to the child's own sense of guilt and complicity. In these poems, the father becomes a specter, censorious and unappeasable, a *doppelgänger* haunting the unworthy son, and by way of compensation, an unimpeachable figure, quasi-divine, whom the child seeks to reconcile. For the death of a parent to create such a profound psychological shock, it must occur when the child's sense of identity is still vulnerable. In such a case, before the child is objectively able to understand his dilemma, fear and guilt have become a part of his sensibility, his way of seeing and his way of life.[6] The damage to the crucial sense of inner security may absolute, creating an existential anxiety which can define the patterns of future life.

With Roethke the psychological scar was obviously intensified by memories of the authoritarian relationship between father and son. Allan Seager has explored this well in *The Glass House* where he describes Roethke as an awkward, introverted adolescent who found little outlet within a stern family milieu for his excessive sensitivity.[7] His parents were of Prussian descent, devoted to the old tradition of *"tüchtig."* In retrospect, Roethke remembered his father as a quick-tempered, taciturn man whose love he doubted, and every childhood memory he recorded tells of his loneliness and sense of rejection. Even at an early age there seems to have been a conflict of personalities, perhaps traceable to a paradox within the father himself. Most often, Otto Roethke presented an exterior of authoritarian order and discipline, and, from Roethke's perspective, little angered him more than the "effeminate" sensibility of

6. For a discussion of depression and its sources in childhood, particularly as related to the death of a loved parent, see Roy Grinker et al., *The Phenomena of Depression*. See also A. Alvarez, *The Savage God: A Study of Suicide*, which traces the depressive disorders of artists as various as Cowper, Chatterton, Cesare Pavese, and Sylvia Plath to traumas in childhood, and in so doing offers a sensitive analysis of the "father complex." Nancy Hunter Steiner, in *A Closer Look at Ariel: A Memory of Sylvia Plath*, p. 45, explores the relevance of this theme to Sylvia Plath.

7. Allan Seager, *The Glass House: The Life of Theodore Roethke*, hereafter referred to in the text as *Glass House*.

his only son. But there was one place, according to his children, where an alternate side of the man was revealed. In the greenhouses he gave expression to a deep sensitivity to the beauty of nature. Apparently it was not a sensitivity he would acknowledge, irreconcilable as it was with his Prussian exterior, and it may be that his gruff manner was an overcompensation for the vulnerable core he suspected in himself. This at least is the paradox Roethke comes to express in the last poems to his father, "Otto" (*C.P.*, p. 224) and "The Old Florist's Lament" (*S.L.*, pp. 226–27), in which he seems to reconcile in his mind his father's harshness and his underlying sensitivity, the violence and the deeper gentleness of the man. He does so by seeing his father as a type of the artist, capable only through violence and the sternest self-discipline of wrenching the chaotic into beauteous form. Certainly the paradox was too much for the young boy to grasp, and from the consequent sense of his own inadequacy Roethke seems to have acquired the burden of fears and guilts which haunted him all his life. Had the relationship of father to son been able to take its course, understanding and reconciliation would have been gradual. As it was, a profound sense of inferiority remained with Roethke and, according to Allan Seager, was the primary source of the later guilt and panic which were features of his adult life. James Dickey has speculated that no amount of praise was ever enough to reassure him or dispel his sense of chagrin and bafflement over his relationship to the father who died before his son could convince him of his worthiness.[8] His continual habit of addressing close friends in authority as "Pa" may have been symptomatic of his uncertainty. It was, as it were, the outward expression of a deeply personal need to recover his father, but more than the lost father of his youth. By this time his father had become a symbol, conflated with poetry itself, of a strength and wisdom superior to his hunger, to which the belief and power of his life could be united. His father's death became the implicit center of all his work. To it can

8. Dickey, "The Greatest American Poet," p. 56.

be traced the sense of ubiquitous, arbitrary death which pervades his poetry, threatening the validity and endurance of the self. His obsessive concern with identity, and his many speculations as to how identity can be found, or maintained or evaded, find their nexus here. And his urgent need to release the pent-up guilts and obscure hostilities accumulated from his childhood impels his poetry through one of its predominant patterns—an exploration of guilt and hostility which leads to expiation, and the lucid acceptance of his own mortality.

If his father's death induced in Roethke a pathological fear of inadequacy, it was the catalyst of that concern central to his poetry—the nature of death and the fundamental relationship between the influential dead, especially the parent, and the living. "Death Piece," "On the Road to Woodlawn," "The Tribute" (*S.L.*, p. 22), and "The Premonition," all efforts to bring meaning to that death, end as sheer statements of blank sorrow. Roethke learned that "fantasies of sorrow breed/Acedia in the active brain" (*S.L.*, p. 54) and that the living can be tyrannized by the dead. Many of the poems of *Open House* are struggles for release from arid sorrow:

> Exhausted fathers thinned the blood,
> You curse the legacy of pain;
> Darling of an infected brood,
> You feel disaster climb the vein.
>
> . . . .
>
> The dead leap at the throat, destroy
> The meaning of the day; dark forms
> Have scaled your walls, and spies betray
> Old secrets to amorphous swarms.
>
> You meditate upon the nerves,
> Inflame with hate. The ancient feud
> Is seldom won. The spirit starves
> Until the dead have been subdued.
>
> [*C.P.*, p. 4]

Roethke describes the dead fathers as fantastical, hallucinatory forms that prey on the confidence of the living. The sons must withstand their assaults but they feel betrayed, and biologically, mentally weak. (One recalls Robert Lowell's *Life Studies.*) The sons' position is precarious. Stirring up secret inadequacies, inordinate sorrow can expose the living to amorphous swarms, the forces of mental disaster. Love must be denied. The dead can be usurped only through hatred and violent rejection.

The young poet wages the same feud with the dead. "Darling of an infected brood," he is weak and frail beside the supreme masters, but he must resist their too powerful, too seductive influence if he is to carve out a style of his own. Most often the young poet struggles against an initial antagonist blocking his way to autonomous creativity: Blake's Milton, Shelley's Wordsworth, or Wallace Stevens' Pater. But with Roethke the battle against engulfment was continuous throughout his life. He seems to have had a personal need to come to terms with the great poets who influenced him, with Eliot, Yeats, and Whitman. The problem was part of the larger difficulty which he acknowledged with a certain amount of self-mockery as his continual looking for a father figure (*S.L.*, p. 223). This was both fruitful and dangerous: fruitful because this aspiration is responsible for the way one feels his poetry was an act of sheer will against the greatest personal disasters; dangerous because it could have led to subservience to the masters. This dilemma was particularly crucial, as will be seen, when, in his own words "daring to compete with papa" (*S.P.*, p. 70), he turned to Yeats's authority in the moving love poems of *Words for the Wind.*

Roethke was compulsive and often self-destructive by temperament. Personal doubts about his own abilities worked continually to undermine his confidence. In a curious poem called "The Victims" he places himself with the introverted and alienated, those terrified by life:

> Infection's bloom expands in secret places.
> They strip themselves of strangeness to survive,

But death puts on a set of falser faces
To lure them down the highway to the grave.

[*S.L.*, p. 67]

In his early poetry, Roethke usually seeks relief behind the impersonal pronoun, but here, in particular, the ruse of displacement breaks down. One feels in the poem what D. H. Lawrence elsewhere called "this strange gentle reaching out to death"—the infectious bloom of despair dissolving the body's resilience slowly from within. It was a dissolution Roethke knew intimately. Excessive drinking and debilitating depression carried him over the precarious edge on which he always balanced into breakdown in 1935. He was twenty-seven. Yet he insisted that the episode was self-induced to reach a new level of reality. In his notebook he wrote: "A descent can be willed. The real danger lies in the preceding euphoria getting out of hand. My first breakdown was in a very real sense deliberate. I not only asked for, I prayed that it would happen." [9] It is possible that this was a self-destructive impulse in response to the burden of fears and guilts accumulated from childhood, giving agency and forwardness to his creative drive. Such a conjunction is not unusual. Sylvia Plath wrote her best work when, like Roethke, she was finally able to tap the destructive resources in her personality, and though Rimbaud derived his theory of deliberate cultivation of mental aberration from other sources, particularly the spiritualist tracts proliferating in France during his time, it is clear that without the demonic energy so apparent in his personality, he could hardly have carried out his spiritual self-immolation so thoroughly. Yet the poetry Roethke was later to write about his psychological experiences clearly indicates that, however terrible at the time, they were to become sources of creative insight. Many existential psychologists, R. D. Laing in particular, insist that breakdown is a derisive term of cultural censure: mental "disorder" is not always a pathological

9. Notebooks, reel 14, no. 194; available on microfilm from the Roethke Collection, University of Washington Library, Seattle. Hereafter cited in the text as Notebooks. John Vernon, *The Garden and the Map: Schizophrenia in Twentieth Century Literature and Culture,* a book which I came across when the present study was largely completed, is rich in suggestive information about the implications of breakdown to Roethke's poetry.

and alienated condition; it can be a creative attempt to break from normative, rational consciousness into intuitive, holistic modes of being. Certainly this was the direction Roethke's experiences took, and it is revealing that Rimbaud became his demonic model.

Seager questioned whether he had read Rimbaud at this time, but it is clear that he had, not only from notebook references but from the clinical statement of self-analysis submitted to his psychiatrist which refers to Rimbaud as his model for the aesthetic of associational thinking (*Glass House*, p. 94). Rimbaud advocated a systematic *"dérèglement de tous les sens"* through drugs and whatever means as a theory of creativity. He was one of the first poets to deliberately cultivate the unconscious psychic processes, viewing the poet's task largely as a pacification of the ego in order to render it susceptible to unconscious influences. He insisted that the poet must make himself a seer by a long, prodigious, and rational disordering of the senses. Of the poet he said: "He searches himself, he consumes all the poisons in him. . . . Because he has cultivated his own soul . . . he reaches the unknown; and even if, crazed, he ends up by losing the understanding of his visions, at least he has seen them! Let him die charging through those unutterable, unnamable things." [10] Roethke's motive in deliberately cultivating mental disaster was precisely this: to break down the conscious ego in order to achieve an expansion of consciousness. Expansion of consciousness, the loss of self, he wrote in 1963, can be induced "simply by intensity in the seeing. To look at a thing so long that you are a part of it and it is a part of you—Rilke gazing at his tiger for eight hours, for instance. If you can effect this . . . you will break from self-involvement, from I to Otherwise, or maybe even to Thee" (*S.P.*, p. 25). On the eve of his breakdown, he recorded an experience of visual intensity like Rilke's. While walking in a wood he stopped in front of a tree and felt that disintegration of the empirical self and reintegration with the world's body that is characteristic of mystical ecstasy (*Glass House*, p. 90).

10. *Rimbaud: Collected Poems*, ed. and trans. Oliver Bernard, pp. 10–11.

His condition was variously diagnosed as manic-depressive psychosis and paranoid schizophrenia. Such clinical phraseology is distressingly abstract, and Roethke's own analysis is more convincing: "If I have a complex, it's a full-life complex" (*Glass House*, p. 94). This is not to underestimate the tragic dimension of his experience, but it is to insist that more was at stake than private anxieties. He was able to see in his experience a potential insight into other thresholds of consciousness. In retrospect, in his notebooks, he outlined his own three-part definition of mania:

Manic: 1. A limitless expanding of the ego with no controlling principle.
2. An intense communion with nature in which subject and object seem identical.
3. Abdication of the ego to another center, the self.
[Notebooks, reel 14, no. 206]

It is quite clear that this experience is behind some of the most beautiful moments of Roethke's poetry: "To have the whole air!" (*C.P.*, p. 67); "Speak to the stones, and the stars answer" (*C.P.*, p. 90); "I could watch! I could watch/I saw the separateness of all things!" (*C.P.*, p. 63). The experience of psychic disorder convinced him of the existence of other forms of consciousness apart from the rational, and the need to explore these forms became the obsessive preoccupation of his poetry. He rejected the false deluding euphoria of breakdown which is often an attempt to escape reality, but remained convinced of the existence of a mystical intuition; that is, of an irrational but undeniable instinct for a reality other than that apparent to the external eye. From this experience some of the persistent themes, one might almost say habits of perception, of his poetry are derived. Ambiguity, the perception of both inner and outer reality as a series of opposites, seems to have become the set cast of his mind. "In my veins contraries skip," he wrote (Notebooks, reel 5, no. 69). The exacerbation of opposites, the swings in his poetry from ecstasy to despair, find their pattern here, as does his desire for reconciliation of opposites into some kind of unity.

Yet Roethke never confused madness and creativity. Breakdown was for him a terrifying and dangerous experience, with recovery never assured. In a letter to James Wright he warns with moving authority against the folly of indulging nervous debility. Artistry demands control. "I want you to stay intact so you can write that piece" (*S.L.,* pp. 220–21). In later years he always insisted that the idea that good writing must come at a heavy, even tragic cost is the most fallacious of doctrines and comes from a distrust of vicarious experience.[11]

The immediate impact of breakdown on Roethke's poetry was negligible, proving that it is no automatic strategy for creativity. A few poems were written in retrospect which offer intimate respect to the hostile powers of the unconscious, acknowledging the way in which unconscious fears are realized in phantastical images:

> Our phantasies, like flies
> That buzz from ear to shoulder,
> Keep just beyond our gaze,
> Too quick for hands to smother.
> We double in our tracks
> Pursuing tails of shadow,
> The atavistic Other
> That jumps on careless backs.
>   [*S. L.,* p. 93]

If he accepted Rimbaud's credo that a thorough self-knowledge would demand physical, intellectual, and spiritual self-mortification, Roethke was more rigorous in his imposition of a stylistic self-discipline. He had to teach himself how to use the intuitions afforded by his experience through a reckless willingness to experiment technically. In *Open House* he had only begun to understand his subject; it would be some time before he could find the voice to articulate it.

Roethke's way of recovery from breakdown was the way of the essentialist. Thus began his disparagement of reason. What good is reason against the things we cannot see? Reason is one with the luxuries like illusion, pride, and honor discarded in a fantasy of disencumbrance recorded in "The Auction" (*C. P.,* p. 21). What is

---

11. *Straw for the Fire: From the Notebooks of Theodore Roethke 1943–63,* ed. David Wagoner, p. 200.

left after all the "rubbish of confusion" is sold is will; not reflective, but pure brute will, intuitive blood longing. In "Assailants," he writes: "You need to resurrect the will/To fight when backed against the wall" (*S.L.*, p. 36); in "Statement," less impassioned and more resolute:

> The body learned its length
> And breadth; my darkest mood
> Was written with my name.
> Now I declare my strength
> And find a proper theme:
> My vigor is renewed.
> [*S.L.*, pp. 57–58]

Through breakdown Roethke learned of the paralysis of the soul without positive force of its own. He sought to escape the self-cannibalism of despair, Rimbaud's "I consume myself," by positive affirmation. In his rejection of the sophistications of the civilized in such poems as "Highway: Michigan," and of "the mind . . . quick to turn/Away from simple faith" (*C.P.*, p. 31), it is nature that provided him with assurances.

Most of the early poems on nature record a conventional fascination with the seasons and cyclic regeneration, but there are a few which hint of the garden master that was to come. In a poem called "The Signals" Roethke writes:

> Often I meet, on walking from a door,
> A flash of objects never seen before.
>
> As known particulars come wheeling by,
> They dart across a corner of the eye.
>
> . . . .
>
> They slip between the fingers of my sight.
> I cannot put my glance upon them tight.
>
> Sometimes the blood is privileged to guess
> The things the eye or hand cannot possess.
> [*C.P.*, p. 8]

Here Roethke records one of those peculiar experiences when old familiar objects are drained of their familiarity and become strange flashes of light and dark, "tail flicks from another world." These naturalistic signals were his initial intimations of an intuitive order of experience, what D. H. Lawrence called experiences we can feel but cannot know.

"The Heron" describes the incredible insouciance and antic dignity of that bird. What fascinates the poet is its singleness of spirit. Without disorder or distress, one easy wing-flap carries the bird into that realm Roethke longed for in the line "more pure than flight/Of curving bird, I'll walk the night" (*S.L.*, p. 24). The heron is the first of those pure sensuous forms which were to become a constant theme of his poetry.

It is in "Genesis" that he first records the intuition which was to serve him throughout life:

> This elemental force
> Was wrested from the sun;
> A river's leaping source
> Is locked in narrow bone.
>
> This wisdom floods the mind,
> Invades quiescent blood;
> A seed that swells the rind
> To burst the fruit of good.
>
> A pearl within the brain,
> Secretion of the sense;
> Around a central grain
> New meaning grows immense.
>   [*C.P.*, p. 18]

"Genesis" makes the fundamental discovery that there is a continuity of energy between organic and human nature, an identity of being. This intuition would be extended to the point where he would reject the barrier between self and other and, by a power of "sympathetic" apprehension, seek to enter intuitively into the subliminal irrational world of nature. The capacity he was to develop for a compassionate flow of self into the things of his experience, what Stanley Kunitz was to call his metamorphic grace, was to become his poetic signature. Poems like "Genesis" sent him back to his childhood to that point of most intimate contact with nature in the greenhouses to recover what he called "singleness of spirit above all else" (*C.P.*, p. 24) and "quiet at the core" (*C.P.*, p. 20).

In *Open House* Roethke was engaged in the long arduous task of evolving a personal style, but as he complains in "The Gentle": "The sleep was not deep, but the waking is slow" (*C.P.*, p. 29). He always insisted that his Saginaw, Michigan, background accounted for this tardiness. Timid and withdrawn by temperament, he became more than most a victim of that isolation of the American writer outside the large metropolis. Had he had the assurance which comes from a literary background he might have broken through this, but in his Midwestern environment serious intellectual interest was conspicuously absent and artistic ambition was scarcely tolerated and certainly ignored. Within his family, the idea of wanting to become a writer was itself disloyal and he suffered some guilt for failing to become the lawyer his father would have wished. This profound apathy to aesthetic values not only retarded his poetic growth; when he did turn to poetry it was with a timidity and deeply rooted sense of inadequacy which made it more difficult for him to assert his individuality. It is difficult to overemphasize the isolation of his early years. In his notebooks he wrote: "I think no one has ever spoken about the peculiar, the absolute—can I say—cultural loneliness of the American provincial creative intellectual." [12] In retrospect he remembered his apprenticeship as intolerably confused: "It was literally astonishing the rubbish I devoured and tried to emulate. I was all wrong about everything and there was no one to tell me otherwise" (Notebooks, reel 14, no. 196).

Even after he had escaped the Midwest, habits of isolation were

12. Ibid., p. 228.

hard to break. He seems to have gained little as a poet from the year he spent as graduate student at Harvard beyond a chance and momentary meeting with Robert Hillyer. His later love affair with Louise Bogan and the strong friendships he formed with Rolfe Humphries and Stanley Kunitz must have helped considerably to increase his sophistication, as his correspondence with these writers attests. Yet until he could tolerably order the emotional tumult within him it seemed impossible to tap the profounder resources of feeling on which his later mastery would depend. He was always convinced that it was rhythm that unmistakably identified a poet, was a clue to the energy of his psyche. To discover his own rhythm, his personal voice, he would, by an inevitable necessity, have to discover his own psyche. This was not to happen in *Open House*. In this first book he seems to be marking time building up a technical resourcefulness for the period when he would be ready to use it.

The book is a workshop of experiments like the ones he used to set for his students of verse form: poems in pentameter and tetrameter couplets, heroic quatrains, ballad forms and free verse with internal assonantal patterns. His method was always one of imitation and assimilation, and at this point in his career he found the models for his rhythmic experiments among his lesser known contemporaries. On this matter of influence he wrote:

Eliot said, "Bad poets imitate; good poets steal." . . .

All true, but in some ways a terrifying remark for the beginning writer, who is often neither bad nor good, but simply, as yet, unformed. He isn't sure whether he is a thief or a fake. . . . Particularly if he is a provincial . . . [he may turn to] the immediately preceding literary generation, or the more precocious around his own age . . . to the over-neat technicians who simplify experience by forcing it into an arbitrary order. [*S.P.*, pp. 62–63]

In search of cadences, Roethke turned to the "over-neat technicians" Elinor Wylie, Leonie Adams, and, with greater reward, to Louise Bogan and Emily Dickinson. The poem "No Bird" is a careful imitation of Dickinson's "On this long storm the Rainbow rose." The last stanzas of the two poems bear comparison:

> Slow swings the breeze above her head,
> The grasses whitely stir;
> But in this forest of the dead
> No bird awakens her.
>   [*C.P.*, p. 17]

> The quiet nonchalance of death—
> No Daybreak—can bestir—
> The slow—Archangel's syllables
> Must awaken *her!* [13]

As Jenijoy La Belle pointed out in her essay on Roethke's use of tradition,[14] the phrase "forest of the dead" is taken from Dickinson's "Our journey had advanced":

> Our pace took sudden awe—
> Our feet—reluctant—led—
> Before—were Cities—but Between—
> The Forest of the Dead—[15]

Roethke uses the allusion as a kind of tribute. Only when it is recognized, and the imitative style of "No Bird" identified, does it become clear that the poem is actually an epitaph written for the elder poet who once "knew/The secret heart of sound."

In "Epidermal Macabre," Roethke is quite clearly indebted to Louise Bogan's "The Alchemist." [16]

He borrows the absolutely regular quatrameter couplet and the rhetorical pose:

> Indelicate is he who loathes
> The aspect of his fleshy clothes,—
> The flying fabric stitched on bone,
> The vesture of the skeleton,
> The garment neither fur nor hair,
> The cloak of evil and despair.
>   [*C.P.*, p. 19]

13. *The Complete Poems of Emily Dickinson,* ed. Thomas H. Johnson, 1 (no. 194): 139.
14. Jenijoy La Belle, "Theodore Roethke and Tradition: 'The Pure Serene of Memory in One Man,' " *Northwest Review,* 11 (no. 3): 1–18.
15. *Complete Poems of Emily Dickinson,* 2 (no. 615): 473.
16. Louise Bogan, *Collected Poems,* p. 21.

But the younger poet's technique is not entirely adequate to the rigid structure. In the fourth and fifth lines, the rhyme scheme and catalogue form force him into banality. Diction is labored— "flying fabric"—and the poem's cry becomes rhetorical resentment. W. H. Auden has said that wit requires a combination of imagination, moral courage, and unhappiness. Roethke was in the process of discovering these in the recesses of his own personality, and they were to stand him in stead in later poems like "I Knew a Woman." Initially, however, metaphysical witticisms were a barrier to personal statement. What is important here is his sensitivity to rhythmical subtleties, though he had not yet sufficient control of diction or metaphor to escape banality. In these early poems he ran the danger and learned the risk of borrowing another poet's rhythm. It was a skill that would bring him much criticism in the future.

In the later poems of *Open House* he was seeking a simplification of rhythmic techniques and a new sincerity. Wit and the strictures of rhyme were abandoned for the casual tone of simple narrative. "The Premonition" was written in 1938.

> Walking this field I remember
> Days of another summer.
> Oh that was long ago! I kept
> Close to the heels of my father,
> Matching his stride with half-steps
> Until we came to a river.
> He dipped his hand in the shallow:
> Water ran over and under
> Hair on a narrow wrist bone;
> His image kept following after,—
> Flashed with the sun in the ripple.
> But when he stood up, that face
> Was lost in a maze of water.
> [*C.P.*, p. 6]

He warned John Ciardi: "Be careful of the 'big theme' " (*S.L.*, p. 72). Here he relies totally on a single image to carry the full burden of his father's death. There are few articles and no adjectives, except for the moving "narrow wrist" bone. This economy, the fluidity of the feminine rhyme endings, and the isolation of "bone" from the rhyme sequence, make this one of the most effective poems in the book.

His sense of metaphor was also deepening throughout *Open House*. With remarkable persistence and increasing sophistication, the poems seek to detail the internal landscape of the mind through naturalistic imagery. In this way he was consciously evolving a personal symbolism. In the poem "Orders For the Day," the necessary maturation from innocence, the confrontation of hatred, and the anticipation of ease are described in an allegorical journey:

> Feet, bear the thin bones over
> The stile of innocence,
> Skirt hatred's raging river,
> The dangerous flooded plain
> Where snake and vulture hover,
> And, stalking like a crane,
> Cross marshland into clover.
> [*C.P.*, p. 7]

The images are obvious, but Roethke is searching for a system of correspondences—the long-legged crane is offered as an image of the self seeking to escape contamination; hatred is a bog-land; moral peace is clover. The metaphoric process is more subtle in "The Light Comes Brighter," where the psychic landscape itself begins to be imagistically detailed:

> And soon a branch, part of a hidden scene,
> The leafy mind, that long was tightly furled,
> Will turn its private substance into green,
> And young shoots spread upon our inner world.
> [*C.P.*, p. 11]

Roethke's drive was ever toward a rediscovery of the intimate relationship between the creative self and nature. From the beginning he knew that he was to be, as James Dickey wrote, one of the "Empathizers" like Rilke and Lawrence who make poetry out of a deeply intuitive response to the organic. But not until he recovered the image of the greenhouse world in his second book of poetry could he really probe this intuition. In the greenhouse lyrics, he discovered that cultured botanical growth and the slimy sublife of slugs and other such creatures provided the right imagistic focus his poetry needed to channel and concentrate the emotional tumult he felt within his own riotous psyche. In *Open House,* he was paring his craft, discovering a personal style that would breathe, move, and be unpredictable; a style convincing the reader, as Robert Lowell once said, that the journey has been honest.

❧ II ❧

Lean to Beginnings
POEMS 1942–48

When sprouts break out,
Slippery as fish,
I quail, lean to beginnings, sheath-wet.
[*C.P.*, p. 37]

Theodore Roethke's father, Otto Roethke, was a florist owning what were at one time the largest and most beautiful greenhouses in the state of Michigan. As a child Roethke worked and played alongside his father in the greenhouses just behind the family home. It was the kind of world which could shape a child's imagination, a primitive microcosm demanding constant attention and even a childish sense of loyalty. Roethke spoke of it as "several worlds, which, even as a child, one worried about, and struggled to keep alive" (*S.P.*, p. 9). It was in fact, a universe, complete, exhaustive, with its own eschatology of heaven and hell, a moist artificial womb of fecund growth, and a place of death, with the father-gardener, all-powerful, all-ordering, at its center. Roethke came into his own as a poet in his second book, *The Lost Son and Other Poems*, when he was able to recover this greenhouse world. He was to call it "my symbol for the whole of life, a womb, a heaven-on-earth" (*S.P.*, p. 39). Reclamation was a dangerous process since it inevitably meant reactivating the fears and guilts haunting him from his childhood; but for this very reason it was crucial to the poet. The ordeal of recovery was excruciatingly slow. A chronological study of the publication of individual poems in the *Lost Son* volume indicates that, while most of the poems of Sections 2 and 3 were written between 1941 and 1943, much of the

22

sequence was begun in a burst of creativity in 1944, after what seems a considerable fallow period.

According to Jim Jackson, a colleague at Bennington College where Roethke was teaching, the years between 1944 and 1946 were a time of "much surge, much lassitude," a gestation period during which he was working out a new personal style of poetry. Later Kenneth Burke was to call this period the "cult of the breakthrough." [1] "On days when he was not teaching, he moped around Shingle Cottage alone, scribbling lines in his notebooks, sometimes, he told me, drinking a lot as a deliberate stimulus . . . popping out of his clothes, wandering around the cottage naked for a while, then dressing slowly, four or five times a day" (*Glass House*, p. 144). This was not exhibitionism, as Allan Seager makes clear, but a kind of ritual stripping down to the skin as an effective act of purgation to get back to first things, irreducible life—the poet groping, only vaguely conscious that he searches for the metaphoric world that will correspond to the needs of his sensibility. Roethke said of the greenhouse sequence: "In those first poems I had begun, like the child, with small things and had tried to make plain words do the trick" (*S.P.*, p. 10).

When he returned to the greenhouses, his attention was riveted on growth, on the willful, tenacious struggle of plants into being in a drive against death. In effect, he went to the vegetal world to penetrate to the root sources of life and in that way to redefine himself. His initial discovery was of a world of multiplicity, terrifying and degrading to human sensibility. He described the greenhouse as a bifurcated universe—an underworld of orchids like adder-mouthed devouring infants, of shoots lolling obscenely from mildewed crates, of lewd monkey-tails hanging from drainholes, and an upper inviolate world above the benches of pale lilies, cyclamen, and roses, with the poet trapped down below in the fetor of weeds "alive, in a slippery grave" (*C.P.*, p. 39).[2] Roethke

---

1. Kenneth Burke, "Cult of the Breakthrough" (review of *Selected Letters*), *New Republic*, 159 (21 September 1968): 25–26.
2. Only Stanley Kunitz, in his essay "Roethke: Poet of Transformations," *New Republic*, 152 (23 January 1965): 23–29, has adequately emphasized the deep ambivalence of

found the greenhouse symbol an objective correlative for his own disgust and hatred of life and his feeling of defilement by organic processes, emotions inextricably woven with desperate insecurities which were the legacies of childhood.[3] But the greenhouse symbol is more than simply a projection of sexual anxiety. He has, as it were, mythologized it into a microcosmic symbol, taking advantage of inherent conceptions involved in the idea of a greenhouse. After all, as Kenneth Burke remarked in his essay "The Vegetal Radicalism of Theodore Roethke," what is a greenhouse? Neither sheer nature like a jungle, nor regulated nature, like a formal garden, it is in fact both—a precarious balance of natural and artificial: "All about one, the lovely, straining beings, visibly drawing sustenance from ultimate, invisible powers —in a silent blare of vitality—yet as morbid as the caged animals of a zoo."[4] In fact, as a microcosmic symbol, "my symbol for the whole of life," the greenhouse is largely negative. Life beneath its plenitude is mechanical and deterministic, administered by an implacable father inaccessible to the child. It is an image of a fallen world of materiality and death. The impulse of the volume is for transplantation, transcendence—not, however, through evasion of the material, but by a deeper penetration into the meaning of process, time, and change. By an intuitive, intensely personal investigation into nature, Roethke sought to understand the bond between his human nature and the subliminal world which had made him, and

Roethke's attitude toward the greenhouse, in one aspect a nostalgic world of order lost to childhood, in another, a terrifying world of organic processes degrading to human sensibility.

3. Much attention has been devoted to the sexual implications of Roethke's symbolism—see particularly Karl Malkoff, *Theodore Roethke: An Introduction to the Poetry,* pp. 47–58. I have therefore chosen to concentrate on the metaphysical implications of the sequence. Furthermore I would agree with William Meredith in "A Steady Storm of Correspondences: Theodore Roethke's Long Journey out of the Self," in *Theodore Roethke: Essays on the Poetry,* ed. Arnold Stein, p. 41: "I might say first that I think [these poems] can be damaged by overt sexual interpretation. Insofar as we are sexual beings—and happily that is quite far—things lurk in our minds. But insofar as a skillful artist speaks of experience other than the sexual, we must suppose that he intends to treat other experience, and pay attention to that."

4. Kenneth Burke, "The Vegetal Radicalism of Theodore Roethke," *Sewanee Review,* 58 (Winter 1950): 82.

in that way to recover his attachment to life. Henri Bergson may have been helpful in his intuitive investigations into nature. A copy of Bergson's *An Introduction to Metaphysics,*[5] dated 1938, is one of the few philosophical works retained among his annotated volumes. It may have been the metaphorical implications of intuition that interested him. Bergson insisted that apart from human understanding there are other forms of consciousness, immanent and essential to understanding the full meaning of life, and that if these were brought together and amalgamated with intellect, the result might be a consciousness as wide as life. These other forms are the intuitive, pulsative attachment to life of the biological and the animal, types of consciousness capable of complete self-surrender to an external object—not abstracted from life, but completely absorbed into its creative impulse. This form of consciousness is not entirely foreign to the human being because, around the luminous nucleus of the intellect, there is, as a vestige of the biological evolution, a vague nebulosity of intuition—that propulsive a priori sudden apprehension of complexity which is the source of all original creativity. Bergson's yearning to see beyond intellect terminates inevitably in a desire for a mystical apprehension of reality. If the human being could complete his consciousness by recovering intuition, "such a consciousness, turning around suddenly against the push of life which it feels behind, would have a vision of life complete . . . even though the vision were fleeting."[6] Roethke sought to recover this intuitive consciousness—this supra-intellectual knowledge of life not externally apprehended but experienced from within. When he returned in his poetry to the greenhouses of his childhood, it was "not the intricate tracery of the leaf or the blazonry of the completed flower" which absorbed him,[7] but the essentially creative impulse compelling life. He sought through the intuitive power of sympathy to

5. Henri Bergson, *An Introduction to Metaphysics,* trans. T. E. Hulme. However, no strong claims are made for direct influence. The similarity may be one of vision.
6. Henri Bergson, *Creative Evolution,* trans. Arthur Mitchell, p. xii.
7. Stanley Kunitz, "News of the Root," *Poetry,* 73 (January 1949): 223. Kunitz emphasizes that Roethke was attracted to "invincible Becoming" in plant life, a word crucial to Bergsonian philosophy.

place himself within the object of his contemplation in order to coincide with it, to achieve an experience of identity. It is significant that his interest in nature rarely extended far into the animal kingdom. What concerned him were slugs and snails, snakes and frogs—animals which represent the extremity of instinct alien to the human condition. When he went to the biological it was to discover through intuitive vision the coincidence between his own human nature and the naked processes of life—it was a response to his rage for order.

After *Open House* Roethke was always meticulous about the order and arrangement of poems within each book, often deleting poems because they did not fit into a sequence. He wrote: "I believe a book should reveal as many sides of a writer as is decent for him to show: that these aspects be brought together in some kind of coherent whole that is recognizable to the careful reader. This means that some poems will sometimes support other poems, either by being complements to them, or by providing contrasts" (*S.P.,* pp. 57–58). The first section of *The Lost Son and Other Poems* falls into three distinct parts: (1) the eye close on the struggle into growth; (2) the world outside the greenhouse; (3) the desire for change, transplantation, transcendence of the greenhouse world.

Roethke once described the greenhouse as a tropics in the savage climate of Michigan. The first six poems of the greenhouse sequence show it to be precisely this: a closed artificial world concentrating and accelerating growth, in itself a morbid metaphor for the degrading biological processes of life. "Cuttings" is a poem written in two sections—an early and a later view of severed plants struggling to recover life. With a compulsive fascination, the poet watches, or rather imagines, the desperate effort of the delicate slips for growth beneath the seemingly dead and dried surface of sticks-in-a-drowse. With slow, tenacious energy, the plants penetrate the barrier into life in an atmosphere of pure suspension, as if the silent process had no relation to human time. As Roethke himself said: "Intensely seen, image becomes symbol" (*S.P.,* p. 122). "Cuttings" discovers the unobtrusive, mysterious coming into being of all life as it "Pokes through a musty sheath/Its pale tendrilous horn" (*C.P.,* p. 37).

"Cuttings (later)" recovers the process at a more advanced, more violent stage of pure incipience. Here, creation is a humiliation, with the plants "sucking" and "sobbing" in a struggle which the poet feels at the core of his own anatomy: "In my veins, in my bones I feel it" (*C.P.,* p. 37). Roethke's analogy to the saint is remarkable, as though the biological struggle were a penitential process. The dead stems struggling to regain vitality are engaged in a naturalistic resurrection which he wishes to duplicate: "Slippery as fish,/I quail, lean to beginnings, sheath-wet" (*C.P.,* p. 37). For the first time, he uses the metaphor of the fish, the irreducible denominator of all life, the half-way point, as it were, between plant and animal, which defines the interdependence of all living matter. It is as though he wishes to recover from the biological the pure unidirectional impulse toward life, but it is an impulse which is, at present, terrifying to him in its sheer tenacity.

This is the theme of "Root Cellar," the darkest, dampest part of the greenhouse, where roots are left exposed and dormant, to grow larger before planting. Descent into the root cellar is like a descent into a violent inferno of creation:

> Nothing would sleep in that cellar, dank as a ditch,
> Bulbs broke out of boxes hunting for chinks in the dark,
> Shoots dangled and drooped,
> Lolling obscenely from mildewed crates,
> Hung down long yellow evil necks, like tropical snakes.
>
> . . . .
>
> Nothing would give up life:
> Even the dirt kept breathing a small breath.
>   [*C.P.,* p. 38]

Life, the sheer tenacious impulse to live, is terrifying and perverse. The cause of Roethke's terror is clear from the images—this is severed, disjointed, voracious growth, a chaos of aimless and bewildering multiplicity. Even "Orchids" are described as ruthless, vicious life. Behind a delicate pose, they are "devouring infants," part of the Darwinian universe where the law of survival reduces even the loveliest natural growth to "Nature red in tooth and claw." The closer one comes to the instinctive world, the more violent is the urge to shy away from it. Sexuality drags the human being back into the sultry abyss and therefore Roethke rejects it as perverse and voracious, a degradation to the spirit. Inevitably the impulse is to reject the physical entirely. In "Forcing House," the hottest part of the greenhouse, where heat, moisture, and manure are used to accelerate maturation, all types of plant life, from mildews to delicate cyclamen tips, are caught in a concentrated cycle of growth, a cannibalistic cycle in which putrified life—lime, dung, and ground bones—goes to feed life soon to die. The analogy to human organicism is deftly underlined in the adjective "live" heat.

In "Weed Puller," Roethke coalesces his images into an overview of the greenhouse. We discover that it is a fallen world of material growth, a slippery grave of death, and he is an animal in it, "crawling on all fours." He may have said in *Open House,* "Long live the weeds that overwhelm/My narrow vegetable realm!" (*C.P.,* p. 18), but here he is caught in that low life, hacking, digging, tugging, crawling, unable to control the violence of growth. Alliteration and diction ("lewd," "coiling") effectively convey his repulsion, which is equally directed against his own sexuality. In particular, "dripping smilax" inevitably recalls its homonym "smile" to underline the sinister perversity of growth. The desire for transcendence comes as a longing for the "crisp hyacinthine coolness,/Like that clear autumnal weather of eternity" (*C.P.,* p. 43) of the later poem "Carnations." But again, this will prove a fantasy not long satisfying. He could not abandon his vegetal realm. He had to achieve an integration, to penetrate more deeply into the biological until he could say:

> Such quiet under the small leaves!—
> Near the stem, whiter at root,
> A luminous stillness.
>
> [*C.P.,* p. 221]

There was only one possible direction for recovery—metaphorically downward and under, to penetrate even further to the root sources. The poem "Moss-Gathering" extends this investigation. It recalls the young poet's sensations while collecting moss in the marshlands. It was like stripping skin from the live plant and plunging into the yellowish flesh to the elbows. This is a primitive world in which the human is alien, but, far from repelled, Roethke is humbled, sensing a rhythm "old and of vast importance" (*C.P.*, p. 40), about which he knows nothing.

The last six poems of Section I all record the desire to master or transcend the greenhouse world. In "Child on Top of a Greenhouse" the poet as a child climbs to the top of the chrysanthemum house. In a letter to Kenneth Burke, Roethke wrote: "This act of being up on top of this greenhouse was something that even the most foolhardy older kids condemned because if you slipped you pitched through the glass to if not certain death, a broken back or neck and bad cuts . . . (*S.L.*, p. 119). In the poem, the feat is an act of defiance against the greenhouse world with the "half-grown chrysanthemums staring up like accusers" (*C.P.*, p. 43). In part the chrysanthemums are the adolescent (half-grown) kids and the climb is the foolish act of the child to prove himself to his peers. But it is also more than this. It is a daredevil transcendence of the vegetal for the world of the "few white clouds," those plunging "horses" freed from the tether. This childish bid for freedom is therefore an expression of an eminently human impulse to be released, to be distinguished from the lower physical world. "Flower Dump" also reproduces the hierarchical image of the former poem, and confirms the desire for transcendence. Here whole beds of bloom are pitched on a pile, the root-veins twined like fine hair, with one tulip on top, "One swaggering head/Over the dying, the newly dead" (*C.P.*, p. 43). The theme is clear, a defiance of mortality.

Several poems express a nostalgia for order, for the father-master of the greenhouse world, or for Frau Bauman, Frau Schmidt, and Frau Schwartze, who, like three transcendent fates, could sew up the air with a stem, "keeping creation at ease." [8] They could even "coax" a seed into life which the cold kept asleep. The poet, cold in his bed, would be similarly directed, but these are all figures from a "first sleep." New direction would demand willful transplantation.

"Transplanting" insists that there is something to be learned from the vegetal world:

> The sun warming the fine loam,
> The young horns winding and unwinding,
> Creaking their thin spines,
> The underleaves, the smallest buds
> Breaking into nakedness,
> The blossoms extending
> Out into the sweet air,
> The whole flower extending outward,
> Stretching and reaching.
>
> [*C.P.*, p. 42]

The sheer mindless movement into life in a sensitive response to creative sun energy, so that nakedness becomes part of a natural process—this is Roethke's aim. "Will I stretch out of wretchedness? Yes. . . . the last least parts of me strain/When I see maimed roots grappling granitic stones." [9] He wishes to recover vital energy from the vegetal realm, and a re-initiation into that rhythm, "old and of vast importance." In these last few poems, he finally rejects his idealization of withdrawal and desire for abstract transcendence, and identifies himself with the generative reality of the here and now. Opening himself to crude and violent energies, he begins to find his creativity and art in precisely those forces which first appeared most repulsive to him. The upward movement of the greenhouse sequence in a concerted drive for resolu-

8. "Frau Bauman, Frau Schmidt, and Frau Schwartze," *Collected Poems* (published only in the English edition), p. 44, was not part of the original greenhouse sequence; it was first published in 1952, and added to the sequence in *The Waking: Poems 1933–1953*.

9. This poem "Could I spiral like this, like these strings," though completed in 1946, was never included in the greenhouse sequence. Roethke sent it in a letter to Kenneth Burke, apparently with misgivings as to whether the ideas and symbols were completely realized. His analysis of the poem offers an interesting example of his working methods. See *Selected Letters*, p. 118.

tion is to become a characteristic of his work, repeated in every book he wrote.

A thematic change in Roethke's poetry is always accompanied by a corresponding change in rhythmic structure. In the greenhouse sequence, he freely adapts the techniques of Hopkins' sprung rhythm. Lyrics like "Cuttings" and "Forcing House" do not yield to regular metrical scansion, but must be measured in terms of stresses. The technique is that of *The Wreck of the Deutschland* where the number of stresses varies per line, rather than of the sonnets, where each line has an equal number of stresses within syllabic variation:

> This urge, wrestle, resurrection of dry sticks,
> Cut stems struggling to put down feet,
> What saint strained so much,
> Rose on such lopped limbs to a new life?
> [*C.P.*, p. 37]

The principle of sprung rhythm is accent or stress. Feet are regarded as of the same length or beat, no matter what the number of syllables. The seeming inequality of additional syllables in one foot is balanced by pausing or stressing. Hopkins called this the principle of "equal strengths." [10] In a line like "Under the concrete benches," "Under the," a three syllable unit, is given the same stress as the two syllable units "concrete" and "benches." This technique, working throughout the greenhouse poems, produces that remarkable surge or blood-pulse of energy which imitates the compressed intensity of plant growth. With the flexibility afforded by the use of sprung rhythm, Roethke could completely vary effects within the same stanza. In the line "This urge, wrestle, resurrection of dry sticks," the increasing number of syllables per stressed foot allows the line to release its energy, and the words stumble over one another in a rising rhythm until the affirmation of the last spondee. The effect is entirely different in "The small waters seeping upward." The absolutely regular divi-

10. W. H. Gardener, *Gerard Manley Hopkins: A Study of Poetic Idiosyncrasy in Relation to Poetic Tradition*, pp. 44–45.

sion of syllables drags the line, imitating the slow tenacious struggle of plants into growth. This was exactly the rhythm Roethke
needed to produce the greenhouse pulse, a rhythm that could, as
Hopkins said, turn a stanza into one long strain. All of the poems
are either one or two, at the most three, sentences—alliteratively
controlled units that surge in a single onrush, creating a mobile
impression of the energy that Roethke wished to explore, that
"rhythm old and of vast importance" which his intuition disclosed
to him in nature.

Hopkins himself was trying, through sprung rhythm, to reproduce the sensation of instress which comes when an object is
viewed closely. When one goes to the essence of an object, sees its
inscape, its individually distinctive rhythm and beauty, one feels
an attendant experience of instress. For Hopkins this was a frankly
religious experience of the pressure of God's grace in and through
material objects. The greenhouse poems form a naturalistic variant
of the experience of instress, and Roethke was finally to define this
instressing of the creative pulse of nature as a mystical experience.

In the third section of *The Lost Son and Other Poems,* written between 1941 and 1943, Roethke undertook a deliberate apprenticeship in the use of evocative imagery. He described this section
as an attempt to use the image of water to suggest a "relation between visible and invisible reality" (*S.L.,* p. 114), between natural
and psychic experience. His later comments on technique in poetry are pertinent: "We all know that poetry is shot through with
appeals to the unconsciousness, to the fears and desires that go far
back into our childhood, into the imagination of the race. And we
know that some words, like *hill, plow, mother, window,
bird, fish,* are so drenched with human association, they sometimes can make even bad poems evocative" (*S.P.,* p. 80). Roethke
is obviously thinking of Jung's theory of the collective unconscious—that below the personal psyche, with its welter of private
experience, exists the common residue of primal instincts which
are the evolutionary heritage of the race from its earliest origins.
He insisted that he had read little psychology, but this was a kind
of subterfuge, perhaps to ward off single-minded interpretations of

his work according to psychological formulae. His notebooks indicate that while he may have read little Freud or Jung, he was familiar with certain of their disciples.[11] More importantly, he had
intimate knowledge of the aggressive powers of the psyche from
his own harrowing experiences of mental breakdown. He was interested in how to tap these for poetic images and it is probable
that his intense reading of Maud Bodkin's *Archetypal Patterns in
Poetry* helped him toward this end. In her book, Maud Bodkin
studies the way in which certain universal, elemental images, ordered in particular patterns, will turn the mind back to its primitive origins. She speaks of these as archetypal patterns of experience within us that "leap in response to effective presentation in
poetry of an ancient theme." [12] Her analysis of the cavern images
of "Kubla Khan" and *Paradise Lost* are particularly pertinent to
Roethke's poetry.[13] She explains that the image of the dark stream
which surges from the underground cavern into the light sounds a
responsive chord in the human being, awakening a deep affinity
to, yet paralyzing fear of, his subhuman origins. She indicates that
images like that of the cavern operate almost cylindrically,
through complex layers of associations: cave—womb—cistern of
the mind. After Jung, she calls these archetypal or universal
images (as opposed to archetypal patterns like rebirth) that tap a
core of elemental feeling which transcends the personal. The existence of natural, organic patterns of symbolism, evocative juxtapositions that do not depend solely upon rational explanation, is
obviously of crucial significance for poetry. If certain words can tap
deeply into the roots of the mind, evoking continuous chain reac-
tions of associations, the poet has at hand spontaneous threads of
images from which to weave his poetry for maximum evocation.

11. Titles in Roethke's early notebooks include C. G. Jung, *Psychology and Religion;*
Karen Stephen, *The Wish to Fall Ill: A Study of Psychoanalysis and Medicine;* and Karen
Horney, *Self-Analysis;* this last is included among Roethke's annotated volumes. For his
disavowal of having read much psychology see *Selected Letters,* p. 260.
12. Maud Bodkin, *Archetypal Patterns in Poetry: Psychological Studies of Imagination,* p.
4. Stanley Kunitz indicated in "Poet of Transformations," p. 25, that this book was one
of Roethke's most important sources for *The Lost Son* sequence.
13. Bodkin, *Archetypal Patterns,* pp. 112–14.

Roethke's drive was ever toward the intuitive. He was not interested in the social inheritance of meanings stored in language. He wanted to pare away the progressive encrustations of meaning to recover the power of language to evoke primal emotions—desires, fears, passions that are seldom felt, yet eternally significant. He began to build up patterns of images: bird, tree, water, hill, tunnel—most often used for their symbolic counterpart (soul, body, death or flux, release or aspiration, submergence) but with a simplicity and grace that are most moving. In "Last Words," he says good-bye to the old encumbrances: "The psyche writhing and squirming in heavy woolen" (*C.P.*, p. 48). What he needed was a root language of fundamental simplicity.

In "Night Crow" there are only three objective images: a clumsy crow, a wasted tree, and night; yet they touch off unconscious associations—a dark bird-shape flowing back into the deep recesses of the mind. The point of the poem is that an unconscious fear, in this case the primal fear of death (the bird flaps from a "wasted tree," the image Roethke often uses to refer to the body), can be activated by an external object. The poem's power comes from the poet's ability to balance the correspondence—between the clumsy crow and the sinister incorporeal bird-shape, half sensation, half phantom, which penetrates to the unconscious. As he indicated, he was attempting to keep two realms, visible and invisible, psychic and material, in equilibrium. Here, the psyche within the external world exists as one cylinder within the other, both infinitely extensive.

In "Night Crow" the correspondence is literally outlined. "The Minimal" is more ambiguous. The dark world of caves, bogs, and ponds, in which the direction is downward and under, has a long romantic heritage as symbolic of the cistern of the mind. But Roethke intends a precise correspondence. The world of stone-deaf fishes, squirmers, and bacterial creepers is the unconscious, harboring both sinister shapes of primal fears and anxieties, and magical healing instincts that can be of aid to the human being. The protagonist of *The Lost Son* sequence will later say: "My mission became the salvation of minnows" (*C.P.*, p. 90). It is as if, in

the depths of the self, lies a core of power, a redemptive memory
that must be brought to the surface, fished out (night-fishing is a
continual motif in his poetry). The nature of this power is at least
suggested by the minimal life, those sleepers, nudgers, squirmers,
wriggling, kissing, cleansing, caressing, creeping, healing. What
they have and what the poet wants is the wisdom of silent
things—their quiet, continuous, unobtrusive intensity which the
human being can only know in rare moments of self-transcendence.

In "River Incident" the poet explores the unconscious forebod-
ing which always seizes him at the river's edge:

> A shell arched under my toes,
> Stirred up a whirl of silt
> That riffled around my knees.
> Whatever I owed to time
> Slowed in my human form;
> Sea water stood in my veins,
> The elements I kept warm
> Crumbled and flowed away,
> And I knew I had been there before,
> In that cold, granitic slime,
> In the dark, in the rolling water.
>   [*C.P.*, p. 49]

Immersed in the water, Roethke discovers his own subhuman origins. The human form becomes expendable, a graft onto a more
basic substance, the cold granitic slime. Time is a human expedi-
ency which measures a finite existence. The intuition is terrifying.
Roethke may say: "I knew I had been there before" but how can
this personal "I" be defined in the dark rolling waters. Where is
the line to be drawn between individuality and this primitive unconscious substance that is its irreducible mould.

In these three poems, Roethke was trying to recover emotion at
its primitive level, to articulate the inherent, as it were, organic
responses to certain elemental experiences—such as the fearful sensation of anonymity felt when gazing into water, or the uplifting
of the spirit with the rising of the wind. Such a belief in arche-

typal experience is the inherent principle of myth—the symbolic projection onto nature of the psychic drama universal to all human beings. He saw language as a storehouse of such primitive correspondences which had become obliterated through continual encrustations of meaning. His linguistic experiments were directed to pare away these sophistications. His belief in the evolutionary continuity of human existence must be kept in mind. He saw man as:

> A prince of small beginnings, enduring the slow stretches
> of change,
> Who spoke first in the coarse short-hand of the subliminal
> depths.
> [*C.P.*, p. 170]

He sought to articulate this shorthand by an elliptical use of words, so that they become as instinctive as the cry of an animal. He expected to be able to put down the natural image and take the unconscious association for granted. His faith was founded on an infinite confidence in the unity of all human experience. He would write, "Remember an old sound. Remember water" (*C.P.*, p. 59), and expect the reader to know that the correspondence intended was between the flow of water and the sensation of release of the spirit so often conveyed through this metaphor. Sometimes such an expectation seems unfounded, almost a shirking of poetic responsibility. But most often Roethke was fully justified in throwing the reader back on his own resources. Turning next to the writing of one of his finest poems, "The Lost Son," he was now prepared to allow his subconscious free rein, content to create out of this upswelling a genuine imaginative order.

❧ III ❧

Ordnung! Ordnung!
THE LOST SON SEQUENCE

> Scurry of warm over small plants.
> Ordnung! ordnung!
> Papa is coming!
>
> A fine haze moved off the leaves;
> Frost melted on far panes;
> The rose, the chrysanthemum turned toward the light.
> Even the hushed forms, the bent yellowy weeds
> Moved in a slow up-sway.
>
> [C.P., p. 57]

Roethke's deliberate cultivation of his own past in the greenhouse poems posed terrible psychic risks. By returning to the greenhouses of his childhood he became once again the lost son. Kenneth Burke has made it clear that willfully entwining himself in the mental tangles of his youth helped to precipitate his second breakdown in December 1945.[1] "The Lost Son" and its three companion poems were completed after this episode in a period of recovery.[2] T. S. Eliot has stressed the ambiguous connection between mental disorder and creativity. Probably alluding to the breakdown which preceded the writing of *The Wasteland*, he indi-

---

1. Burke, "Cult of the Breakthrough," p. 25.
2. There is some dispute as to whether "The Lost Son" was written before or after Roethke's illness. He was writing to the Ford Foundation of a poem called "The Lost Son" as early as February 1945, but the poem as we know it seems to have been completed in May 1946, after the impact of his breakdown, and published in *Sewanee Review*, 55 (Spring 1947): 252–58. However, even were its gestation previous to his illness proper, the experience of mental terror which is its subject was all too familiar from earlier disorders.

cated that certain forms of ill health can stimulate poetry by breaking down habitual barriers and repressions normally frustrating composition.[3] This was clearly Roethke's experience. He wrote: "The speed with which ideas, good and bad, slipped out of my mind was fantastic" (Notebooks, Reel 5, no. 66). He published *The Lost Son* sequence over a period of a year, a fluency which was remarkable since he usually found composition a laboriously slow process. This second illness seemed to have given him the breakthrough into his past for which he had been waiting, and at precisely the time when he was ready with a craft sophisticated enough to take advantage of it. It also gave him the thematic pattern of the poems themselves. "The Lost Son," "The Long Alley," "A Field of Light," and "The Shape of the Fire" are imaginative, symbolical transcriptions of the experience of psychic disintegration.[4] They are desperate poems, each beginning in negative, life-denying solipsism which is gradually and painfully transcended until the poet achieves an exultant experience of wholeness and relation. The early lyric "The Return" is their prologue:

> A cold key let me in
> That self-infected lair;
> And I lay down with my life,
> With the rags and rotting clothes,
> With a stump of scraggy fang
> Bared for a hunter's boot.
>   [*C.P.*, p. 47]

In Roethke's description, breakdown is an interior journey into complete and terrifying self-absorption in which all outside be-

3. T. S. Eliot, *The Use of Poetry and the Use of Criticism: Studies in the Relation of Poetry to Criticism in England*, p. 144.

4. These four poems were originally published as a sequence in *The Lost Son and Other Poems*. They were inserted in Roethke's next book as the middle section of the *Praise to the End!* sequence. As I am interested in the development of Roethke's poetry, I have preferred to study them in their original order of composition as they appear in the *Collected Poems*. Because the latter is the most readily available text, I have referred to it throughout. However mention should be made of discrepancies in the margination of stanzas between this and earlier volumes, particularly in the poems "The Lost Son," "Where Knock Is Open Wide," and "A Field of Light." Though these are slight, they do distort the psychic shifts of mood and pace that Roethke always indicates by a change of margins, and comparison should be made with earlier volumes.

comes alien and aggressive, while the self within is loathsome and infected. To lie down with his life in order to come to the core of the psychic wounds which had made present existence impossible, he began "The Lost Son." He said: "I have tried to transmute and purify my 'life,' the sense of being defiled by it, in . . . poems which try in their rhythms to catch the very movement of the mind itself . . ." (*S.P.*, p. 15). He called these poems the record of "miseries and agitations which one has been permitted to escape by the act of creation itself!" (*S.P.*, p. 36).

When Roethke returned to explore his relationship to his father, the greenhouse confronted him. In the privacy of his notebooks he asks: "What was this greenhouse? It was a jungle and it was a paradise. It was order and disorder. Was it an escape? No, for it was a reality harsher than . . ." (*Glass House*, p. 166). In the greenhouse lyrics he had described his father's world as a bifurcated world and had consigned himself to the slimy realm of smuts and stems, the wildly organic which focused his sense of guilt and inadequacy before his father. Yet his mind always returned nostalgically to this first world as an ideal of paternalistic order and security. In brief, the greenhouse image defined an oscillation he lived—between his fear and hatred of life as physical process so intimately tied to his filial sense of inferiority, and his regressive longing for the idealized self-contained world lost to childhood, his father's ordered world. He struggled to extricate himself from this dualism. As a poet, he saw in the seeds of his struggle a basic human problem—the need to reassert independent value for man as a spiritual being. His emotional relationship to his father became the model for his sense of relation to a higher transcendent power—a coercive, fearful longing, tormenting in its frustration, which was gradually purified through inward reconciliation into an experience of silent communion. *The Lost Son* sequence re-enacts this struggle symbolically. He called it "a struggle out of the slime; part of a slow spiritual progress; an effort to be born, and later, to become something more" (*S.P.*, p. 37).

Roethke was well aware of the amorphous character of much autobiographical poetry. Therefore he sought a structural principle which would give his sequence order. While there were yet only four poems to the sequence, he defined this order as regressive: "I believe that to go forward as a spiritual man it is necessary first to go back. Any history of the psyche (or allegorical journey) is bound to be a succession of experiences, similar yet dissimilar. There is a perpetual slipping-back, then a going-forward; but there is some 'progress' " (*S.P.*, p. 39).[5] He later amplified this statement in a letter to Kenneth Burke: " 'One must go back to go forward.' And by back I mean down into the consciousness of the race itself . . . any regression does go back or repeat what has happened before and not merely in the individual man" (*S.L.*, p. 116).

Roethke probably came to his theory of a racial consciousness through Jung's literary disciple Maud Bodkin, in her *Archetypal Patterns in Poetry*. Jung had insisted that there are primordial thought patterns, which are collective structural elements of the human psyche reaching back eons into the evolutionary process. Bodkin devotes much of her book to the most central of these— rebirth. According to Jung, the psyche is engaged in a continual process of psychological adaptation to life, which can be frustrated. When this happens, vital feeling disappears, the impetus toward the real world collapses, and the mind falls back on itself, its life currents hemmed and split. Maud Bodkin describes this process imagistically:

It may be felt by the sufferer as a state of compulsion without hope or aim, as though he were enclosed in the mother's womb, or in a grave—and if the condition continues it means degeneration and death. But if the contents which during the introverted state arise in fantasy are examined for the hints, or "germs," they contain "of new possibilities of life," a new attitude may be attained by which the former attitude . . . [is] transcended.[6]

---

5. This idea of a repetitive cycle is similar to the Freudian theory of the repetition-compulsion pattern of the psyche—a repetitive return to a traumatic experience in order to meet it again, each time achieving a new control. See Freud's "Beyond the Pleasure Principle," *Complete Psychological Works,* ed. and trans. James Strachey et al., vol. 18. Roethke may have come upon the theory through Kenneth Burke. For a study of Burke's influence on his poems see Brendan Galvin, "Kenneth Burke and Theodore Roethke's 'Lost Son' Poems," *Northwest Review;* 11, (no. 3): 67–96.

6. Bodkin, *Archetypal Patterns,* p. 72.

This is precisely the pattern of the four poems: "The Lost Son," "The Long Alley," "A Field of Light," and "The Shape of the Fire." An intense state of spiritual introversion focused through womb, cave, and grave images is transcended either by means of a healing memory from the past or through sheer assertion of will. Roethke attempts to objectify the very ebb and flow of the libido or vital life energy through a peculiar "water" language: "This slag runs slow"; "Remember an old sound./Remember/Water" (*C.P.*, p. 59); "An old scow bumps over black rocks" (*C.P.*, p. 64)—each a precise notation, a kind of psychic shorthand for a mental state.

At first sight, the poems appear to be surrealistic juxtapositions of nursery rhymes, riddles, songs, and chants. Viewed more closely it becomes clear that Roethke is imitating an Elizabethan tradition, that of the Bedlam Beggar, the natural man, stripped of all pretenses, who stands on the edge of incoherence, courting madness as a recovery of sense. Thus the rants and ravings, attempts to convey the mind's extremity, can always be translated naturalistically, but of course at the price of their vigor. For they are an attempt to force language to convey the very rush and thrust of emotive impulse, to make language instinctive. The experiment is part of a purgative quest to get back to elemental emotions, what he affectionately called "mutterkin's wisdom," learned with the ear close to the ground. If we look to the core of the introverted state with which each poem begins, we discover that what is damming the vital life energies is a fear of organic processes and of death, projected onto nature that is stagnant and implacable. To exorcise this fear Roethke underwent a purgative cleansing, a ritual stripping away of all encumbrances until he achieved, in the state he called "Pure Mind," a fervent, intuitive attachment to, and re-absorption in, life.

One of the most important poems Roethke wrote is "The Lost Son." It brings us to the core of his sensibility—a paralyzing fear of death and a harrowing doubt that the frail "I" will prove powerful enough to oppose it. The poem is an appeal for order, "Ordnung! ordnung!" to the symbol of the father, a request for spiritual survival in the primal sucking waters. It is patterned on the immemorial night journey: "We must surely go the way of the waters, which always go downward, if we would salvage the treasure, the precious legacy of the father." [7] The treasure, pearl, or lotus is the immortal self submerged in the turgid waters of the unconscious. As Jung has said: "Dealing with the unconscious has become a matter of life for us. It is a matter of spiritual being or nonbeing." To recover the soul-treasure at the bottom of the river, we must become "fishers who catch with hook and net what floats in the water." [8]

The poem begins with the "Lost Son" at Woodlawn where his father lies buried. Not only personal loss but also the dread impersonality of death harrows him as he feels in himself the acquiescent pull toward death. The slamming of iron, whether the sound of shovels or of the cemetery gate, is lulling, hypnotic to his ears. Shaking the "softening chalk" of his bones, he sets out on a therapeutic quest for identity, an "I" to assert against this disintegration. He turns for solace to the subhuman:

> Snail, snail, glister me forward,
> Bird, soft-sigh me home.
> [*C.P.*, p. 53]

In his essay "On Identity" (*S.P.*, p. 25) Roethke insists that in calling upon the snail, he is calling upon God as would the primitive mind, but there is no answer, no oracular voice or miraculous sign, only vague riddles. [9]

> Dark hollows said, lee to the wind,
> The moon said, back of an eel,

7. C. G. Jung, *The Integration of Personality*, trans. Stanley Dell, p. 67. It is not important whether Roethke actually read this, since Maud Bodkin is very explicit on the theme of the night-journey. In addition, his notebooks of this period contain a reference to *The Epic of Gilgamesh*, a possible source for the night-fishing motif.

8. Jung, *Integration of Personality*, p. 73.

9. These are a kind of hieroglyphics which point to the unconscious, always symbolized by the element of water. John Lucas, "The Poetry of Theodore Roethke," *The Oxford Review*, no. 8 (1968), p. 49, interprets the moon and eel as mother and father symbols with the caution that too rigid an interpretation will undermine the heightened visionary quality of the imagery.

The salt said, look by the sea,
Your tears are not enough praise,
You will find no comfort here,
In the kingdom of bang and blab.

The Lost Son has proven unworthy and cut himself off from the primitive code of "mutterkin's wisdom." Therefore he begins the terrifying journey through an emblematic landscape of filth and slaughter to the "quick" water, the reed-grown river's edge in the valley of the psyche.[10] What he is seeking in his flight is described in the traditional teasing manner of folk riddle. The motif is familiar in Roethke's poetry and will occur again in the poem "O Lull Me, Lull Me": "For you, my pond,/Rocking with small fish,/I'm an otter with only one nose" (*C.P.* p. 84). In "The Abyss" he insists:

I'm no longer a bird dipping a beak into rippling water
But a mole winding through earth,
A night-fishing otter.

[*C.P.*, p. 220]

The subject of the riddle is the self as night-fisher plunging into the depths of the unconscious.[11] It is described as phallical— lubricous and repugnant, because this is the core of the Lost Son's obsession. His fear of life and desire for oblivion express themselves as a revulsion from sexuality. He descends to "The Pit," a place of elemental questions: "Where do the roots go? . . . Who put the moss there? . . . Who stunned the dirt into noise?" The questions echo Blake's epigram to the "Book of Thel": "Does the Eagle know what is in the pit?/Or wilt thou go ask the Mole." [12]

10. The poem is written almost as a dream sequence in which the dreamer is the whole dream—the landscape, the swamp, the otter are all details that express tendencies in the unconscious of the subject. See Jung's analysis of the river motif in *Integration of Personality*, pp. 66–74.

11. Jung actually identifies the otter as a fantasy image of the self as night-fisher, but arrested at an earlier instinctual stage of development, for example that of the child. Roethke need not have read this since he is writing from the store of his own fantasies. See *Integration of Personality*, p. 73.

12. *The Poetry and Prose of William Blake*, ed. David Erdman, p. 3. The theme of "The Book of Thel" is the willful rejection of life in flight from the fear of death; this may have been in Roethke's mind as he wrote his poem.

The Lost Son's questions carry him to the primal source of existence which he defines, as did Thel, in its negative aspect only—it is "Mother Mildew," the slimy mold sucking all life into unredeemed obliteration; Blake's watery chaos where every natural growth is an imprisoning womb, a world of embowered forms, or grasping tendrils. Terrified, the Lost Son cries: "Nibble again, fish nerves," bitten by the instinctive, sympathetic nervous system that ties him to the evolutionary chain.

In "The Gibber," the child stands at the cave of sexual initiation. His own rampant sexual hunger is felt with guilt and desolation. All nature becomes negative and accusatory, an oracle of death. The Lost Son turns to the Father with a primitive appeal for order: "Hath the rain a father?" and finds only the stern memory of his father, "Father Fear." His guilt and isolation are now most intense, re-activating a grisly adolescent nightmare, symbolically rendered through dream images of flowing water and reflexive sexuality.

> What gliding shape
> Beckoning through halls,
> Stood poised on the stair,
> Fell dreamily down?
>
> From the mouths of jugs
> Perched on many shelves,
> I saw substance flowing
> That cold morning.
>
> Like a slither of eels
> That watery cheek
> As my own tongue kissed
> My lips awake.

This repulsive auto-eroticism leads to sexual frustration, described in surrealistic language:

Is this the storm's heart? The ground is unstilling itself.
My veins are running nowhere. Do the bones cast out their fire?
Is the seed leaving the old bed? These buds are live as birds. . . .
Goodbye, goodbye, old stones, the time-order is going,

I have married my hands to perpetual agitation,
I run, I run to the whistle of money.[13]
    Money money money
    Water water water

In his outline of "The Lost Son" ("Open Letter," *S.P.*, pp. 36–43), Roethke speaks of a period of "frenetic activity" followed by momentary release and blackout. The intense excitability of the lines, the symbols of seed and buds, and the image of the hands married to perpetual agitation would seem to confirm that these lines are indeed a symbolic notation of the masturbatory episode. The consequence of the "frenetic activity" is a "lapsing back into almost a crooning serenity": "How cool the grass is./Has the bird left?/The stalk still sways," but inevitably denial of desire is a kind of self-murder: "Kiss me, ashes, I'm falling through a dark swirl." In the same outline Roethke indicates that throughout the sequence onanism is equated with death. It is a symbol of withdrawal, of the longing to escape sexual responsibility and life. Here masturbation represents a kind of suicidal fantasy or death-wish, a retreat from life as an extreme act of placation and atonement for hostilties toward the father.

The return is achieved through a redeeming memory of the father, not as "Father Fear," but as one who could call the greenhouse world to order. The memory telescopes the imagistic pattern of tunnel and pit of the earlier sections. The Lost Son travels through the long greenhouse, a slippery tunnel of violent organic growth, to the fire-pit, the boiler room where bricks like red roses were burned for fuel. It is a fearful and terrifying place, an imprisoning womb. Into this world comes the father with his cry of "Ordnung! ordnung!" Roethke wrote: "By the *'Ordnung! ordnung!'* I had also hoped to suggest the essentially Germanic character of the 'Papa,' the authority whose Prussian love of order and discipline had been sublimated into a love for, and a creating of the

---

13. Roethke wrote in a notebook draft: "I wooed possession in my father's name" (Reel 5, no. 66). This line "I run, I run to the whistle of money" is probably meant to emphasize the Lost Son's guilt and efforts at placation. Yet it seems to break the dramatic continuity of the poem since we are still, according to Roethke's explanation in "Open Letter," in the mind of the adolescent boy. See *Selected Prose*, pp. 36–43.

beautiful (the flowers). . . . The child, a kind of sentry guarding the flowers, both lolling sleepily, guiltily; but jumping to attention at the approach" (*S.L.*, p. 162). The conflation of child and flower is remarkable. Both respond to the father-sun in a primitive striving toward the light as the mere presence of the paternal principle brings order and assurance to the greenhouse world. It is as though, through the father's cry of order, the redirective will to self-discipline, self-attention, had been discovered, and the terror of dissolution arrested. Earlier, paternal order was seen as terrifying and destructive, but here it is clear that the father's "sublimated" will to order has created the truly beautiful world of the greenhouse. On the personal level, fear and the torment of remorse, raised almost to a mythological level in the childish mind, have been expelled by a recovery of an intimate and benevolent memory of the father. But as Hilton Kramer was the first to insist, there is a further ramification to this image of homecoming: a tension, never stated explicitly, between this image as a private reconciliation with the father, and as an "objective dramatization of a certain situation of the soul." [14] What is described is a "Return" in final terms to a spiritual solidarity, captured in the image of the flowers giving themselves to the light after their nocturnal drowse. The old notion of "Father Fear" is abandoned as life itself is seen to be creative and:

> The rose, the chrysanthemum turned toward the light.
> Even the hushed forms, the bent yellowy weeds
> Moved in a slow up-sway.
>
> [*C.P.*, p. 57]

In a winter, purgatorial world, illumination recurs to the mature man, exactly repeating the interior reconciliation experienced by the child at the father's call. Here the Lost Son sees the weeds, the life so rancorous to him in "Weed Puller," as beautiful surviving bones swinging in the wind. It is of course the Lost Son who has been stripped down to the surviving bones, having arrested the

14. Hilton Kramer, "The Poetry of Theodore Roethke," *Western Review*, 18 (Winter 1954): 140.

softening disintegration of the death-wish ("I shook the softening chalk of my bones"). In a moment of intense light and silence he has an experience of internal communion: "A lively understandable spirit/Once entertained you." The word "understandable" has a remarkably childish simplicity; it gives substance to "spirit" as though to imply a palpable indwelling presence that has entered the self in a moment of visitation. The echo of Eliot's phrase "mid-winter spring" implies the kind of experience Roethke feels he has had, "a moment in springtime, but not in time's covenant." But he refuses it final definition. The light could be external, internal, or transcendent. It will be the object of his entire poetic effort to find out which. All he knows now is that the self has once been satisfied.

In retrospect, "The Lost Son" epitomizes the psychological pattern of rebirth or renewal common to "The Long Alley," "A Field of Light," and "The Shape of the Fire." It is a pattern that depends upon a definition of the unconscious as the receptacle not only of fears and guilts but also of life-directive instincts that come in moments of extremity to sustain the self.[15] If only the paralyzing fear and hatred of life, in all its harrowing negativism, can be endured, healing impulses to love will rise out of the self. The process is really a secular variant of the dark night of the soul. Instead of eschewing the body, the self seeks to purify it in willful contemplation of the organic, until natural life is seen in its beauty and individuality.

Like "The Lost Son," "The Long Alley" is an interior monologue, with the mind in a state of acute psychic distress. Roethke conveys the phantasmagoric immediacy of thought in such states through continual personification, the basic metaphor of the primitive mind. The poem begins with the eye trained on nature as a receptacle of death, but it becomes clear that it is merely a mirror of the interior weather. Thus the image of a stagnant river, "The slag runs slow," conveys psychic stagnation wherein water, the

15. Bodkin, *Archetypal Patterns,* pp. 19–20. This theory aligns Roethke with Jung rather than with Freud. In Jung's system, the unconscious can be creative, harboring redirective impulses to life.

free libidinous flow of life energy, is an old sound. The cause of stagnation is the self's loathing of the body: "What bleeds when metal breaks?/Flesh, you offend this metal"; to which the sulphurous water replies: "There's no filth on a plateau of cinders./ This smoke's from the glory of God" (*C.P.*, p. 59). "Cinders" in Roethke's poetry often refer to the body. Here the sulphurous waters of sexuality claim its divinity. The aim of Roethke's experiment is to pack language with maximum evocation. Thus a word like "cinders" carries overtones of that which is both loathsome and transitory. In the same way, when the self remains skeptical: "What does the grave say?" the reply "My gates are all caves" brings death imagistically before the mind as a dead end, a stultifying enclosure.

In desperation the self seeks dialogue with the soul or spiritual principle, the "kitten-limp sister," "milk-nose," "sweetness I cannot touch" that is locked in the "horse barn" of the body. The technique is closest to the tradition of the Bedlam Beggar: "The foul fiend haunts poor Tom in the voice of a nightingale. . . . Croak not, black angel; I have no food for thee." [16] To the mind in psychic distress, spiritual entities are palpable hallucinatory presences. Thus the self with remarkable pathos cries for the soul as a lover after sexual embrace: "I need a loan of the quick" (*C.P.*, p. 59).

When the appeal fails, the poet is thrown back to the lonely solipsism of sexual hunger. Again Roethke uses wild songs and riddles to convey the mind's frenzy; their theme is sexual. The waiting ghost of frustrated desire warms up the dead self in the old onanistic dance of "barley-break and squeeze." But the lover, the kitten-limp sister, is still locked in the old silo. In a riddle, the self asks what are the consequences of the sexual act (detach the head of a match)? What do we do to the soul? Do we rout death or does the carnal have the last laugh?

The only way out of the mind's torturous rehearsal of this same theme is through a purgative cleansing of the will. The poet turns

16. *King Lear*, act 3, scene 6, lines 29–32.

to the long alleys of the greenhouse, previously the focus of his guilt and terror before the organic. Reaching out penitently to the small brothers, the breathers and winders with their delicate fishways, the self begins to embrace the physical in a moment of mystical translation: "The leaves, the leaves become me!/The tendrils have me!" (*C.P.,* p. 61). The invasion of the very tendrils that were so loathsome and defiling in the greenhouse poems is accepted with delight.

In "A Field of Light," the poet is again in nature which is stagnant and diffuse, but here he is aware of the potential for change. Thus nature is engaged in delicate metamorphoses: "Reached for a grape/And the leaves changed;/A stone's shape/Became a clam" (*C.P.,* p. 62). Life is on the edge of incipience, in a "watery drowse." In this mood, the poet invokes the angel within, the milk-nose of "The Long Alley," and asks: "Did I ever curse the sun?" He turns to the deep, dark underness, the root sources, and in a ritualistic, penitential act, embraces life at its core: [17]

> Was it dust I was kissing? . . .
> Alone, I kissed the skin of a stone;
> Marrow-soft, danced in the sand.
> [*C.P.,* p. 63]

His conquest of the greenhouse world in "The Long Alley" is now extended to the whole of nature, which he experiences not as an oracle of death but as the medium for release of the spiritual being: "The dirt left my hand, visitor":

> Listen, love,
> The fat lark sang in the field;
> I touched the ground, the ground warmed by the killdeer,
> The salt laughed and the stones; . . .
> I could watch! I could watch!
> I saw the separateness of all things! . . .

17. The poem repeats the pattern of Coleridge's *The Rime of the Ancient Mariner* in which the blessing of the water snakes is offered as an extreme act of placation to those forms of life against which the protagonist has sinned. Roethke calls this moment in the poem a penitential act (*S.P.,* p. 25).

And I walked, I walked through the light air;
I moved with the morning.

                                        [*C.P.*, p. 63]

Feeling nature in its minute presences, Roethke has one of those rare moments of enthusiasm when one feels the self consumed and extended into the whole of space. He called this an experience of "intensity in the seeing" (*S.P.*, p. 25), when a very sharp sense of the being of something else, even inanimate life, brings a corresponding awareness of oneself. The vision invests the self with verifiable life: "The weeds believed me, and the nesting birds."

The final poem of the *Lost Son* volume is one of Roethke's most extraordinary works, an attempt to convey the crisis of mental breakdown. If the images are examined, it becomes clear how logical the seemingly surrealistic juxtapositions are. For example, the first line, "What's this? A dish for fat lips," becomes wholly comprehensible when read in conjunction with the later line "My meat eats me." Both refer to the self-cannibalism of psychic distress in which the interior self feels consumed and suffocated by the alien body. The poem attempts to describe the mind on the edge of psychic disaster, using language impressionistically. Thus the mind "scraping bedrock" is described as "An old scow bumps over black rocks." [18] The introverted state is felt as an entrapment in womb or cave. The poet calls to the Mother as the agent of rebirth and nourishing relation:

Will the sea give the wind suck? . . .
Mother, mother, stir from your cave of sorrow.

                                        [*C.P.*, p. 64]

The cause of distress is conveyed elliptically. It is the old hatred of the physical being: "Wake me, witch, we'll do the dance of rotten sticks." But in addition there is an allusion to a state of spiritual aridity, particularly destructive to the poet:

[18]. Burke, "Vegetal Radicalism," p. 95, reports the suggestion of one of Roethke's students that the line "an old scow bumps over black rocks" is meant to echo the heartbeat of the mother "as the foetus might hear it dully, while asleep in the amniotic fluids," but no grounds have been offered for assuming that Roethke is the source of this interpretation.

In the hour of ripeness the tree is barren.
The she-bear mopes under the hill.
Mother, mother, stir from your cave of sorrow.

Roethke usually thought of his muse in the image of a bear. Here muse and mother are conflated in an appeal for ripeness. The course of mental breakdown is outlined in an address to "the flat-headed man," the warder of death or madness "come to unhinge my shadow." The poet insists that, once articulate, he had "slept in the pits of a tongue," in a state of fruitful inspiration: "The silver fish ran in and out of my special bindings." But he had grown tired of the greenhouse ritual, and of his subordinate role as "assistant keeper of the mollusks." "A two-legged dog hunting a new horizon of howls," he looked for new themes. Roethke's early draft of this section had read: "Having exhausted the possibilities of common sense,/I composed the following:" [19]

> Pleasure on ground
> Has no sound,
> Easily maddens
> The uneasy man.

The poet wants to penetrate to subterraneous wisdom, but madness is always a potential hazard on such journeys:

> Who, careless, slips
> In coiling ooze
> Is trapped to the lips,
> Leaves more than shoes;
>
> Must pull off clothes
> To jerk like a frog
> On belly and nose
> From the sucking bog.
> [*C.P.*, p. 65]

He describes the fall into the primeval slime as careless. In order to break free, he will have to lose himself, strip away the man he has become, soiled, lost, and confused. He prays to the Muse-

19. Ibid., p. 100. It is possibly worth noting that Roethke recorded the cause of his first breakdown as being over a line of poetry (*Glass House*, p. 94).

Mother: "Renew the light, lewd whisper." But in Section 3, the poet's state is still one of tense waiting for directives. Caught in the constrictions of contraries, "The edge cannot eat the center," he yet senses immanent revelation: "The grape glistens. . . . An eye comes out of the wave." But the process of transcendence of the flesh is long and harrowing: "The redeemer comes a dark way" (*C.P.*, p. 66). Redemption comes in the form of a regressive memory from the world of childhood where "Death was not." For Roethke, childhood is an intuitive state in which being is acted and unconscious and vision is a process of continual and fluid exchange. One remembers Whitman's child:

> There was a child went forth every day,
> And the first object that he look'd upon, that object he became . . .[20]

It is as though there were an ideal conjunction between the child and his world. The world is made for him: ". . . the sun for me glinted the sides of a sand grain," and is responsive to his will: "My intent stretched over the buds at their first trembling" (*C.P.*, p. 66). Most important, the child's world is one of mutually benevolent presences engaged in a continual creation and becoming whose energizing principle is love:

> Rain sweetened the cave and the dove still called;
> The flowers leaned on themselves, the flowers in hollows:
> And love, love sang toward.

This remembrance from childhood is very important. It is as though the self had been stripped to bedrock, removing the layer of acquisitions which cover nature, and the instinctive impulse to love has been discovered as the mainspring of all life.

This intuition is carried back to the adult world. What was thought to be atomistic and disordered is suddenly seen as a universe of plenitude flowering into beauty, one that had been there all the time only for want of seeing. In a magnificent stanza, Roethke describes all of life moving in a slow response to sun

---

20. "There Was a Child Went Forth," *Leaves of Grass: Reader's Edition*, ed. Harold W. Blodgett and Sculley Bradley, p. 364.

energy, whether it be the rose unfolding spontaneously from within, or a water bead falling with the glitter of the sun's light. The assurance this brings is marvelously primitive:

> To know that light falls and fills, often without our knowing,
> As an opaque vase fills to the brim from a quick pouring,
> Fills and trembles at the edge yet does not flow over,
> Still holding and feeding the stem of the contained flower.
>
> [*C.P.*, p. 67]

The image describes a world of unity and containment in which the pulse of sun energy, like water in a vase, fills the whole of space.

Roethke insisted that in his sequence there is regression but there is also continual progress (*S.P.*, p. 39). We see this progress when the final sections of each poem are juxtaposed. In part, it is a seasonal change from winter to summer, mirroring the soul's weather; but more it is a movement from an intimation of order in a winter world of light where the vegetal realm is quieted, to an acceptance of the constricted organic world of the greenhouse, to a perception of the individually distinctive beauties of the natural world outside the greenhouses, to an intimation of unity and relation, that "rhythm, old and of vast importance," in a fecund world of plenitude. We begin to see that Roethke is truly moving in the direction Bergson outlined. Here he has only an intimation of a natural order through the principle of sun energy, an extension of the intuition which occurred to him in "Genesis" and "Transplanting." Throughout his work he will attempt to penetrate to the core of this illumination until he can assert a spiritual order to existence. Bergson counseled that the human being can come to a true understanding of existence only through the recovery of intuitive vision. If we put ourselves into our wills and our wills back into nature, we will discover the vital creative energy moving through matter, linking the whole series of the living in one continuous flow of perpetual self-creation and self-transcendence. This is a spiritual affirmation Roethke sought. It required an imaginative act of willful self-transcendence that had to be perpetually renewed. In the intervals between imaginative experiences, there was only the chaos of aimless and bewildering multiplicity. As he said: "We go from exhaustion to exhaustion" (*S.P.*, p. 39).

Before we turn to the *Praise to the End!* sequence, mention should be made of one final point—that *The Lost Son* sequence has provoked crucial questions of interpretation; particularly whether an entirely psychoanalytical approach to literature is justified. In his essay "Freud and the Analysis of Poetry," Kenneth Burke studied the relevance of Freudian modes of analysis to literature, and offered a helpful distinction between psychoanalytical interpretation as an essentializing process (the analyst must discover the single essential motive of any action, excluding all other considerations as sublimations), and what he calls the proportional strategy of literary criticism which seeks to define the configuration or synthesis of motives under the category of communication rather than that of wish, with its disguises, frustrations, and fulfillments.[21] The distinction is an important one since many critics, interested in an application of psychoanalytic methods to literature, have attempted to claim the essentializing strategy for literary criticism, reducing a work of art, which depends on formal and thematic principles of proportion and relation, to a single motive, often a neurotic symptom.

Such a mode of criticism has sometimes been applied to *The Lost Son* sequence, particularly to the title poem. Some critics have seen it as an attempt to articulate a private psychological problem, the poet's inability to come to terms with his own sexuality. In deference to the school of Freud, they have tried to discover the one particular offence in the poem. This is usually identified as the "Oedipus complex": repressed childish lust in regard to one parent and hostility toward the other. Karl Malkoff, for instance, speaks of the protagonist's incestuous desires as the source of his guilt and resentment toward the father.[22] The remark may be relevant,

---

21. Kenneth Burke, "Freud and the Analysis of Poetry," in *Psychoanalysis and Literature,* ed. Hendrik M. Ruitenbeek, p. 117.
22. Malkoff, *Theodore Roethke*, p. 81.

perhaps more to the poet's life than to the poem, but it is not a
sufficient comment on the motives of "The Lost Son," as Malkoff
himself admits. To offer the poem only in these terms is reductive,
since Roethke clearly intended to imply a larger debate of values—
the struggle for spiritual identity as over and above sexual identity.

The problem becomes crucial when John Lucas in the *Oxford
Review* dismisses "The Lost Son" as a failure because the poet does
not come to terms with the crisis of discovered sexuality. Instead
he sublimates his feelings to religious escapism, turning his conflict with an "earthly father" into one with a "heavenly father." [23]
There is a tacit assumption of psychological dishonesty—of the
poet, precisely because he fails to come to terms with his sexual
neurosis, resorting to cosmic pieties. There is, of course, an important margin of overlap between the aesthetic and the neurotic,
but there are also important divergencies, precisely because a poem
is a communicative structure (not a dream structure) demanding
that the conscious as well as unconscious motives of the artist be
respected. Roethke has offered the poem as expressive of a moral
dilemma, a search for spiritual value. He uses the theme of reflexive sexuality as a metaphor for a fearful withdrawal from life, a
death-craving or deep organic need for release when the life currents feel hemmed and split. To stave off this impulse to dissolution he begins a quest for meaning which, from the outset, involves final questions of order and authority. The crucial point of
the poem is not the need to come to terms with sexual inhibitions,
but rather the quest for spiritual identity, intimations of which
might stem the fear and hatred of the organic. Thus, there is no
deus ex machina final revelation in the last section of the poem as
John Lucas would insist, precisely because the quest for spiritual
paternity has been paramount throughout. In fact, the reference to
the Oedipus complex seems far too generalized, a mere first approximation in an attempt to explain the private terrors and guilts
of the poem. And to dismiss it as a failure because it does not

23. Lucas, "The Poetry of Theodore Roethke," p. 49.

come to terms with the Freudian formula is to apply terms which are only secondary to the poem as Roethke wrote it.

The problems of unconscious intention, resistance, purposive forgetting, and so on notwithstanding, to search for the sublimated motive of a poem is to conceal, to a large degree, what is important to it as a work of art. It is, as Kenneth Burke remarks, to apply the ideal of science: "to explain the complex in terms of the simple," a reductive process for a work of art which is the expression of a synthesis of motives: "The motive of a work of art can only be equated with the structure of interrelationships within the work itself." [24] Burke's "proportional strategy" helps the critic resist the Freudian tendency to overplay the psychological factor, and concentrate instead on the work of art as an act of communication with moral, intellectual, and aesthetic motives that must be given equal credence.

24. Burke, "Freud and the Analysis of Poetry," p. 121.

❧ IV ❧

A Father's Ghost
THE *PRAISE TO THE END!* SEQUENCE

I'll feed the ghost alone.
Father, forgive my hands.
[C.P., p. 85]

In writing "The Lost Son" Roethke finally freed himself from the constrictions of the lyric form which had forced him to segment experience. For the first time he saw the possibility of recreating in poetry the continuity of a single life. Jim Jackson writes:

> . . . at Bennington during *The Lost Son* gestation, he talked endless of *the long poem.* Meaning by this, as I finally came to see, not the long poem as any particular verse-form, past, present, or future, but as *entry* into the poet's whole lifelong expression (segmented, of course, for certain practical as well as aesthetic reasons) . . . there is a growing, continuing awareness of being your own source, of the uniquity of your material and—even more!—the assurance that the very process of probing the self constitutes an exploration of all human knowledge. [*Glass House,* pp. 144–45]

With this assurance Roethke began the *Praise to the End!* sequence. It picks up many of the motifs and symbols of the four *Lost Son* poems, and is an attempt to record the gestation and evolution of the child's mind. In "The Shape of the Fire" he rediscovered the child as an image of the primitive unity of being for which he always longed, being which is acted and unconscious. He began his latter-day *Prelude* to understand how this unity was lost. To be absolutely faithful to the gestation of consciousness, he wished to view it dramatically from within. His intention was to isolate the process whereby the mind is encrusted with false accumulations that obliterate its natural center.

57

In writing on the theme of the child, he was aligning himself with a long tradition that includes figures as various as Traherne, Blake, Wordsworth, and Emerson—the tradition that offers the child as a symbol of the visionary imagination. From this viewpoint, the child lives in a world that is inseparable from himself, in a state of vivid and nourishing relationship to Nature. As Emerson put it: "[His] mind being whole, [his] eye is as yet unconquered." [1] Eventually however, consciousness intrudes upon the child's power of direct and immediate apprehension of reality: "Man is, as it were, clapped into jail by his consciousness." By consciousness is meant rationalization, abstraction that invents the concepts of time and space separating the individual from the source of his experience. The desire to transcend these barriers, to discover a world neither distinct from nor opposite to the self, is the driving principle of this tradition. The problem lies in vision, in the individual's manner of regarding the world. Childhood becomes a symbol of correct relation to nature. The naïve or innocent eye is deliberately cultivated as a poetic strategy in order to recover the child's reverent passiveness before nature's mysterious plenitude.

The idea is neither sentimental nor a simplification, because Roethke, like Blake, recognizes that the distortion of vision is the consequence of a painful internal process of self-alienation; not as Traherne would have it, of the "Dirty Devices of the World." [2] A complex evolution of anxieties and guilts progressively narrows the child's world in Roethke's scheme. The purging of these guilts and the release into sexual love becomes an essential preliminary to the recovery of innocent vision. As in Blake, a correlative evolution of the spirit is thus implied in the evolution of the sexual self. [3]

1. *The Complete Essays and Other Writings of Ralph Waldo Emerson*, ed. Brooks Atkinson, p. 147.
2. *Thomas Traherne: Centuries, Poems, and Thanksgivings*, ed. H. M. Margoliouth, 1: 111.
3. Roethke cited Blake as one of the major sources of his sequence (*S.P.*, p. 41). In his notebooks he lists two studies of Blake: Emily Hamblem, *On the Minor Prophesies of William Blake*, and Northrop Frye, *Fearful Symmetry: A Study of William Blake*, both of

The *Praise to the End!* sequence is very much Roethke's own spiritual autobiography: a means by which he sought to come to terms with present wounds through an understanding of the complex foundations of personal identity. His concern was entirely with the frustrations to the process of maturation, as is indicated by the passage in Wordsworth's *Prelude* from which the title of the sequence is taken:

> How strange, that all
> The terrors, pains, and early miseries,
> Regrets, vexations, lassitudes interfused
> Within my mind, should e'er have born a part,
> And that a needful part, in making up
> The calm existence that is mine when I
> Am worthy of myself! Praise to the end! [4]

Through his child-hero, the Lost Son, Roethke would understand what regrets, vexations, and early miseries have been formative in undermining the integrity and independence of his sense of self. The initial cause is, of course, the premature death of the father described in "Where Knock Is Open Wide." One of the most important themes of the sequence is the equation between the loss of the father and of existential security. By a complex process of introversion, the hostility felt at the experience of the father's death is introjected into the ego in self-persecution, compromising essential confidence in life. The father becomes an unappeasable *doppelgänger* cutting the son off from independent identity, a "ghost dead in a wall" persecuting, punishing, seeking revenge. Sexuality precipitates the decisive crisis, presenting the child with a choice—between withdrawal into auto-eroticism in guilty retreat from sexual assertion, always a suicidal isolation, and sexual initiation which the child can only achieve by coming to terms with his

which emphasize Blake's sexual ethos. He referred to other sources as "German and English folk literature, particularly Mother Goose; Elizabethan and Jacobean drama, especially the songs and rants; the Bible; . . . Traherne; Dürer."

4. *The Prelude or Growth of a Poet's Mind,* 2d ed., ed. Ernest de Selincourt; rev. by Helen Darbishire, bk. 1, l. 350, p. 22. Most of the titles of individual poems also have literary sources which usually help to define the context in which Roethke's own poem is to be understood.

fear and hatred of sexuality, thus exorcising the censorious ghost of the father. The sequence balances, as it were, between tensions of withdrawal in acquiescence to fear and disgust; and of initiation and celebration of sexuality as the driving source of all natural life. With Roethke, reconciliation with the body is possible only if he can recover the conviction that "the flesh can make the spirit visible"; that "body and soul are one" (*C.P.*, p. 250). The poems are in fact regressive night-journeys into the darker, blinder strata of the unconscious in revulsion from the limitations placed on being: "Reason? That dreary shed, that hutch for grubby schoolboys!" (*C.P.*, p. 92). Roethke would search out a larger vision, one which might accommodate the spiritual self: "The eye perishes in the small vision/ . . . Go where light is" (*C.P.*, p. 90). He is very much in the tradition of the visionary poet seeing his task as the search for and realization of "unknown modes of being." In keeping with these themes, the *Praise to the End!* sequence is ordered into two sections. The first six poems detail the birth of individual consciousness in the crisis of sexual awakening. They are coordinated by an increasing sophistication in the mode of consciousness—from the infant sensibility, still linked to prenatal instincts, to the mind of the young adolescent, initiated into experience. The last four poems are written from the perspective of the maturer mind concerned with the expansion of consciousness and the recovery of innocent vision.

In the first poem "Where Knock Is Open Wide," the poet tries to penetrate the operations of the childish mind slowly coping with the psychic shock of wakening consciousness.[5] He shows how the mind begins to order external reality—first through analogy and association, and, only after long and arduous effort, through conceptualization. The poem begins with a narrative incident, the father's refusal to sing the child a lullaby—"His ears haven't

5. The title is taken from Christopher Smart, *A Song to David,* ed. Edmund Blunden, stanza 77, pp. 50–51. Smart describes a mystical world responsive to personal desire "Where ask is have/ Where seek is find/ Where knock is open wide," a paraphrase of the Beatitudes: "Ask and ye shall have, seek and ye shall find, knock and it shall be opened unto thee."

time." The child tries to order the chaos of his feelings through analogy: [6]

> A kitten can
> Bite with his feet;
> Papa and Mamma
> Have more teeth.

Here pain and teeth have become synonymous—Mamma and Papa have deeply hurt the child; therefore they have more teeth. They have effectively said:

> Sit and play
> Under the rocker
> Until the cows
> All have puppies.
>   [*C.P.*, p. 71]

Later the child will say: "Bullheads have whiskers./And they bite"; "I'll be a bite." "Do the dead bite?" Each time the word carries the previous painful associations. By such accumulations words begin to carry a primitive moral venom, and the arduous evolution of moral conscience is underway. The childish thought process is summarized in the line: "A real hurt is soft." Because the child has no grasp of concept, his attempts to define his resentment at his parents' refusal force him to resort to physical analogy. There is an underlying premise in Roethke's work that such associative thinking is ultimately the most faithful to experience. Thought should be sensed and palpable, a kind of revelation; not something invented but something forced upon us, bringing conviction through its immediate actuality.

In an elaborate sleep-song the child sings of his own conception, Roethke defines gestation as an interruption of some prenatal serenity:

---

6. In a letter to Kenneth Burke (*S.L.*, p. 149), Roethke indicated that he had been reading James Joyce, *A Portrait of the Artist as a Young Man,* and William Faulkner, *As I Lay Dying.* In both instances he discovered not only a theory of the evolution of consciousness through complex patterns of association grounded in physical experience, but also a way in which to render this dramatically through image and symbol.

Once upon a tree
I came across a time,
It wasn't even as
A ghoulie in a dream.

There was a mooly man
Who had a rubber hat
The funnier than that,—
He kept it in a can.
                    [*C.P.*, p. 71]

Still half submerged in unconscious processes, the child remembers the sexual act as a funny, slightly sinister game—a
mooly man (a word in Scottish dialect meaning earth on a burial
mound) beating in a can. Conception means his initiation into
physical dissolution, yet the child can invest the act with no personal reality. Roethke's notion of pre-existence resembles Wordsworth's in the "Immortality Ode." Wordsworth described the
child's entry into the world trailing clouds of glory to explain his
ecstatic responsiveness to nature, and to emphasize that life is a
diminution of this power of empathy. Roethke would concur,
with the emphasis on the paradise forfeited. The culprit is inevitably time:

What's the time, papa-seed?
Everything has been twice.
My father is a fish.
                    [*C.P.*, p. 72]

The father, tied in his sexual role to the long evolutionary ladder,
bears the responsibility for this imposition of creation; later the
child will ask: "Fish me out/Please."

From the moment of conception, the child is engaged in a long
arduous process of self-definition through distinction and analogy.
"I'm not a mouse." "A worm has a mouth" (I have a mouth). "A
ghost can't whistle" (I'm not a ghost). "Who keeps me last?" But
this process is relieved when the child is caught up and absorbed
into a nature of auditory presences: "God, give me a near. I hear
flowers. . . . Hello happy hands." Only at such times are the

hands, the members of self-definition which reach out to life, happy.

The child's fall from psychic innocence comes with the death of the father. For the first time the mind, once so wonderfully intimate and conversant with its world, has to confront cold abstraction—"How high is have?" "Nowhere is out." "Have I come to always?" The intrusion of concept severs the participation mystique in which the child is so beautifully caught up into life. Now, with the primordial snake awake at the core of consciousness, the child's response is aggressive: "I'll be a bite. You be a wink./Sing the snake to sleep." It is life in the figure of the father which has betrayed the child by the withdrawal of love. Therefore the child rejects all paternity: "Maybe God has a house./But not here." That his arrogance is defensive is poignantly emphasized: "Don't tell my hands." The child's sense of integrity of self has been shattered, and fragmentation, the disunion of self and body, has begun. The potential world of security "Where Knock Is Open Wide" is now irrevocably lost.[7]

Roethke never succumbs to romantic and nostalgic notions of childhood. His child—no pre-lapsarian—is cruel, uncompromising, and often arrogantly unjust. But he does posit at the core of human personality a contrary intuition toward otherness, a hunger for relation, ultimately a metaphysical instinct of human nature to extend beyond the self. This idea was clearly confirmed in his intense reading of Traherne's *Centuries*. In the poem "I Need, I Need" this instinct awakens in the child a vague experience of transcendent love: [8]

> Stop the larks. Can I have my heart back?
> Today I saw a beard in a cloud.

7. For an amplified reading of this poem see Malkoff, *Theodore Roethke,* pp. 70–78. I would however disagree with Malkoff's too explicitly Freudian emphasis which sees the child's guilt only in terms of the traditional "Oedipal conflict," involving desire for one parent and hostility toward the other, rather than in terms of a complex process of introjection of the despair and hostility occasioned by the father's death.

8. The title echoes Blake's "I Want! I Want!" from the ninth design of "For the Sexes: The Gates of Paradise," *The Poetry and Prose of William Blake,* p. 261. The designs trace life from childhood to age and death.

> The ground cried my name:
> Good-bye for being wrong.
> Love helps the sun.
> But not enough.
>
> [*C.P.*, p. 76]

Maturation inevitably corrodes this instinct by severing the child's intimacy with nature. Even here the child responds with a vague sense of guilt because he has already denied the sacramentalism of nature: "Maybe God Has a house./But not here" (*C.P.*, p. 74). Consciousness only furthers this severance: "Hardly any old angels around any more." Plaintively the child asks: "Whisper me over,/Why don't you, begonia" (*C.P.*, p. 74). "The worm has moved away" (*C.P.*, p. 73).

The child comes fully to consciousness only with the wakening of sexual desire which begins the harrowing drama of guilt and self-doubt.[9] Initially the sexual impulse is felt to be natural and life-directive. With the first awakening of desire in "I Need, I Need" the child delights in the happy delirium of touch, the entrance to mutuality, and cries his new-found joy: "I know another fire./Has roots." Even "Bring the Day!"[10] begins with a nonchalant ditty of fertilization: "Bees and lilies there were." The first masturbatory experience is frightening but ecstatic: "I'm a biscuit. I'm melted already./The white weather hates me. . . ." "The herrings are awake./What's all the singing between?" (*C.P.*, p. 77). The child feels the oracular voice of nature on his side: "The grass says what the wind says:/Begin with the rock;/End with water." His own sexual fluids unite him metaphorically and actually to the whole of nature, wherein he finds a beautifully simple self-justification:

> A swan needs a pond.
> The worm and the rose

---

9. C. G. Jung, "The Stages of Life," in *Modern Man in Search of a Soul*, pp. 113–14. Jung indicates that full consciousness comes only with the awakening of sexuality.

10. The title is taken from "The Excursion," IV: 115, *The Poetical Works of William Wordsworth*, vol. 5, ed. Ernest de Selincourt and Helen Darbishire, p. 113. The line records a moment of visionary intensity.

Both love
Rain.
[*C.P.,* p. 78]

But such assurances do not last long. In "Give Way, Ye Gates" Roethke describes how natural timidity and repression drive the innocent vision into the subconscious, perverting sexual energy and creating a furnace of frustrated desire beneath consciousness.[11] Desire can be sublimated for a time in the fantastical images of the dream world, but against this wars the ravenous sexual need.

A detailed examination of "Give Way, Ye Gates" is not out of place since this poem records the central climax of the first half of the sequence. The poem opens with a rhapsody to the phallus, a common motif from fairy tale, in which the boy delights in his potency:

> Such music in a skin!
> A bird sings in the bush of your bones.
> Tufty, the water's loose.
> Bring me a finger.

The address changes to cat and moon, images of the dream-lover who is the object of the boy's need:

> And you, cat after great milk and vasty fishes,
> A moon loosened from a stag's eye,
> Twiced me nicely,—
> In the green of my sleep,
> In the green.
> [*C.P.,* p. 79]

Blake said: "Out of our awakening love we create amorous images." Jung defined these images as the projections of the anima, lures by which the soul seduces matter into life which would rather follow the impulse to quiescence.[12] Both insights are

11. The title is taken from Robert Herrick, "The Wassaile," *The Poetical Works of Robert Herrick,* ed. L. C. Martin, p. 178. The poem's theme is the deprivation of the senses through fear. It ends with an appeal to enter into and celebrate the world of fertility and fecundity.

12. Jung, *Integration of Personality,* pp. 75–76. The anima as Jung defines it implies the soul, but not in the dogmatic sense; rather in the sense of the living, a priori element

ultimately the same. The female lover is the fascinating and luminous expression of the soul's longing for fulfillment. Indeed, in Roethke's poem "The Long Alley," the cat is offered as an image for the soul or true self with which the poet longs to unite.

The second stanza begins with a prayer for aid and companionship, to Nature: "Mother of blue and the many changes of hay" and then a return to the dream image, "May I look too, loved eye?" The two figures are conflated, emphasizing the archetypal nature of the vision. When the child insists: "I'll risk the winter for you," we see that desire is a life-directive impulse—he won't hibernate; he'll stay out.

The mood of the second stanza changes as the boy again addresses the phallus:

> You tree beginning to know,
> You whisper of kidneys,
> We'll swinge the instant!—
> With jots and jogs and cinders on the floor:
> The sea will be there, the great squashy shadows,
> Biting themselves perhaps;
>
> [*C.P.*, p. 79]

Now the horrifying aridity of sexual frustration becomes the dominant motif. The dream visions are nightmare phantoms of reflexive sexuality, and the sexual need, repressed and unsatisfied, a ghost dead in a wall. The ghost awakens the memory of the dead father censuring the onanistic act. In a later poem the boy will say: "I'll feed the ghost alone./Father, forgive my hands" (*C.P.*, p. 85). The gates of the title are clearly symbols for the repressive barriers of guilt that prevent the vital, sexual evolution of the spirit, trapping it in onanistic self-absorption. The danger is that the individual's whole creative being, if it succumbs to sexual repressions, will remain embryonic, shrouded in the darkness of dream and private fantasy.

The poem ends with a horrifying repudiation of onanism: "The dead crow dries on a pole . . . Who stands in a hole/Never

---

in man, the life behind consciousness that cannot be completely integrated with it, but from which, on the contrary, consciousness arises.

spills." The familiar figure of Onan, punished for wasting his seed, linked here with voracious life, becomes a symbol for all refusal to embrace life.[13] The poem offers no solution, merely a quiescent waiting, with the consolation:

> The deep stream remembers:
> Once I was a pond.
> What slides away
> Provides.
> [*C.P.,* p. 80]

Again we return to the wisdom of water. It becomes clear that Roethke uses water to image the libidinous flow and ebb of the creative life current at the core of being. Here he insists that, to the mind submerged in the welter of unconscious processes, the memory of a past clearness and lucidity becomes a source of assurance. In such a way, the past provides.

In the later poems, the drama of guilt and frustration is only intensified. Roethke conveys this by the adolescent's radical reversals from ecstasy to self-doubt (indicated by changes in stanzaic indention) that betray an essential instability at the core of self. In "Sensibility! O La!" as the title anticipates, the image of the loved one is extended into a naïve version of the divine muse herself, "A true zephyr-haunted woodie," a Venus from the waves speaking to the awakening sensibility: "Thy soft albino gaze/Spoke to my spirit" (*C.P.,* p. 81). But a quick depression of mood undermines this early confidence and the spell is broken. It seems that a new tension has arisen to shatter the vision, emblematically expressed: "Can a cat milk a hen?" Roethke occasionally uses hen or hen house to refer to the unconscious (*S.L.,* p. 116; *S.P.,* p. 89). The potential poet, wakening to sensibility, may be asking if he will ever milk the core of his own being.

We begin to see more clearly that the dialectic of Roethke's sequence is one familiar from Blake. Withdrawal into sexual fear is a refusal to embrace the creative potential of being. The innocent acceptance of sexuality is a necessary preliminary to the recovery of

---

13. Roethke refers to Onan's folly (*S.L.,* p. 147).

innocent vision. Thus it is consistent that section 3 of "Sensibility! O La!" plays out the dramatic conflict between reflexive and potent sexuality. The section is addressed to "You all-of-a-sudden gods," a primitive description of the state of onanistic ecstasy. The boy complains to them, "There's a ghost loose in the long grass!" He has only succeeded in awakening the phantom of his guilt and frustration, and the memory of the censuring father. The self-absorption is terrifying. An Adam, the boy is alone with his ribs, his incipient desire trapped in the cave of the unconscious. Defiantly he confronts his own guilt and hatred of the sexual:

> You've seen me, prince of stinks,
> Naked and entire,
> Exalted? Yes,—
> By the lifting of the tail of a neighbor's cat,
> Or that old harpy secreting toads in her portmanteau.
> [*C.P.*, p. 82]

Renewed by defiance, the boy seeks to escape his solipsism: "Mamma! Put on your dark hood:"—the sorrowful headgear for the long arduous journey out of the self. The mother is invoked as a protective, sustaining spirit, arising out of the unconscious as such images always rise to the immature mind thrown back on itself. The boy is caught on the verge of immanent revelation: "The light turns." Like a mythic hero, he sets out into life, "the sun under my arm," insisting that his quest out of the dark world of dreams has been successful: "I insist! I am."

"O Lull Me, Lull Me" repeats the pattern of oscillation but ends with a willful acceptance of the dream:

> A wish! A wish!
> O lovely chink, O white
> Way to another grace!—
> I see my heart in the seed;
> I breathe into a dream,
> And the ground cries.
> [*C.P.*, p. 83]

The affirmation of desire is a "white way to another grace," the other becoming a means to embrace the core of one's own sexual

being. The lost son is finally prepared for initiation: "I'm all ready
to whistle;/I'm more than when I was born" (C.P., p. 84). But
more is implied in the image of the lover. The anima is the projection of the soul's striving for the idealizing, transforming power of
love. Through acceptance of this image, the transition is made
from infantile fear, binding and tormenting in its frustration, to a
love that can more truly exercise and fulfill the many-sided aspirations of the spirit. This first part of the sequence ends with an ecstatic overture to nature echoing the delight of William Strode's
poem "In Commendation of Musick": "O lull mee, lull mee,
charming ayre,/My senses rock with wonder sweete!" [14]

It is helpful to remember that while Roethke was writing the
Praise to the End! sequence, he was also working on some of
the poems for his children's volume *I Am! Says the Lamb.* In
fact the title poem is based on the nursery rhyme:

> *Dear Sensibility,* Oh la!
> I heard a little lamb cry, baa!
> Says I, "So you've lost your Mamma?"
>
> The Little lamb, as I said so
> Frisking about the field did go,
> And, frisking, trod upon my toe. [15]

Problems like the loss of serenity seem to be of the order of sensibility, not a part of the nonchalance of the animal world. At least,
this is how Roethke reinterprets the poem.

> The Lamb just says, I AM!
> He frisks and whisks, *He* can.
> He jumps all over. Who
> Are *you?* You're jumping too!
> [C.P., p. 182]

Existence is not quite so simple for the human being who has lost
the wisdom of innocence through consciousness, the ability to
embrace life without having to know it. Even the child does not

14. *The Poetical Works of William Strode*, ed. B. Dobell, p. 2.
15. *The Annotated Mother Goose*, ed. W. S. Baring-Gould and C. Baring-Gould, p.
301.

consistently achieve such self-transcendence, except in nature, when he is marvelously caught up into life. And these moments recede under the impact of full consciousness. Guilt and fear of sexuality initiate a withdrawal from nature that must be impeded if the wisdom of innocence is to be recovered.

The last four poems of the *Praise to the End!* sequence are meant to carry the poet through to a new wholeness, a final resolution. They are written from the perspective of a maturer mind coursing back over past memories and dreams in quest of spiritual identity. In his notebooks Roethke outlined the primitive dialectical theme which can be seen to be their premise: a distinction between "Eros," as "embracer of life," and "Narcissus," as "rejector of life" (Notebooks, Reel 13, no. 185). The poems are dramatic expressions of the antagonism between these two forces. Onanism is the primary symbol for the narcissistic principle. The impulse to onanism implies a violation of the natural order by a refusal of life, a soul- and body-destroying breach with the necessary principle of love. The acceptance of Eros, on the contrary, implies a willing celebration of life.[16] The sexual metaphors would seem to be a way of objectifying the impulse to withdrawal, activated by anxiety and guilt, which is one of the principle temptations confronting the protagonist. To this is associated the yearning for a world of essences, for the imperishable and uncorruptible, which is really a perverse longing to be released from the demands of nature. Wholeness and health can only be achieved by participation in the actual and verifiably human.

Roethke always insisted that he read little psychology. From his notebooks, it is clear that this was a subterfuge. But his poems never follow abstract psychological formulas. They are intuitive investigations into what was obviously a profoundly personal crisis in the evolution of the sexual self, shaping his general vision. For throughout his poetry we find a vision of life, and of the establish-

16. Roethke's antithesis seems to be a poetic counterpart to the Freudian theory of the antagonism between the life and death principles, implying a human drive which makes of death a final and desired goal. Roethke calls this latter narcissism which, to him, is a negative, life-denying impulse to self-absorption, implying a refusal of life. See Freud's "Mourning and Melancholia," *Complete Psychological Works*, 14: 237–59.

ment of personal identity, as involving short critical periods where the process of growth or change converts a previous cycle of protection into one of confinement, activating a struggle between antagonistic desires for dependence and release. The first such revolution is a purely biological one—the change at birth when the child is forced from the benign protection of the womb, which has become a malignant circle of confinement, into a world of aggression and differentiation, a change that Roethke dramatizes in "Where Knock Is Open Wide." Adolescence is another such crisis, activating opposite impulses to withdrawal and initiation, the physical alteration demanding a corresponding change in personal structures of value and meaning. In the process of maturation, there are many other jolts of a less purely biological nature; for Roethke there is especially the one pivotal crisis, the death of the father, which precipitates a complex of fear and guilt impeding the son from an essential assertion of independent identity. The tensions which these crises create between impulses to regression and participation, initiation and flight, seemed to provide the archetypal pattern of his experience.[17] There is no more typical pair of images in his work than the retreat of the snail into its shell, and the free flight of the bird before water, the symbol of unimpeded movement. Resolution between these antagonistic impulses, and consequent initiation into life, comes in his poetry only with the assurance of spiritual identity that can stem the fear of dissolution aroused by the memory of the dead father. But spiritual self-hood was something he had to achieve and re-achieve continually. He called himself a perpetual beginner, making the quest for rebirth through the death of the old self the central preoccupation of his entire work.

"Praise to the End!" is the classic enactment of this struggle between impulses to regression and initiation, fear and love. It begins with an onanistic dance familiar from fairytale in the figure

17. My analysis of this pattern is derived from Burke, "Freud and the Analysis of Poetry," pp. 122–23. Burke was Roethke's intimate friend and advisor during the period when his two major sequences were written and it is highly probable that Roethke found the psychological pattern for personal tensions between regression and initiation through him.

of Bumpkin or Tom-of-the-thumb. The complaint of the poem is by now an old theme—the macabre pettiness of conception, the indignity of incarnation. As expected, the father bears the brunt of the son's indignation. The speaker sings to the phallus:

> My dearest dear my fairest fair,
> Your father tossed a cat in air,
> Though neither you nor I was there,—
> What footie does is final.
>
> [*C.P.*, p. 86]

The old self-detestation and hatred of organic life floods in to overwhelm the self into retreat: "I've been asleep in a bower of dead skin . . . I can't stay here." Two flashbacks from childhood follow, one seemingly a remembrance of catastrophe, probably the father's death; the other the protagonist's dream of his own death and release from desire. Thoughts of eternity comes as fantasies of regression which resolve into a euphoric death-wish: "This grave has an ear." The onanistic ecstasy of the next section is an attempt to escape reality entirely:

> I know the back-stream's joy, and the stone's eternal pulseless longing.
>
> . . . .
>
> Many astounds before, I lost my identity to a pebble; . . .
>
> Wherefore, O birds and small fish, surround me.
> Lave me, ultimate waters.
> The dark showed me a face.
> My ghosts are all gay.
> The light becomes me.
>
> [*C.P.*, p. 88]

In his commentary, Roethke defined this passage as an experience of sublimation—onanistic release leading to a kind of self-suicide, a desire for oblivion in the "annihilation" of ecstasy (*S.P.*, p. 40). What distinguishes this ecstatic experience from other seemingly similar ones is that the euphoric ride leads to dissociation of per-

sonality and a loss of identity which is not followed by reintegration. The protagonist ends alone, isolated from all that is human.
The poem is clearly a dramatization of the regressive instinct for
withdrawal that Roethke knew intimately, a craving for death as a
deep organic need for release when the life currents feel hemmed
and split.

If "Praise to the End!" concludes in an impasse, the other three
poems turn to life, and love, to the verifiable and the actual for a
solution to the dilemma of spiritual identity. In "Unfold! Unfold!" Roethke records the regressive journey into the self: [18]

> I was far back, farther than anybody else.
> On the jackpine plains I hunted the bird nobody knows;
> Fishing, I caught myself behind the ears.
>
> . . . .
>
> I met a collector of string, a shepherd of slow forms.
> My mission became the salvation of minnows.
>   [*C.P.*, pp. 89–90]

In Roethke's work, minnows are part of the minimal life still on
the threshold of beginnings, the extremity of instinct that corresponds to the darting multitudinous life of the mind beneath the
rational. Salvation depends upon contact with this part of the self.
The implication is that the unconscious, if it harbors desperate
fears and guilts, nevertheless will unleash natural, redirective impulses to life. It should not surprise that penetration to the unconscious recovers the transcendental powers of the self. Roethke, following Jung, would insist unequivocally that the psyche, in its
deepest reaches, participates in a form of existence beyond space
and time.[19] Nature is now discovered to be symbolic:

18. The title is taken from Henry Vaughan, "The Revival," *The Complete Poetry of
Henry Vaughan*, ed. French Fogle, p. 419—the last lines of which are revealing: "Un-
fold, unfold! take in His light . . . /And here in *dust* and *dirt*, O here/ The *Lilies* of
His love appear!"

19. Jung, *Two Essays on Analytical Psychology*, in *The Collected Works*, vol. 7, trans.
R. F. C. Hull, p. 202. See also *Psychology and Religion*, the title of which appears in
Roethke's notebooks.

Sing, sing, you symbols! All simple creatures,
All small shapes, willow-shy,
In the obscure haze, sing!

A light song comes from the leaves.
A slow sigh says yes. And light sighs;
A low voice, summer-sad.
Is it you, cold father? Father,
For whom the minnows sang?

A house for wisdom; a field for revelation.
Speak to the stones, and the stars answer.
At first the visible obscures:
Go where light is.

[*C.P.*, p. 90]

It has been advanced that Roethke's notion of nature as symbolic bears on the Swedenborgian theory of correspondences, but it is improbable that he had read either Swedenborg or Boehme by 1952.[20] Rather, he derived a personal version of the theory from Blake and Yeats. While he rejected the neo-Platonic belief in explicit correspondence—that every physical entity corresponds to a spiritual essence (an idea that tempted Yeats and Blake into occult philosophy in search of analogy), he gave the theory psychological ramifications. He affirmed a profound correspondence between mind and nature offering primitive life as a precise notation for the interior workings within the subworld of the unconscious. This was more than a literary convention; it was an expression of the primitive, animistic cast of his mind. He regarded nature as sacramental. In moments of intensity natural objects could sound deep responses within the individual, convincing of a coinherence of interior being and exterior world in a relation which he called worshipful. In one instance he wrote: "If the dead can come to our aid in a quest for identity, so can the living, . . . including the sub-

20. See Malkoff, *Theodore Roethke,* pp. 101–3. None of the works of these philosophers are mentioned in Roethke's early notebooks. It is always dangerous to tie him too closely to philosophical sources at this early date when his influences are largely from literature, folklore, mythology, and psychology.

human. This is not so much a naïve as a primitive attitude: animistic maybe. . . . Everything that lives is holy" (*S.P.*, p. 24). Roethke's description of nature as symbolic is less a philosophical conception than an animistic belief in a single creative propulsive energy, the soul of things, animating all living matter, including the human and subhuman in its embrace. In the stanza in question, he is asking, simply, delicately, whether the directive instinct at the core of his being, which is one with the impulse which moves all nature, is a cry for the father, the ultimate transcendent Father as creative progenitor. When he writes, "At first the visible obscures:/Go where light is," it is simply because "The eye perishes in the small vision." A greater comprehensive vision can bring life to a cosmic unity: "Speak to the stones, and the stars answer." In this directive lies a program of recovery: "I'll seek my own meekness./What grace I have is enough" (*C.P.*, p. 91). To his aid come the dead, the terror of their plight goading him on to discovery:

> In their harsh thickets
> The dead thrash.
> They help.
> [*C.P.*, p. 91]

The next poem "I Cry, Love! Love!" [21] is the most affirmative poem of the sequence, the cry of love coming through the muse of William Blake, one of the ancestral dead to whom Roethke has appealed: "I proclaim once more a condition of joy./Walk into the wind, willie!" (*C.P.*, p. 92). His new-found assurance comes from a readjustment of personal vision, allowing him to reject reason, which searches after metaphysical assurances, in favor of intuitive vision:

> Reason? That dreary shed, that hutch for grubby schoolboys!
> The hedgewren's song says something else.
> [*C.P.*, p. 92]

21. This title comes from "Visions of the Daughters of Albion," *The Poetry and Prose of William Blake*, p. 49. This title was initially intended to be the title of the whole sequence, indicating that the movement into life and love is its primary concern.

It says that there is another order of existence lived by the animal but also by the child—a condition of unity and simplicity in which they seem caught up in something larger than themselves. From such moments comes a conviction of the essential unity of all existence. The instinctive tie to the evolutionary chain, so repellent in "River Incident," becomes the assurance of verifiable life: "Hello, thingy spirit." The poem ends with an invocation of the "Other," the "sweetness I cannot touch," which brings an intuitive assurance of the a priori indivisibility of body and soul in an image from prenativity:

> Who untied the tree? I remember now.
> We met in a nest. Before I lived.
> The dark hair sighed.
> We never enter
> Alone.
>
> [*C.P.*, p. 93]

The last poem "O, Thou Opening, O" is offered as a kind of coda or synopsis of the progress that the poet feels has been made in the sequence as a whole.[22] It begins with the old hatred of the body: "I'm a draft sleeping by a stick," and the quest for meaning: "Dazzle me, dizzy aphorist./Fling me a precept" (*C.P.*, p. 97). The need to move forward is paramount: "A true mole wanders like a worm." The impediment is again the human propensity for self-delusion. The Lost Son castigates himself:

> And now are we to have that pelludious Jesus-shimmer
> over all things, the animal's candid gaze . . .
> I'm tired of all that, Bag-Foot. I can hear small angels
> anytime. Who cares about the dance of dead underwear, or
> the sad waltz of paper bags? Who ever said God sang in

---

22. In two previous volumes, *The Waking: Poems 1933–1953* and *Words for the Wind*, this entire poem is italicized. Only the posthumous *Collected Poems* omits this. Roethke usually used italics to isolate a coda or summary statement as in "The Swan," and this seems his intention here. "O, Thou Opening, O" was added to the sequence almost as an afterthought in *The Waking* in 1953. Two other poems were written in this style but wisely excluded from the sequence: "The Song," *Botteghe Oscure*, 8 (Fall 1951): 282–83, and "The Changeling," *Botteghe Oscure*, 10 (Fall 1952): 239–41; rpt. in *Collected Poems*, pp. 258–61.

your fat shape? . . . And don't be thinking you're simplicity's
sweet thing, either. A leaf could drag you.

[*C.P.*, p. 98]

There is an element of pose and of vanity in even the most rigorous attempts to face the self. But close to nature, humility is
endless: "Stand by a slow stream:/Hear the sigh of what is." Listening in delight to creation, the Lost Son learns that "The dark
has its own light./A son has many fathers" (*C.P.*, p. 98). He
embraces his own sexuality, his chance to "be a body lighted with
love." Rejecting the regressive tendencies of the sequence, he
breaks through to the outside world, dreaming of "be." Though in
many ways this is the least rhythmically successful poem of the
sequence, its diminishing code is a moving climax:

> Going is knowing.
> I see; I seek;
> I'm near.
> Be true,
> Skin.
> [*C.P.*, p. 99]

The revelation that is near is described in the poem "The Light
Breather," which Roethke called the epilogue to the sequence.
Once he had felt that the spirit was defiled by life, that it became
a "foulness, a disgusting thing from which we should be delivered," and that the only solution was to keep the spirit spare
through a saving rage. Through the harrowing process of psychic
purgation, he has come to see that the spirit "can grow gracefully
and beautifully like a tendril, like a flower" (*S.P.*, pp. 21–22).

> The spirit moves,
> Yet stays:
> Stirs as a blossom stirs,
> Still wet from its bud-sheath,
> Slowly unfolding,
> Turning in the light with its tendrils;
> Plays as a minnow plays,
> Tethered to a limp weed, swinging,
> Tail around, nosing in and out of the current,

Its shadows loose, a watery finger;
Moves, like a snail,
Still inward,
Taking and embracing its surroundings,
Never wishing itself away,
Unafraid of what it is,
A music in a hood,
A small thing,
Singing.

[*C.P.*, p. 101]

In "Unfold! Unfold!" Roethke had said, "My mission became the salvation of minnows." Here, the soul is a minnow "Tethered to a limp weed, swinging/Tail around, nosing in and out of the current." But the limp weed is no longer an impediment; it is the medium for unity of being, an indispensable part of the soul's movement. In the greenhouse sequence, Roethke had wished to escape the body, that "animal on all fours." Therefore he had bifurcated reality into the world of rank weeds beneath the benches and the world above, where flowers opened into the "crisp hyacinthine coolness of eternity." Here the process of change, including dissolution, becomes the very life of being; you take from what is not yourself and you participate in what changes you. Changing, you share in the creative life of the universe: "Great Nature has another thing to do/To you and me" (*C.P.*, p. 108). He once wrote in his notebook, "In the very real and final sense, don't *know* anything." [23] Instead, think by feeling, what is there to know? The antagonism is age-old: Cogitation versus Sensibility. Roethke placed his faith in the latter, believing that in moments of deep emotion more meaning adheres than in years of speculation. And he liked to quote Marianne Moore for authority: "Once we feel deeply, we begin to behave" (*S.P.*, p. 26).

The Lost Son and *Praise to the End!* were greeted with enthusiasm when they were published in 1948 and 1951. As unique as they were, they were yet part of a tradition of experiment. Initially they

23. Wagoner, ed., *Straw for the Fire*, p. 21.

were interpreted as a poetic transcription of the stream of consciousness technique of Joyce and Faulkner. Certainly this held true for the early *Praise to the End!* poems, recording the evolution of consciousness of a very young child. In fact, "Where Knock Is Open Wide" borrowed its central motifs of "sleep-song" and "fish" directly from *A Portrait of the Artist as a Young Man* and *As I Lay Dying.* But it soon became clear that in the earlier *Lost Son* poems, as well as in the later poems of the *Praise to the End!* sequence, Roethke was less interested in a literal transcription of the processes of consciousness and more in the welter of psychic processes at the infinitely deeper level of fantastic logic that has been called primary thinking and that is reached by the mind on the extreme edge of psychic distress. One might better call his technique the stream of subconsciousness deriving its motifs from myth and folklore. Perhaps his own phrase is best. The poems speak in the "coarse short-hand of the subliminal depths" (*C.P.,* p. 170). One might claim for Roethke Beckett's praise of Joyce: he is a "biologist" of words, seeking to desophisticate the language by returning the mind to its more primitive patterns. A comparison might be made to *Finnegans Wake* with the reservation that Joyce is much more of a verbal alchemist. Roethke was content to turn to folk tale and nursery rhyme to replenish his language.

He was steeped in Russian, English, and German myth, fairy tale, and nursery rhyme. Not only are his poems full of their primitive protagonists—cats, rats, Tufty, Bumpkin, Wee Willie Winkie, Algy, ducks, snakes, witches—but they also prove the source of many of his formal techniques. As in myth, the natural world of his poems is one of mystical presences, a place of unknown terrors and hidden demons, where objects have become answering subjects and the dead are aggressive antagonists. In part, as Kenneth Burke has noted in his essay "Vegetal Radicalism," such an atmosphere is created by verbal contrivance. He continually applies communicative verbs to natural objects:

> The weeds whined,
> The snakes cried,

> The cows and briars
> Said to me: Die.
>   [*C.P.*, p. 55]

> Snail, snail, glister me forward,
> Bird, soft-sigh me home.
> Worm be with me.
>   [*C.P.*, p. 53]

The verbal patterns are borrowed from familiar nursery rhymes: "Snail, snail, comes out of your house," but Roethke turns to them for more than their rhythmic neatness. The appeals to nature are meant to be taken literally. He believed in a primitive kind of animism; even the material world is articulate with meaning:

> Dark hollows said, lee to the wind,
> The moon said, back of an eel,
> The salt said, look by the sea,
> Your tears are not enough praise,
> You will find no comfort here,
> In the kingdom of bang and blab.
>   [*C.P.*, p. 54]

Again in one sense this is a linguistic riddle of reflexivity to turn the mind inward. Yet it is also a statement about the natural world, insisting that there is a language in which nature speaks to human beings, the key to which the protagonist has lost by a sacriligious denial of nature's beneficence. Roethke's notebooks indicate that he may have augmented his knowledge of primitive thought through marginal reading in anthropology. One source was Levy-Bruhl's popular *The Soul of the Primitive.* Levy-Bruhl defines animism:

To the mind of the primitive there is, existent and permeating, on earth, in the air and in water, in all the diverse forms assumed by persons and objects, one and the same essential reality . . .

Like air, wind, it could manifest its presence. It was the soul of things . . . a living principle, that which enables everything to exist as we know it, yet also distinct from things, too, which exist by it.[24]

24. Lucien Levy-Bruhl, *The "Soul" of the Primitive,* trans. Lilian A. Clare, p. 17.

Thus in the primitive world nature is continuously animated, and personalized, so that the individual lives in a mystique of participation. This tendency to anthropomorphism is probably the cardinal rule of mythology, and Roethke uses it continually. But when he fails to particularize nature, the technique can slip into formula:

> The wasp waits.
> 　　　　The edge cannot eat the center.
> The grape glistens.
>
> 　　　　　　　　[*C.P.*, p. 66]

When natural image is sacrificed to the emblematic psychic equation, the effect is thin.

Roethke borrows many of the symbols of the *Praise to the End!* sequence from the fairy-tale and nursery rhyme tradition. Most central is his division of his world into maternal and paternal principles. At the basis of this vision of life is the Mother, the warm moist subliminal world of the womb that sponsors all being, in one aspect appealed to for sustenance, in another dreaded as the sucking bog. Over against this is the Father, the external principle of light, the bringer of order which can be both rewarding and punitive. The fairy lover, a "zephyr-haunted woodie," is a dream image, the numinous expression of the soul's longing. Her opposite is the witch, the hostile power of the unconscious associated with sexuality and guilt, who threatens carnal metamorphosis: "I've been asleep in a bower of dead skin./It's a piece of a prince I ate" (*C.P.*, p. 86). Jung points out that in mythology, psychic figures are always duplex, with a positive and negative aspect, which only emphasizes the authenticity of Roethke's personal symbolism.[25]

Roethke has an elaborate symbolism for the antagonism of body and soul, one of his central preoccupations. The spirit is often a bird, while the body is a tree: "O small bird wakening,/Light as a hand among blossoms" (*C.P.*, p. 78). "Is he a bird or a tree?" (*C.P.*, p. 64). Sometimes the bird represents an ephemeral spiri-

25. C. G. Jung and C. Kerenyi, *Essays on a Science of Mythology: The Myths of the Divine Child and the Divine Maiden,* trans. R. F. C. Hull, pp. 75–76.

tual self which the protagonist is seeking: "On the jackpine plains
I hunted the bird nobody knows" (*C.P.*, p. 89). Again the self can
be purely corporeal, without spiritual existence: "A dead mouth
sings under an old tree" (*C.P.*, p. 59). Roethke has other ways of
expressing the dichotomy of body and soul which are nuances on
this theme: "I'm a draft sleeping by a stick" (*C.P.*, p. 97). "The
soul resides in the horse barn" (*C.P.*, p. 59). Usually the body is
associated with the inert: stalk, silt, cinders. Sometimes it is the
phallus itself that is addressed as tree or stalk: "The stalk still
sways" (*C.P.*, p. 56). Traditional to folk tale, the child in the
womb is emblematically a fish: "Fish me out/Please" (*C.P.*,
p. 72). By extension, the father in his procreative role is also a
fish. The childish desire giving rise to onanistic activity borrows
from this image: "The herrings are awake" (*C.P.*, p. 77), or "I've
played with the fishes/Among the unwrinkling ferns/In the wake
of a ship of wind" (*C.P.*, p. 80). Fishing can also mean plunging
into the unconscious depths in search of minnows. In their mi-
nuteness, the minnows represent the extremity of instinct that
must be integrated with consciousness. The most difficult symbol
in Roethke's poems is the stone. In primitive mythology, stones
are endowed with animistic powers. They are the bones of the soil,
the stasis of the earth as the skeleton is of the body.[26] Roethke
drew on this equation; he always uses stones in his poetry to herald
moments of mystical revelation: "Speak to the stones and the stars
answer" (*C.P.*, p. 90).

The only problem with Roethke's symbolism is the danger of
reductivity—sometimes it can become merely a grammar of sub-
stitution:

> This frog's had another fall.
> The old stalk still has a pulse;
> I've crept from a cry.
> The holy root wags the tail of a hill;
>   [*C.P.*, p. 99]

At other times it stretches even intuitive comprehension:

26. Levy-Bruhl, *"Soul" of the Primitive*, p. 27.

Loo, loo, said the sulphurous water,
There's no filth on a plateau of cinders.
This smoke's from the glory of God.
                    [*C.P.,* p. 59]

Though a connection is certainly implied through "sulphurous," "cinders," and "smoke," one cannot be certain of the holocaust represented. One can only assume from the context of the lines, and from Roethke's symbolism elsewhere, that a vindication of the body is somehow in progress. The problem is that associations have descended to an entirely private level and, because the original tenor of the metaphor has been suppressed, the reader has no possible way to understand its meaning.

Roethke's poems are verbally, as well as psychologically, regressive. He is after an emblematic, aboriginal language in which objects and emotions are confounded in a kind of surreality. By way of analogy, one can think of Wallace Stevens' passion to see the sun in its first idea, to put the world in parentheses so that at last it becomes immediate sensuous experience, the world as it first appeared to Adam before he began naming it. Roethke's notion of decreation is much more psychological and much less sophisticated. His desire is to recover the primitive analogical mode of thinking, a mythopoeic confrontation of the world in which abstraction has no place. Evanescent psychic happenings could then be experienced and expressed in concrete sensuous images with all the inevitable clarity of primitive inarticulation.

The notebooks of this period are filled with linguistic experiments. In an attempt to simplify his language, Roethke writes continually, phrase after phrase, until an elemental tone begins to enter his work—usually obtained by concrete words, invocations, and effects of synaesthesia. He writes long lists of botanical plants and vegetal imagery, and cultivates a kind of pun logic, dependent on principles of personification: "In a maze of hedges" becomes "an amaze of hedges"; "Bonfire"—"bone fire"; "Will the steps change"—"in the steps of change." He condenses continually, always with a view to animating his images. "A snail's glister sighing me forward" becomes "Snail, snail, glister me forward."

Nouns are used as verbs where possible, and active verbs are replaced by ones of reciprocity: "The steam kissed the leaves awake"; "I leaned my ear into the elemental." All these techniques are a concerted drive to recover what psychologists call the primary thought processes characteristic of the child, the primitive, and the sophisticated mind in states of mental intensity or stress, when the logical or secondary thought processes are weakened or overpowered.

The quality Roethke values most at this stage is concrete immediacy. Consequently he turns continually to natural imagery to imply mental states. But his technique is unique. To explain it one might say that the tenor and vehicle of metaphor are deliberately separated, and the reader must discover the two coordinates for himself. For instance, "The dark flows on itself" (*C.P.*, p. 59), is meant to conjure up the terrifying state of introversion. Only the reflexive or regressive movement of the "flowing" dark is isolated. Context, the sequence of images which surround the line, determines its association to psychic tension. In the line "An old scow bumps over black rocks" (*C.P.*, p. 64), only the sensation of scraping rock bottom is offered. But juxtaposition, the mainspring of the technique, soon makes it clear that this is one of a sequence of images describing a mental state. The effect is to throw the reader back continually on his own intuitive resources. Often he is assisted by the fact that Roethke draws his associations from folklore or American slang, as in the above instance where "scraping rock-bottom" is a familiar expression. A similar dependence on folk literature is clear in the lines:

> The ear hears only in low places.
> [*C.P.*, p. 59]

> Those close to the Ground
> —Only stay out of the Wind.
> [*C.P.*, p. 97]

> A low mouth laps water.
> [*C.P.*, p. 64]

Lowness comes to imply a state of innocence, a closeness to nature. The technique is borrowed from proverbs where an abstraction is always rendered concrete in action.

Roethke will often imply the interior state of his protagonist only indirectly by offering it projected in naturalistic image. "Will the sea give the wind suck?" (*C.P.*, p. 64), is a desperate appeal for relationship. The technique is obviously borrowed from biblical metaphor: "Can the rush grow up without mire? can the flag grow without water" (Job 8:11). In such cases the images stand by themselves and the reader must determine the implicit subjective associations. Sometimes, however, natural images are taken over wholesale for subjective requirements. Thus the line: "A dry cry comes from my own desert" (*C.P.*, p. 93). Moods are often conveyed succinctly through appeal to the appropriate animal without need for further amplification. The protagonist is alternately a rat, frog, mouse, dog, and serpent. Sometimes the analogy intended is clear only after repeated references, as with the image of wasps, "great lords of sting," which one discovers most often represent the rational processes. The rewards of such concision are obvious: value judgments are conveyed impressionistically. By often appealing to words in their generic character, Roethke achieves an interesting effect of universality. Thus the phrase "Mother me out of here" (*C.P.*, p. 64) using "mother" as a verb immediately calls up the archetypal protector. The effect is similar with "Rub me in father and mother" (*C.P.*, p. 56) so that relationship is reduced to instinctive drives.

Denis Donoghue has pointed out one of the pitfalls of these techniques. As he explains, Roethke's concretions have a strangely abstracted air. Things become emblems before they become themselves. "Often everything is eliminated from nouns except their emblematic direction." [27] Of course, the most powerful natural images never lose their palpability. The coiling ooze, no matter what it also stands for, is present in its seething brutality. But as

27. Denis Donoghue, "Aboriginal Poet," *New York Review of Books,* 22 September 1966, pp. 14–16.

Mr. Donoghue points out, Roethke's method can sometimes fail him when images are reduced to an emblematic status.

> The sea has many streets;
> The beach rises with the waves.
> I know my own bones:
> This doxie doesn't do.
>
> [*C.P.*, p. 83]

The effect is an arid accumulation of signs, where the images have ceased to have any but generic reference to the natural object. The problem is that words have become ideas and, in the process, have been husked of any sensuous freshness, the very thing Roethke wanted to avoid.

As a poet Roethke deliberately cultivated the unconscious. His criterion of honesty in poetry was whether a poem seemed to be "an upswelling from the unconscious" (*S.P.*, p. 130). Allan Seager records his deliberate, fantastic flights of free association. "Any object, a refrigerator, a tree, a house, seemed to be to him not only itself but the sum of the associations he could wreathe around it, a microcosm, in fact, and out of these exercises came his symbols and many new word combinations" (*Glass House*, p. 189). Psychic automatism is thus the basic aesthetic behind the poems, it being the nonrational aspect of language, rich in intimation, suggestion, and indirection which interests Roethke. But he is architect of his fantasies; his intention is to give a truly imaginative order to the contents of the unconscious through rigorous artistic control. A relationship has often been drawn between the technique of these poems and the tenets of surrealism, the implication being that the poems adhere to the theory of automatism which characterizes surrealistic poetry. Roethke was certainly familiar with surrealism, and was in fundamental agreement on one point, that the logical, rationalistic response to experience had been overvalued, and that the unconscious could be harnessed as an alternate source of power, of mysterious and unknown modes of being. Here the comparison ends. Surrealism is essentially concerned with the automatic outpourings of the unconscious in the absence of formal control and outside the preoccupations of aesthetics and morality. Its aim is the "pure poem" that derives its power from the haphazard connections of the mind running without restraint. But surrealism is fundamentally limited in that it contains an inherent fallacy. Allowing the unconscious free play results in mere description and superficial exposure, never in a penetration of the complex and deep resources of unconscious processes. Surrealism can accidentally release striking images and violently incongruous juxtapositions (as in Lautréamont's famous "the chance meeting, on a dissecting table, of a sewing machine and an umbrella"), but it will never channel unconscious processes into a form in which they can be understood. Roethke deliberately sought to reproduce the mind's internal tensions in states of deep psychic distress, its quick shifts from tension to release, ecstasy to despair. This required a manipulation, selection, and technical control anathema to the "pure poem."

Like most poets, he kept elaborate notebooks of single memorable lines. During the composition of the *Praise to the End!* sequence, it was his habit to reread his notebooks constantly, often dating the rereadings. Whole sections of the poems written at the time are mosaics of lines taken from different parts of his notebooks. He defined his method:

Much of the style (in these pieces) and elsewhere is based on shifts in association. Now, either these are imaginatively right or they're not. Plenty of times chances are taken. . . . But think: it is one thing to make amazing metaphors as opposites on a string;—this Thomas does, but rarely does he go in for real *jumps* in association. . . . Eliot does.

[*S.L.*, p. 251]

Eliot introduced to modern poetry a way of composing a poem by juxtaposing poetic fragments without indicating their logical relations. His technique, according to W. H. Auden, can be explained as follows: "To 'understand' a poem was not a logical process, but a receiving, as a unity, a pattern of coordinated images that had sprung from a free association of subconscious ideas." [28]

28. Quoted by Richard Hoggart in *Auden: An Introductory Essay*, p. 46.

Eliot took his pattern of images from history and tradition. Roethke turned to the absolute privacy of his own psyche. This has led some critics to dismiss these poems as unintelligible because dependent on too private, too febrile associations. Yet within the technique of fantastic juxtaposition, he always attended to the overall unity of the poem.

Jim Jackson, a colleague of Roethke's at Bennington, describes how he always "made a 'brief' for each verse in progress. An analytical substructure; a reasoned-out girding of his thoughts." He explains that what continually surprised him about the poems in their rough drafts was their "obvious duo-structure: the legal or the logical co-existing side by side with the intuitive, the associational: the former being most in evidence in the presence of certain abstract nouns, generalized epithets or crudely personified ideas, which almost without exception disappeared in the later drafts" (*Glass House,* p. 145). The girding of "Praise to the End!" is described in a letter to Kenneth Burke:

(1) Act
(2) Reaction to Act (quiet, sense of impotence)
(3) Song: reasons for act
      reaction again
(4) Two flashbacks related to act, then the present again.
(5) Sublimation (The fact that there are few human symbols here isn't accidental.)

                                 [*Glass House,* p. 187]

"Praise to the End!" is faithful to this structure, resulting in a psychic logic which orders the poem within the juxtaposition of lines. *The Lost Son* has a similar order. According to Jim Jackson, it "was written in huge swatches. With run-on chants, dirges coming forth pell-mell. Sense of continuity uppermost at all times—even though particular poems in *Lost Son* were later detached and presented as individual poems. . . . poems were organized structurally along simplest lines of Place, dramatic shift-of-event, etc." (*The Glass House,* p. 146). From the notebooks one can see the title poem "The Lost Son" beginning as a Ginsbergian dirge which was gradually refined into stanzaic patterns. A narrative continuity seemingly began to appear out of the morass of images until Roethke was able to identify each section according to place or state of mind: "The Flight," "The Pit," "The Gibber," "The Return." Though no other poems are as precisely ordered as this, they all have a psychological continuity which indicates that he was not writing in submission to the unconscious, but was its master.

The question for the critic remains whether the poems are finally intelligible. Their difficulty arises from the fact that Roethke has made no concessions of judgment or generalized comment within the poems themselves; but they do follow an intuitive logic which is revealed to persistent scrutiny. He wrote that in this kind of poem the artist

works intuitively, and the final form of his poem must be imaginatively right. If intensity has compressed the language so it seems, on early reading, obscure, this obscurity should break open suddenly for the serious reader who can hear the language: the "meaning" itself should come as a dramatic revelation, an excitement. The clues will be scattered richly—as life scatters them; the symbols will mean what they usually mean—and sometimes something more. [*S.P.,* p. 42]

Praise to the End! marks, as it were, an extremity in Roethke's poetry. The almost Elizabethan formality of his next book seems to be the product of a new equanimity achieved in the purgative act of writing the *Praise to the End!* sequence. Only once does he return to this early aboriginal language (in "The Abyss"). This is not surprising since it is less a style than a way of seeing, an attempt to explore his own past in the only way that would be authentic for poetry—at the archetypal level of experience.

The Pure Fury

POEMS 1952–58

That appetite for life so ravenous
A man's a beast prowling in his own house,
A beast with fangs, and out for his own blood
Until he finds the thing he almost was
When the pure fury first raged in his head . . .

[*C.P.*, p. 133]

In 1952, after what he describes in his essay "On Identity" as a long dry period, Roethke embarked on a new direction in his poetry, indicated by the long poem "Four for Sir John Davies." After the experimentation of the *Praise to the End!* sequence, the almost neo-Elizabethan formality of the new love poems seems hardly less than extraordinary. Yet there is a deeper continuity between these two periods of his development than is generally assumed, a continuity at the level of sensibility. Even in this new guise, the poet's voice remains primitive, elemental, defined on the one hand by his unthinking delight in nature confronting him dramatically in the body of the woman, and on the other by his fear that love may entangle him in the defilements of the body: the old guilts, muted it is true, expressing themselves again as an antagonism between spirit and flesh. Underestimating this continuity, many critics have been puzzled to understand what is felt to be the violent disjunction in Roethke's poetry, but the explanation for the contrast lies less in themes than in his conviction of the poet's obligation to experiment. He believed that a poet should play continually with the language, that each new book should be written in a new style. He held to the formalist theory of poetry which insists that a poem's form is organic, dictated by the demands of the subject;

90

and he counseled younger poets to develop a sense of what the material needs, what kind of treatment.

In the *Praise to the End!* sequence, Roethke had sought a style that would be an effective instrument for the exploration of the subconscious self. He ended by creating what he called a psychic shorthand, a language of sheer intuitions that could dramatically reproduce the disordered, associational processes of prethought. The *Praise to the End!* sequence, which had traced the evolution of consciousness from infancy, including prenativity, to maturity, effectively exhausted his subject matter. Further experimentation in this style would almost inevitably have meant repetition. Stanley Kunitz put the dilemma most succinctly when he insisted that after *Praise to the End!* the alternatives were either gibberish or silence.[1]

In his search for a new formal technique, Roethke turned to Yeats as model. This was natural as Yeats was always the poet who engaged his imagination most effectively and with whom he felt the greatest temperamental affinity. What seems to have interested him was the rhetorical, "public" quality of Yeats's poetic voice. Roethke's poetry had already been accused of solipsism. Kenneth Burke, in his essay "Vegetal Radicalism," had pointed out the failure of the poetry to extend itself into the realm of deeply felt, personal relationships. It was all "personification" not "personalization"; was exclusive, self-involved. Burke called for a greater individualizing of human character and human relations.[2] In his letter of January 1952 to Kenneth Burke (*S.L.*, p. 171), Roethke acknowledged the point. Clearly, he felt more than is generally supposed the pressures toward a poetry of social concern. He tried to extend the range of his poetic commitments beyond the self by turning to dramatic monologue, and later to the theme of love. As he put it, "going to school to Yeats," he hoped to bring the accent of public concern to his own work. This direction has occasioned much criticism, particularly accusations of imitation and subservience to a master.

1. Kunitz, "News of the Root," p. 225.
2. Burke, "Vegetal Radicalism," p. 107.

With Roethke, however, the question of imitation must always be confronted at a deeper level, for there were always psychological ramifications to his dependence on other poets. William Meredith remarked that it is hard to think of another instance where a first-rate poet engaged so personally, and what is more important, in maturity, a talent as formidable and distinctive as Yeats.[3] Meredith insisted that this was typical of Roethke. Having, as it were, won through to his own identity in the *Lost Son* sequence, it was characteristic of him to want to match his voice against that of his master. In an early essay Roethke wrote that the young poet feels "the big names of his own time [as] awesome, and overwhelming" (*S.P.*, p. 63). The feeling never left him. On the subject of imitation he wrote: "True 'imitation' takes a certain courage. One dares to stand up to a great style, to compete with papa" (*S.P.*, p. 70). In another context he referred to Eliot as his "super-ego" (Notebooks, Reel 13, no. 176), his censor setting the highest and most exacting standards. In a letter to Ralph J. Mills, he admitted that his strategy of imitation was, to a considerable extent, arrogant and aggressive: "I thought: I can take this god damned high style of W. B. Y. or this Whitmanesque meditative thing of T. S. E. and use it for other ends, use it as well or better." (*S.L.*, p. 231). It should be mentioned that this letter was written in June 1959, during a period of illness. Such periods were times of intense anxiety and self-doubt requiring considerable bombast in order to recover confidence. Roethke seems to have had a personal need to come to terms with the poets who influenced him. The problem was part of that larger difficulty which he termed his continual looking for a father figure. It was a complex impulse. His deep admiration for Yeats, mirroring his attitude toward his father, expressed itself as an aggressive longing to compete, to achieve the Yeatsean standard of excellence. Such an impulse would have been disastrous to a lesser poet, but Roethke's sense of judgment was impeccable. He could count upon his intuitions to mark the delicate line between discipleship and imitation. Yet, it

3. Meredith, "A Steady Storm of Correspondences," p. 51.

must be admitted that this technique led to instances of failure when he allowed his work to be infected by the voices of other poets.

This impulse to compete was intrinsic to Roethke's sensibility, since he made of poetry a radical experience of self-justification. For example, after what appears to have been a long dry period, he wrote "Four for Sir John Davies." The experience was cathartic. In a commentary he wrote: "He, they—the poets dead—were with me" (*S.P.*, p. 24). Arnold Stein, a close friend of Roethke's, says that he lacked the common talents for sustaining himself at the ordinary level of living. "One had the frequent sense that the whole range of wit, knowledge, imagination, and sensitivity hung in the balance; that if the poetry stopped . . . the whole personality would lose its recognizable shape." [4] Roethke was an exacting taskmaster in matters of personal style and technique, but he rarely felt easy or fluent. As a craftsman he thought of himself as a perpetual beginner. He abhorred repetition and complacency, and had continually to feel that his work was progressing. Add to this the implicit dependence of his self-esteem as a man upon his continuation as a poet, and the situation becomes explosive.

He was most susceptible to the impulse to imitate in matters of rhythm and cadence. His greatest power as a poet—that of compassionate flow of self into the things of his experience—was perhaps the very quality that made him most vulnerable to infection. Certainly it was difficult for him not to be influenced by poems that moved him deeply. Of Leonie Adams' poetry and her early influence over him, he wrote, "I loved her so much, her poetry, that I just *had* to become, for a brief moment, a part of her world. . . . I had to create something that would honor her in her own terms" (*S.P.*, p. 66).

His working methods seemed only to have aggravated his propensity for imitation. He would copy out in his notebook long sections of poems that interested him at the time; these included large parts of the *Four Quartets,* the whole of "Ash Wednesday,"

4. Stein, ed., *Essays on the Poetry,* p. xiii.

sections of "Notes towards a Supreme Fiction," and many of
Yeats's poems. It was a discipline which he felt was necessary if
one was to know a poem thoroughly. Yet this habit made him
perilously susceptible to assimilating the rhythms of other poets.
He persisted in it because it remained the best method of extend-
ing his control over previously alien rhythmic patterns. Only occasionally, when he was working out a new style, did he allow his
debt to appear in the finished work.

The question remains of how deeply Roethke realized his debts
and allegiances. It seems that those who complain of imitation or
even of plagiarism in his work often include in that category
allusions to other poets which are deliberate and functional. His
habit of using lines from other poems as titles in the *Praise to the
End!* sequence should have alerted readers to this strategy. His intention was quite clearly to call on echoes outside the poem for re-
verberations, ironic and otherwise—a strategy which, if more limited, is not unlike Eliot's use of allusions in his own poetry. In the
"North American Sequence," for instance, echoes of Eliot in the
lines, "Old men should be explorers" (*C.P.*, p. 189), and "There
are those to whom place is unimportant" (*C.P.*, p. 202), serve by
contrast to emphasize Roethke's theme: his rejection of asceticism
and his commitment to seek an ideal order in the predatory world
of death and decay. This sense of the immediacy of literary tradition is apparent throughout his poetry. In fact, a close reading will
indicate how continuously he refers the reader to a heritage of
poetry—to Wordsworth, Blake, Yeats, Sir John Davies, Eliot—to
identify the cultural or emotional ambience in which his own
poems must be understood.[5] This continual awareness of a living
community of ancestors to whom the poet can appeal served to extend the range and power of his poetry. It is arguable that without
it, his poems might have remained private, even opaque.

The identification of deliberate allusions, however, does not entirely answer the accusation of imitation. Roethke also resorted to

5. For an exploration of Roethke's use of tradition see Jenijoy La Belle, "Theodore
Roethke and Tradition: 'The Pure Serene of Memory in one Man' " (Ph.D. diss., University of California, San Diego, 1969).

the work of other poets in order, through assimilation, to find his own poetic voice. He believed that to imitate was not to limit one's own abilities; it was rather a method of self-realization. He wrote: "The very fact he [the poet] has the support of a tradition, or an older writer, will enable him to be more himself—or more than himself" (*S.P.*, p. 69). For critics, the success or failure of this theory is determined in the matter of his debt to Yeats. The question remains whether in *Words for the Wind,* as W. D. Snodgrass maintained, Roethke created a voice all but indistinguishable from Yeats; [6] or whether, as he himself would assert, he was able, through Yeats, to create a new identity. An affirmative involves both a precise definition of what he borrowed, and a justification.

As he acknowledged in "Four for Sir John Davies," Roethke was attracted by the cadence, the high style or public manner of Yeats's poetry:

> I take this cadence from a man named Yeats;
> I take it, and I give it back again: . . .
>   [*C.P.*, p. 105]

The Yeatsean cadence is technically a matter of a marvelous use of balanced syntax, often within a pentameter rhythm, creating that sense of assurance so ponderable in his poems:

> All men live in suffering,
> I know as few can know.

> Who can distinguish darkness from the soul?

> Man is in love and loves what vanishes,
> What more is there to say?

> How can we know the dancer from the dance?

> He that sings a lasting song
> Thinks in a marrow-bone.[7]

6. W. D. Snodgrass, " 'That Anguish of Concreteness'—Theodore Roethke's Career," in *Essays on the Poetry,* ed. Arnold Stein, p. 82.
7. *The Collected Poems of W. B. Yeats,* pp. 358, 265, 234, 245, 326.

Yeats loved the play of repetition within the line, the ability of syntax literally to reproduce the balance and reconciliation of opposites which was the favorite cast of his mind. Roethke picked up this habit easily so that balance and repetition of sound within the line is one of the most characteristic devices of his verse:

> I breathe alone until my dark is bright.
> [C.P., p. 155]

> I love the world; I want more than the world, . . .
> I shall undo all dying by my death.
> [C.P., p. 155]

> All lovers live by longing, and endure.
> [C.P., p. 107]

Often he uses the device with a lighter hand than Yeats, for the delicate humor the technique can command:

> But who, faced with her face,
> Would not rejoice?
> [C.P., p. 122]

> Loving, I use the air
> Most lovingly: I breathe.
> [C.P., p. 123]

> The shapes a bright container can contain! . . .
> (She moved in circles, and those circles moved).
> [C.P., p. 127]

He learned from Yeats the power of the rhetorical question, of strong driving verbs, and arrogant imperatives. For him, Yeats stood for the imperious note, concentration, and magnificent rhetoric, an example of how to bring language back to bare, even terrible, statement.

Besides a theory of syntax, Roethke learned a technique of symbolism: how to erode the boundary between the figurative and the literal in symbolic language. In creating his own symbolism, Yeats had defined his aim as a union of the cry of the flesh and the cry of the soul: metaphysical abstraction expressed in terms of physical action. His symbol for unity of being is palpable and concrete:

> O chestnut-tree, great-rooted blossomer,
> Are you the leaf, the blossom or the bole?
> O body swayed to music, O brightening glance,
> How can we know the dancer from the dance? [8]

Roethke used this technique in his own poetry. In the line "What sensual eye can keep an image pure,/Leaning across a sill to greet the dawn?" (*C.P.*, p. 154), he crisscrosses intricately between physical action and spiritual vision until metaphysical experience becomes dramatized in sensation. This is a constant feature of his work. He always resorts to a symbol, and one usually based in physical action such as dancing, to avoid abstract conceptualization.

Since it is usually alleged that the influence of Yeats is greatest in "Four for Six John Davies," it will be helpful to turn to that poem to identify debts and dependencies.

> Is that dance slowing in the mind of man
> That made him think the universe could hum?
> The great wheel turns its axle when it can;
> I need a place to sing, and dancing-room,
> And I have made a promise to my ears
> I'll sing and whistle romping with the bears.
>   [*C.P.*, p. 105]

Resemblance to Yeats rests in the use of the rhetorical questions, the rhymed pentameter stanza, and in the stripping of the language to monosyllabic intensity. The dance, no Yeatsean dance, is the shuffle of the circus bear, caged and ridiculous, yet somehow poignantly moving. This image focuses the difference between Yeats's and Roethke's voice. In Roethke, there is always an anguished, powerful energy pushing against the line, making the ordered line buckle. As William Meredith wrote he is alternately more tender, more blustery, and more humorous than Yeats. His sensibility is unique, wild, and passionate in a desperate, awkward

---

8. Ibid., p. 245.

way with a nobility which is entirely personal, and not, as in Yeats, derived from a comprehensive tradition. What makes Roethke seem more dependent on Yeats than he actually is, is that he sometimes borrowed Yeatsean conventions, such as in the line "Dream of a woman, and a dream of death" (*C.P.*, p. 134), and words like "daemon," "inner eye," and "coursing blood." These can be distracting, but they in no way inhibit his personal voice.

Roethke resorted to Yeats's stylistic devices with varying intensity, more determinedly in "Four for Sir John Davies" and "The Dying Man," intermittently in the love poems. He used them as one poet borrows from another, taking what is hard and most substantial from his model and avoiding what is entirely idiosyncratic. And he assured his independence of the borrowed mode by retaining his own stylistic idiosyncrasies, in particular the habit, which he had perfected in his earlier work, of continually shifting metaphor, and a complementary technique of always end-stopping his lines. Both these devices have a radical effect on his style. End-stopping the pentameter line, and thereby depending upon juxtaposition and evocation for effect (even in the more elaborate pieces like "Four for Sir John Davies") eliminates all those leisurely, discursive passages so copious in Yeats. It also assures that the poems will depend more on symbolic language, since it is in the symbols that juxtaposition achieves its impact. More than any other modern American poet, Roethke writes almost entirely in symbols. These become increasingly potent through repetition so that his language always carries a suggestive force of meaning that veils at the same time as it reveals. The resultant ambiguity is often very fruitful.

Roethke also has his own characteristic imagery which assures his independence from his master. A poet's imagery is usually culled from a discipline, a literal or imaginative faith, a leaning toward a certain form of revelation of such seminal importance to his work that without it he could hardly have written.[9] Yeats found his discipline in occultism and in Irish history. This does

9. R. P. Blackmur, *Language as Gesture: Essays in Poetry*, p. 82.

not mean that these figure in every poem he wrote; but they are the core of meaning around which his sensibility ordered itself. Roethke placed his faith in the natural subliminal world that held little interest for Yeats. It is here he discovered metaphors for the primitive unity of being he sought: "The fury of the slug beneath the stone" (*C.P.*, p. 156); for the lover who wakes the ends of life; for the God he sensed in nature: "God's in that stone, or I am not a man" (*C.P.*, p. 149). "His personality is defined by a few objects, by stones, flowers, sunlight, wind, woman, darkness, animals, fish, insects, birds." [10] Here rests his greatness and originality as a poet: in his ability to elevate the organic world to a condition where it could be rehearsed and understood in permanent form, and in so doing, to create a new sensibility.

In 1953, Roethke married Beatrice O'Connell. Marriage seemed to have amounted to a revolution of sensibility. In his notebooks he wrote: "Love's the true surprise." The love poems of *Words for the Wind* were written in the next five years. Roethke felt that they achieved something very different from Yeats's poems—a deeply personal, sexual celebration of love. Many of Yeats's love poems, like the "Crazy Jane" sequence, or the poems of the "wild old wicked man," are polemics on the theme, marvelous propaganda pieces to correct an imbalance. They are meant to whip the mind to frenzy in a delighted acceptance of the bodily imperative. When Yeats wrote in a personal voice, as in poems to Maud Gonne, it was usually of the frustrations of love, or, as in "Adam's Curse," of the failure of desire. Even in poems celebrating the beloved, there is always a note of distance in his tone. Roethke's love poems are of another order. Some are sheer epithalamium to the beloved, rampantly, triumphantly sexual. In these, as James Dickey wrote, he accepts love with the unthinking delight of a creature half-man, half-animal, and there is some mindless, elemental quality in the sound of his voice, something primitive and animistic. His beloved is a green elemental creature "as easy as a beast," half in and half out of nature. Her symbols are wind and water, elements

10. James Dickey, *Babel to Byzantium*, p. 148.

of fluidity and change. Yet, like Rilke's lover, she carries immemorial sap in her veins:

> I met her as a blossom on a stem
> Before she ever breathed, and in that dream
> The mind remembers from a deeper sleep
> [C.P., p. 119]

Seeing her as a manifestation of archetypal beauty, Roethke embraces her with the timidity of one who submits willingly to the
mysteries of nature: "Nature's too much to know" (C.P., p. 130).

   Other love poems, however, are more sophisticated and more
problematical. Love is sought as a principle of order, a means of
overcoming the intransigence of being:

> The flesh can make the spirit visible.
> [C.P., p. 106]

> We two, together, on a darkening day
> Took arms against our own obscurity.
> [C.P., p. 106]

But another foreign note often obtrudes:

> Must I stay tangled in that lively hair?
> Is there no way out of that coursing blood?
> A dry soul's wisest. O, I am not dry!
> [C.P., p. 140]

> When figures out of obscure shadow rave,
> All sensual love's but dancing on a grave.
> [C.P., p. 154]

The urge which informs both attitudes is single: the urge to
wholeness and completion as against the divisiveness of being; but
the allegiances claimed are different. From one perspective,
Roethke sees the body as the possible threshold of immanence. In
the ecstasy of love, the body may be transformed momentarily into
its ideal identity, the intangible spirit. The problem is that this
vision can never be sustained beyond the instant of ecstasy. The
other attitude is based on a fear that entanglement in life, that

"coursing blood," will blur the casement to the world of essences. But here the ties to the tangible must be abandoned altogether, and possibly for a chimera. The cleavage is desperate given the value that Roethke placed in both realms, the organic and the spiritual.

If Roethke's poems have any precedent, it is in the Elizabethan love lyric. That peculiar mixture of sensual delight and emotional skepticism is nowhere more familiar than in Donne, particularly in such poems as "The Ecstasy." Love must prove itself a mystical channel to the spirit and a bulwark against an obsessive preoccupation with death. Roethke's vision, like Donne's, is based on an instinctive dualism tending to view nature and spirit as fundamentally opposed. Love is sought as a means to reconcile this antagonism.

He first turns to the problem in "Four for Sir John Davies." Here love is sought as a principle of order, a way of pressing back the pressures of reality. The poem pivots around the central image of the dance. Dancing-mad, Roethke is thinking of the dance in the Elizabethan sense as Sir John Davies defined it in his poem "Orchestra." Creation is a dance to music. The earthly, celestial, and divine hierarchies speed to the same harmonies, the whole rising in exultant chorus. The notion is appealing to the poetically and mystically minded because it has love as its impetus. It was creative love that first persuaded the warring atoms to move in order. Human love is thus the earthly entrance into divine harmony. Roethke invokes the notion as an appealing fiction out of the past. Instead, he finds himself a caged bear, dancing all alone. The bear image was used by Sir John Davies to refer to the divine order of the constellations to which the human order corresponds:

> [Love] taught them rounds and winding hays to tread,
> And about trees to cast themselves in rings;
> As the two Bears, whom the First Mover flings
> With a short turn about heaven's axletree,
> In a round dance for ever wheeling be.[11]

11. "Orchestra," *Silver Poets of the Sixteenth Century*, ed. Gerald Bullett, p. 330.

Without the directives of a dancing master, Davies' persuading "Love," the poet is reduced to the poignant antics of the caged animal, trapped in a world without inherent order where the reality of universals does not obtain:

> I think with pride:
> A caged bear rarely does the same thing twice
> In the same way: O watch his body sway!—
> This animal remembering to be gay.
>   [*C.P.*, p. 105]

Because he must dance out his rage for order, Roethke seeks a partner, but if all the old myths have lost credence, the myth of love may be implicated too. The question becomes "Was I the servant of a sovereign wish,/Or ladle rattling in an empty dish?" In "Orchestra," Davies had eulogized the dance of love as the soul's means to escape the temporal:

> A gallant dance! that lively doth bewray
> A spirit and a virtue masculine;
> Impatient that her house on earth should stay,
> Since she herself is fiery and divine.
> Oft doth she make her body upward flyne,
> With lofty turns and caprioles in the air,
> Which with the lusty tunes accordeth fair.

Roethke would reproduce this motion but the dance the modern lovers achieve is only a frustrating approximation of its Elizabethan counterpart, for it is danced in desperation against the backdrop of a dark world of obscurity and death: the world which has resulted from the breakdown of the universal harmonies which could subsume Davies' lovers into a higher order of symbolic meaning. In Roethke's poem, only when the body is hurried violently, deliberately to the boiling point of sexual ecstasy can the flesh for a desperate instant make visible the "wraith," the ethereal self:

> What shape leaped forward at the sensual cry?—
> Sea-beast or bird flung toward the ravaged shore?
> Did space shake off an angel with a sigh?

This climax comes in the form of a question because the poet must face the possibility of self-delusion—that the vision of the spiritual self which the dance revealed might be false:

> Dante attained the purgatorial hill,
> Trembled at hidden virtue without flaw,
> Shook with a mighty power beyond his will,—
> Did Beatrice deny what Dante saw?
> All lovers live by longing, and endure:
> Summon a vision and declare it pure.

Roethke is certainly thinking of the transfiguration of Beatrice as type and image of the divine in the *Purgatorio,* Canto 30; but he may also have in mind Yeats's humorous portrait of Dante as the lecher who found in his poetry the most exalted lady loved by man, for here he accepts the possibility that the glorification of the lover as a means to self-transcendence is a willful act of the imagination based on longing rather than on truth. The poem ends with an acceptance of the inevitable failure to sustain the vision: "Who rise from flesh to spirit know the fall:/The word outleaps the world, and light is all." If the fall to flesh is inevitable, yet the pun on "word" contains reservations. Surely the implication is that the flesh, momentarily made word, the body made spirit, outleaps the world; the gesture toward meaning in the act of love offers the only possible means to escape the temporal and finite. If Roethke claims that "light is all," he uses the word not in the sense of understanding or knowledge, but to refer to the bright blaze of being experienced in the sexual act. This elemental intensity, this shining, is the most profound human experience he knows, and if he cannot explain or define it, it yet has the power of a sacramental act.

The poem concludes without making any monumental claims to certainty. He would have the sexual dance guarantee his immortality, but the vision of the ethereal self which it affords both is and is not real. Instead the poem is a willful celebration of love as the nearest "approximation" to the Elizabethan dance. It has sometimes been implied that the ambivalence of this attitude is not intentional,[12] but surely the poem is full of questions to which Roethke refuses to give final answers. If he had been more dogmatic, the poem would have lost much of its power. As Yeats said, "The struggle for complete affirmation in the face of skepticism, may be, often must be, [a poem's] chief poignancy." [13]

But faced with death, "the thick shade of the long night" (*C.P.,* p. 134), the confidence that love may prove a means to self-transcendence begins to waver entirely, and the lover searches for other, deeper assurances:

> Stupor of knowledge lacking inwardness—
> What book, O learned man, will set me right?
> Once I read nothing through a fearful night,
> For every meaning had grown meaningless.
> Morning, I saw the world with second sight,
> As if all things had died, and rose again.
> I touched the stones, and they had my own skin.
>   [*C.P.,* p. 133]

So many of the poems speak of this mindless, brooding state of exhaustion and undirected desperation that is only escaped by a sudden breakthrough into a completely different dimension of the self. He calls this experience of breakthrough the "Pure Fury," when the self blazes into being; when, paradoxically, a sharp sense of the "identity of some other being . . . brings a corresponding heightening and awareness of one's own self, *and,* even more mysteriously, in some instances, a feeling of the oneness of the universe" (*S.P.,* p. 25). He insisted that the switchover into meaning must come suddenly; when it comes "it is either total loss of consciousness—symbolical or literal death—*or* a quick break into an-

---

12. See Malkoff, *Theodore Roethke,* p. 121. Malkoff complains that "in spite of this apparently unambiguous conclusion, no clear-cut philosophical position emerges from this poem; the central paradox—the vision that is both real and not real—is neither resolved nor completely assimilated as a final perception of reality." I would agree with John Lucas ("Poetry of Theodore Roethke," p. 54), who insists that " 'Four For Sir John Davies' is a better poem if we admit its hesitancies and doubts."

13. Quoted by Richard Ellmann, *The Identity of Yeats,* p. 240.

other state, not necessarily serene, but frequently a bright blaze of consciousness." [14]

"The Pure Fury," was written after a period of illness and intense anxiety in the fall of 1957. In his letters, Roethke comments on the sense of desperation which characterized his depressions (*S.L.*, p. 219). In terms of the poem, this desperation is occasioned by the fear of "Nothingness," against which neither philosophy nor the beloved can afford consolation.

> The pure admire the pure, and live alone;
> I love a woman with an empty face.
> Parmenides put Nothingness in place;
> She tries to think, and it flies loose again.
> How slow the changes of a golden mean:
> Great Boehme rooted all in Yes and No;
> At times my darling squeaks in pure Plato.
>
> [*C.P.*, p. 133]

This stanza, which has given critics such difficulty, is taken from a passage in Paul Tillich's *The Courage to Be*, which refers to the philosophical concept of nonbeing.[15] While the stanza itself is none too clear, the poet's tone is obviously ironic. All this philosophizing about "nothingness," this "stupor of knowledge lacking inwardness," is mere verbiage to a man in extremity who has actually confronted the awareness that the self can be totally, utterly annihilated. His humor is mordant, but none the less terrifying, and he willingly acknowledges the senselessness, even the inhumanity, of his situation:

> A man's a beast prowling in his own house,
> A beast with fangs, and out for his own blood
> Until he finds the thing he almost was
> When the pure fury first raged in his head . . .

It is the very rage for life that moves him to the self-cannibalism of despair in his efforts to recover the pure fury—the bright blaze

14. "On 'In a Dark Time,' " in *The Contemporary Poet as Artist and Critic*, ed. Anthony Ostroff, p. 52.
15. Paul Tillich, *The Courage to Be*, pp. 30–31.

of consciousness, itself an experience of "inward" knowledge; a mystical intuition of meaning which, if it cannot be articulated, is nonetheless overpowering. I would thus disagree with Karl Malkoff (*Theodore Roethke*, p. 135) who feels that the "pure fury" is a negative experience of anxiety. The word "first" of 1.20 of the poem links the pure fury with the state of perfection of the previous line, when the poet "almost was" the thing for which he had been longing, a bright blaze of being.

In contrast to this intensity love can be felt as a loss of the purity of self, even as a contamination in the other: "Dream of a woman, and a dream of death: . . . /When will that creature give me back my breath?" (*C.P.*, p. 134). Love can be felt as an encroachment of the sacred solitariness of being. At the core of Roethke's attitude is a familiar vacillation which has been called one of the conclusive secrets of the Western psyche: [16] the vacillation between the celebration of love as essential to self-transcendence: "And see and suffer myself/In another being, at last" (*C.P.*, p. 126); and the recoil from love in the search for a purity higher than any available in the human world. The struggle between the mystic and the lover is easily recognized. It is simply that the aspiration toward a final purity of being stands over and above the momentary ecstasy of love.

Malkoff has pointed out that Roethke was reading Martin Buber at this time, a fact confirmed in his notebooks. This must certainly have stimulated his interest in the metaphysical implications of the I—Thou relationship, particularly in the individual's need for authentication through the other. But Roethke's response to love is more equivocal than this. He is deeply sensitive to the risks of involvement, the precarious threat to identity implied in association with the other. From "The Dying Man," part of the problem would appear to be the familiar guilt and fear of sexuality aroused by the indignant father's ghost. But much more important is the quest for purity which is a continuous theme of his poetry. He had two kinds of images for its achievement: the abstract

16. Denis de Rougement, *The Myth of Love.*

image "O, I would be a thinking star," and the pure sensuous form, fish, snake, or bird. These two images identify a private dialectic—what he called his own personal dialogue between self and soul. The question is whether the search for perfection is to be achieved by withdrawal from life into abstract isolation, the lure that death seemed to have held for him; or whether perfection could be discovered in life itself. The crux of the problem, as defined here, is the terrible idea of death. Death threatens to prove self-identity meaningless. As he wrote in his essay "On 'Identity' " in 1963: "The human problem is to find out what one really is: whether one exists, whether existence is possible. But how? 'Am I but nothing, leaning toward a thing?' " (*S.P.*, p. 20). The vacillation in his attitude toward the lover is inextricable from this debate. He can only move toward love when he can find the conviction that the "flesh can make the spirit visible" (*C.P.*, p. 106). Only then can he accept the "burden" of the other, "And see and suffer myself/In another being, at last" (*C.P.*, p. 126).

"The Renewal" is one of the first poems to integrate these themes into a kind of resolution. Roethke describes his state as one of immanent rebirth: "The night wind rises. Does my father live?/Dark hangs upon the waters of the soul." By now it is clear that, in most of Roethke's poems, a call to the father is an appeal to both natural and divine progenitor—here an appeal for order. Expectant, the poet turns to love as the deepest paradox he knows:

> Love alters all. Unblood my instinct, love.
> These waters drowse me into sleep so kind
> I walk, as if my face would kiss the wind.
> [*C.P.*, p. 135]

But as vital and beautiful as the sexual experience may be, love is not without its terrors:

> Sudden renewal of the self—from where?
> A raw ghost drinks the fluid in my spine;
> I know I love, yet know not where I am;

The familiar ghost of guilt and fear saps the energy at the core of self. The experience of love becomes an experience of loss: "Will the self, lost, be found again? In form?" The appeal to form is a cry to the will to thwart the disintegrating impulse to madness: "I walk the night to keep my five wits warm." By form Roethke means a unique and bounding sense of order opposing the meaninglessness of existence. In a moment of intense illumination, when the "pure fury" blazes into the head, he finds that form:

> I see the rubblestones begin to stretch
> As if reality had split apart
> And the whole motion of the soul lay bare:
> I find that love, and I am everywhere.

He wrote in his notebooks: "The only uninterpreted life is the life of a stone" (Notebooks, Reel 13, no. 179). The stone is his symbol for absolute mystery; its appearance always heralds moments of mystical illumination. Here a dynamic, substantializing force of love is felt as mystically immanent in external creation.

Such mystical moments were states of feeling rather than of intellect. Perhaps William James offers the most precise definition of them when he describes general mystical experience as involving a sense of enlargement, of expansion, of access to a new center of psychic energy, the keynote of which is the sense of reconciliation of opposites. He speaks of a state of insight into deep truths unplumbed by discursive intellect; revelations of noetic quality which, though they cannot be explained or even articulated, have a curious sense of authority. The experience itself, however, is a transient state, involving a perception which seems immanent, but which never completes itself.[17] In this lies its vulnerability. It is an overpowering sensation which yet has no specific intellectual content. That is, it affords insight into consciousness—into the existence of nonrational forms of perception, potential though rarely actualized, but leaves unanswered Roethke's essential question: "Where is the knowledge that/Could bring me to my God?" (*C.P.*, p. 139). The fall from assurance, the oscillation between

---

17. William James, *The Varieties of Religious Experience: A Study in Human Nature*, pp. 379, 388.

moments of ecstasy and despair, is thus almost inherent in the experience itself.

Roethke's was not a sacrificial temperament. He did not feed on religious intuition as a negative principle of humiliation and privation; the soul's happiness gaged in proportion to the intolerableness of external condition. But he was profoundly convinced of the existence of a reality deeper than the quotidian. In his notebooks he wrote: "I always wanted to step in and out of reality," and later, in accents of self-castigation: "To be more than man; that German desire, that is my curse.[18] His attitude toward love was necessarily implicated in his search for purity. The dark maze of carnal attraction could be felt as a contamination. In "The Sensualists," and "The Surly One," love becomes a sensual pen in which the self is either lost or dissipated. In "Love's Progress" and "The Swan," love is a threat, a violence to the self, a distraction in the quest for identity: "Is there no way out of that coursing blood?/A dry soul's wisest. O, I am not dry!" (*C.P.*, p. 140). As a sensual man, Roethke is moved from his skepticism to accept love even as it implies diminution of being: "A man alive, from all light I must fall" (*C.P.*, p. 140). Paradoxically this very acceptance can sometimes afford him a vision of the final purity for which he had been waiting, here expressed in an image of the lover as a silver swan, that sea-beast or bird, the wraith of the ethereal self released in the act of love.

Despite such momentary reversals, the love sequence ends desperately with the poem "Memory." Roethke always insisted that a sequence must be a coherent whole in which poems are placed so as to support each other by complement or contrast. It cannot be without meaning that he places this poem last. In "Memory," the poet has won through to an affirmation of love—"Love's all. Love's all I know"—as a mystical experience of release: "The outside dies within." But the experience is evoked as a memory which is fixed and impenetrable in a world of dream:

18. Wagoner, ed., *Straw for the Fire*, pp. 219–20.

A doe drinks by a stream,
A doe and its fawn.
When I follow after them,
The grass changes to stone.
                [*C.P.*, p. 141]

Throughout the sequence, the lover has had her animal surrogates: swan, dove, deer, cat, bird. Here the poet would follow her, but the memory hardens and he is left in isolation.

Somehow the maze of sensuality has proven too much for Roethke. His strength and attention have been dissipated by doubts and uncertainties, so that both love and mystical illumination have eluded him. He locates his failure in his disregard of elemental questions. His discovery, as always, is focused through his attitude toward the "fearful small," his minimal world of snails, snakes, and frogs. It is always through them that he finds his particular regeneration. The question put in "Plaint" is "Where is the knowledge that/Could bring me to my God?" He finds himself further from that answer, the further he moves from deep roots:

I lived with deep roots once:
Have I forgotten their ways—
The gradual embrace
Of lichen around stones?
Death is a deeper sleep,
And I delight in sleep.
                [*C.P.*, p. 139]

He has lost self-possession, and "plain tenderness." The whole of the "Voices and Creatures" section is an attempt to escape from the sense of isolation and dislocation which he has imposed upon himself by his search after final assurances. He wishes to recover his sense of union with nature's presences. "The Beast" is a moving allegory of his exclusion. The images are enigmatic but not esoteric. Behind a door overhung with burr, bramble, and thorn, is a meadow, the green "meadow of fulfillment" as John Wain has called it.[19] Here a great beast plays—"A sportive, aimless one"

19. Wain, "The Monocle of My Sea-Faced Uncle," in *Essays on the Poetry*, ed. Stein, p. 59.

(*C.P.*, p. 145). In a moment of empathy, the poet recognizes in the animal what is perhaps his own primordial self, caught fleetingly in the racial memory. The door is open but it is impossible for him to penetrate. This oneness of powerful, innocent being which the beast promises is forever lost to the self. In "The Exorcism" exclusion is more terrifying, driving the poet to the edge of madness. Roethke described the poem as one of several on the "theme of flight and the dissociation of personality that can occur in states of terror." [20] The poem derives its power from the urgency, the sense of obsessiveness which propels it. The only hint of the source of terror is the line: "A cold God-furious man" (*C.P.*, p. 147). Elsewhere he wrote: "Running from God's the longest race of all." Here he is "furious" in his anxiety for meaning, and tormented by an existential sense of isolation: "And I was only I" (*C.P.*, p. 143). He describes his anxiety as a physical exorcism:

> I turned and turned again,
> A cold God-furious man
> Writhing until the last
> Forms of his secret life
> Lay with the dross of death.
>
> I was myself, alone.
> [*C.P.*, p. 147]

As Kenneth Burke wrote in another context, resolution can only be a matter of avoiding being undone. Here the poet survives, having sweated out his old selves, but without final resolution. In "The Song," a similar flight from reality occurs, here initiated by a vision of a "ragged man," possibly the poet's mortal self, what he calls his shadow, "my Other . . . reminder that I am going to die." [21] But the flight carries him into nature where he turns to the subliminal world in one of his most beautiful, penitential acts:

> I sang to whatever had been
> Down in that watery hole:

20. Introduction to "The Exorcism" in *Poems in Folio*, vol. 1, no. 9.
21. Roethke, "On 'In a Dark Time,' " p. 50.

I wooed with a low tune;
You could say I was mad.
And a wind woke in my hair,
And sweat poured from my face,
When I heard, or thought I heard,
Another join my song
With the small voice of a child,
Close, and yet far away.

Mouth upon mouth, we sang,
My lips pressed upon stone.

[*C.P.*, p. 146]

On the extreme edge of sanity, he turns to the fearful small to save him. What he seeks and finds is the humility of the child that can efface itself before mystery; indeed, never feel the need to know. Such humility is the only solution to the divisiveness of consciousness straining for metaphysical assurances. As he says in "A Walk in Late Summer": "What is there for the soul to understand?/The slack face of the dismal pure inane?" (*C.P.*, p. 149). The culprit is the evil will which moves the mind in the pursuit of assurances always achieving only that "stupor of knowledge lacking inwardness." Roethke has been criticized for his attacks against reason, but in this he is only following all romantics before him. What is unique in Roethke's case is that, instead of turning to the imagination, he seeks another order of knowing altogether. His teachers are the bacterial small, the soft-backed creatures:

Bring me the meek, for I would know their ways;
I am a connoisseur of midnight eyes.
The small! The small! I hear them singing clear
On the long banks, in the soft summer air.

[*C.P.*, p. 149]

What he learns from them is beautifully summarized in an image from "The Dying Man":

I've the lark's word for it, who sings along:
What's seen recedes; Forever's what we know!—
Eternity defined, and strewn with straw,
The fury of the slug beneath the stone.

[*C.P.*, p. 156]

Roethke finds in the slug, opening in a blind empathic response to his timeless world, an image of an eternal order of existence which might be duplicated in the human sphere. How this is possible becomes clear in one of his epigrams, "The Advice." [22]

> A learned heathen told me this:
> Dwell in pure mind and Mind alone;
> What you brought back from the Abyss,
> The Slug was taught beneath his Stone.

Two orders of existence—the fury of the slug and pure mind—are offered as equivalent orders of consciousness, one innate, the other learned after the long arduous descent into the abyss.

It is clear that Roethke's notion of pure mind has little to do with intellection. Rather it is something like the state of pure being when

> Knowing slows for a moment,
> And not-knowing enters, silent,
> Bearing being itself,
> And the fire dances
> To the stream's
> Flowing.
>
> [*C.P.*, p. 221]

At least this is the order of consciousness recovered from the abyss in the poem by that name. And this "not-knowing," bearing being itself, Roethke finds epitomized in the slug's potent fury. If verification is needed appeal can be made to the philosophy of Henri Bergson. Bergson insists that the insect responding to instinct, the slug in its fury, answers an impulse or imperative received from the depths of being; that instinct is an order of consciousness, unified and intensified, not abstracted from existence, but a response as with a knowledge from within. Only in the phenomenon of feeling, of unreflecting sympathy or antipathy, do we experience, even if in a slight form, something of this consciousness. At its most intense we know it as intuitive vision, that "enthusiasm which can fire a soul, consume all that is within it, and

22. "The Advice," *New Statesman,* 65 (9 August 1963): 176.

henceforth, fill the whole of space . . . [so that we become] simplified unified, intensified." [23] At such times we are introduced into another order of existence, beneath time and space. In "A Walk in Late Summer," Roethke dares for the first time to trace the affirmative fury of the fearful small to its ultimate source: "God's in that stone, or I am not a man!" Bergson would concur, insisting that the order of consciousness in nature's particulars is a minute segmentation of the *"élan vital"* moving matter to the condition of form. In his *Morality and Religion,* he would even go so far as to define this immanent creative consciousness as mystical love, of the very essence of divinity.

Facetiously, we might be tempted to trace Roethke's affirmations to the doctrines of philosophical pantheism, or through Yeats, to the pseudo-Hermetic treatises of the twelfth century which defined god as immanent in each grain of sand, and each squeaking mouse in the corn. But with Roethke, it is always dangerous to resort to labels. In fact, he wrote humorously of himself: "There are few people who have had a more sincere hatred of thinking." [24] His affirmations come not from his readings, but in moments of extremity when stakes are highest—between affirmation and madness. His idea of god is a primitive, animistic notion based largely on intuition, the source Bergson advocated for all such revelations. It will gradually become more sophisticated as it is shaped by his mystical readings. In "A Walk in Late Summer" it brings the assurance that "Existence moved toward a certain end—" and what prevents continual illumination is only the physical being: "A tree thinned by the wind obscures my sight." With the assurance of ultimate meaning, Roethke can find value in intimations of mortality and change. "A Walk in Late Summer" ends with a moving confidence:

> Being delights in being, and in time.
> The evening wraps me, steady as a flame.
> 							[*C.P.*, p. 150]

23. Henri Bergson, *The Two Sources of Morality and Religion,* trans. R. A. Audra and Cloudesley Brereton, p. 216.
24. Wagoner, ed., *Straw for the Fire,* p. 217.

Referring to the *Praise to the End!* sequence Roethke insisted that the struggle for spiritual identity is one of perpetual recurrence. This also applies to the poems of *Words for the Wind* where the falls from assurance are continual. In most of these poems, he struggles to an affirmation that must be perpetually renewed. It is to be expected then that the battle for meaning must be fought again in "The Dying Man."

"The Dying Man" is, as it were, the climactic poem of *Words for the Wind.* It repeats the vacillation between body and soul, mystic and lover, which is the epitomal movement of the volume, and brings it to some sort of resolution. Yeats is the spirit behind "The Dying Man." Echoes of his poems deliberately recur almost as fragments Roethke has shored against his ruin. The theme of the poem is the dramatic engagement of these two poetic minds, or rather the struggle of one sensibility to reach the "affirmative capability" of its spiritual mentor, a phrase used by Richard Ellmann to describe Yeats's demand for affirmation against skepticism in an effort to transcend his human limitations. Truth thus becomes "dramatic," a vision of reality that satisfies the imagination.

The poem begins with Yeats's last words as Roethke imagines them to have been, written in the trimeter rhythm Yeats reserved for final statements. It is a remarkable précis of Yeats's philosophy. The core of the argument is that if the body is a dying animal, yet it is only through the body that the eternal rose can be widened. The rose, as Roethke drew it, rooted in stone, is the miracle of pure centrality, pure equilibrium, balanced in perfection in the midst of time and space, neither temporal nor spatial—which Yeats called "Unity of Being," when "All thought becomes an image and the soul/Becomes a body." If death has "possibilities," and Yeats rehearsed them all, yet faith and value are placed in the human situation. Learning to sing, the dying man brings to memory one of Yeats's greatest moments:

> I am content to follow to its source
> Every event in action or in thought;
> Measure the lot; forgive myself the lot!

> When such as I cast out remorse
> So great a sweetness flows into the breast
> We must laugh and we must sing . . .[25]

Roethke intends this first section of the poem to mark the high point of confidence which the rest of the poem struggles to recover and which is achieved when its tropes begin to be repeated in the last section "They Sing, They Sing."

The crux of the dialogue is the irreconcilable claims of the soul and body, brought to climax before the inevitability of death. Faced with the fact of death, Roethke's immediate impulse is to turn against the body as animal. "I thought myself reborn./My hands turn into hooves./I wear the leaden weight/Of what I did not do" (*C.P.*, p. 154). But this hatred and self-loathing, a memory of the self-cannibalism of *Open House,* only plunge the mind into the solipsism of mental despair. Roethke has no illusions about mental illness. If the unconscious threshold is opened to the free passage of the "ghost," "the atavistic Other/That jumps on careless backs" (*S.L.*, p. 93), there is no breakthrough into meaning. The divisive wall, the barrier to vision, only looms larger out of "this small dark." Roethke finds himself in the dilemma of a Rimbaud, caught in his own hell instead of the heaven he had anticipated. Yet escape into the white dawn of sanity is not enough. He borrows a metaphor from Henry Vaughan—"a deep but dazzling darkness" [26]—to insist that his search is for mystical illumination:

> Dawn's where the white is. Who would know the dawn
> When there's a dazzling dark behind the sun?
>   [*C.P.*, p. 155]

Effectively the poet has reached an impass; his fear of death has led him to an irreconcilable hatred of life. Resolution begins when echoes of assurances from Yeats's poems come to the mature poet to sustain him. One thinks particularly of Yeats's poem "Death." [27]

25. *Collected Poems of W. B. Yeats,* p. 267.
26. "The Night," *Complete Poetry of Henry Vaughan,* p. 325.
27. *Collected Poems of W. B. Yeats,* p. 264.

Goaded by the arrogance of Yeats and the memory of his father's audacity before death, the son is shamed into confidence. He begins to build his own metaphysical deductions: "I die in to this life, alone yet not alone. . . . By dying daily, I have come to be. . . . I shall undo all dying by my death." It is possible that Roethke remembered this from his reading of *The Courage to Be.* Tillich writes: "Since every day a little of our life is taken from us—since we are dying every day—the final hour when we cease to exist does not of itself bring death; it merely completes the death process." [28] Tillich is speaking of the stoical capacity to overcome a fear of death by facing it and reducing it to comprehensible proportions. Death is not a final climactic blow; it is merely the completion of a process. But Roethke's deduction is more ambiguous. His last line: "I shall undo all dying by my death," has all the audacity and power of Yeats's rhetoric—it lays claim to nothing and to everything. Dying may be the last death, or the release from death to another life. With his new-found arrogance, his "affirmative capability," he can face his own mortality: "I bare a wound and dare myself to bleed." He turns to life and to love with a new equanimity, hearing the first strains of defiant song, humorously from the Yeatsean bee-loud glade.

In "They Sing, They Sing" we find that one of the sources of complaint all along has been the longing for eternity, the far fields of forever. Instead Roethke finds an eternal order within life in the metaphor of the slug in its fury. "What's seen recedes; Forever's what we know." The temporal and the spatial norms can be taken in stride; eternity is not simply their opposite but rather the absence of these notions altogether in the purity of emphathic response to life's energy.

"The Dying Man" ends with a climactic summary image in Yeats's style:

> The edges of the summit still appall
> When we brood on the dead or the beloved;
> Nor can imagination do it all
> In this last place of light: he dares to live

28. Tillich, *The Courage to Be,* p. 13.

> Who stops being a bird, yet beats his wings
> Against the immense immeasurable emptiness of things.

Roethke has always offered the bird as a symbol for the soul. Here the paradoxical directive is for the individual to stop being a bird, yet beat his wings. It is a lovely paradox, an appeal for that delicate equilibrium "When neither soul nor body has been crossed." If no final questions have been answered, at least the struggle for meaning has been validated. We are no longer with Matthew Arnold's "beautiful and ineffectual angel beating in the void his luminous wings in vain."

In *The Lost Son* and *Praise to the End!* volumes, Roethke regressed, at a considerable risk, to a language of sheer intuition in his search for essential motives. In the love poems, his intention seems to have been to achieve a larger measure of intellectual content and a broader symbolic dimension that could include the realm of ultimate motives. Kenneth Burke has analyzed Roethke's early language in his essay "Vegetal Radicalism," indicating the absence of all abstractions. He contrasts his vocabulary with Eliot's in *The Four Quartets* to conclude that Roethke deliberately tried to avoid abstractions by such devices as a continual application of communicative verbs to inanimate objects, and by replacing eschatological concerns with the concrete notions of womb heaven, and primeval slime. Here, Roethke tries to incorporate the realm of abstractions within his own aesthetic, without abandoning the spontaneous immediacy that is his greatest strength. His solution is to turn to the lessons of the metaphysical poets: to yoke the abstract to the concrete image. In the love poems we find an entirely new vocabulary and technique of metaphor. Characteristic words are "incomprehensible," "purgatory," "chaos," "death," "unconscious," "sensual," "eternity," "instinct"—all of which would have been anathema in the earlier poems. These abstractions are now made palpable through metaphors of physical action. The poetic rage for order is a dance of bears—bears because Roethke saw his poetry as having an earthly, animal quality. Love as an assertion of order is a dance which undoes "chaos to a curious sound"—*curious* meaning careful as well as strange. "Unblood my instinct, love" is an appeal to love's great paradoxical strength—through blood to unblood. These are representative examples of Roethke's wit, the fundamental principle of which he defined as thinking with the body, bringing the whole sensory equipment to bear on the process of thought. When we think of Eliot, we think of the disembodied voice in the deep throes of meditation. When we think of Roethke, we think of the physical animal image which is usually the vehicle of metaphor.

The other order of language in Roethke's love poetry is the sensuous, elemental, directly felt word from which most of the actualizing strength of his poetry is drawn—words like "stone," "fish," "leaf," "vine," "star," "water," "wind," "moon," "bone."

> Love, love, a lily's my care,
> She's sweeter than a tree.
> Loving, I use the air
> Most lovingly: I breathe;
> [*C.P.*, p. 123]

Language has been honed to the essentials, but rendered evocative in combination so that there is an excitement in the words beyond the excitement of meaning. It is largely the effect of a moving control of rhythm achieved through internal rhyme, alliterative repetition, and the delicate balance of syntax. But it is also more than this. The words of the poem have been injected with the *élan* of a primitive, animistic voice.

In the early aboriginal poems, Roethke had sought to force poetic form into a fluidity capable of adaptation to any emotion. This was because he wanted to reproduce as many of the mind's rhythms as were available to verse. Thus in a single poem, he ranged from the concise stanzas of nursery rhyme, to imagistic passages of free verse, and finally to purely prosaic passages. After this free, experimental attitude toward versification, the formal precision of the love poems seems an extraordinary reversal. Perhaps he felt that this kind of munificent form had to be cultivated by the poet who sought to concern himself with the metaphysical

rage for order. Certainly the departure accords with the distance
between the child's world of *Praise to the End!* and the adult world
of *Words for the Wind:*

> I knew a woman, lovely in her bones,
> When small birds sighed, she would sigh back at them;
> Ah, when she moved, she moved more ways than one:
> The shapes a bright container can contain!
>
> [C.P., p. 127]

The poem is built on the scaffold of an elaborate syntax. About
half of its lines depend on caesural pause so that the voice is continually halting in the lingering satisfaction of adulation. Each
half line is elaborately balanced against its complement—"sighed," "sigh"; "moved," "moved"; "container," "contain." Each single line is an end-stopped unit, which swings into
the next, usually by the association of some quality. The consequent feeling is of a continual, spontaneous elaboration of the
lover's graces.

Sometimes the effect of the end-stopped line is more obtrusive:

> All women loved dance in a dying light—
> The moon's my mother: how I love the moon!
> Out of her place she comes, a dolphin one,
> Then settles back to shade and the long night,
> A beast cries out as if its flesh were torn,
> And that cry takes me back where I was born.
>
> [C.P., p. 156]

Though the metaphors seem disparate, they are all associated with
the themes of birth and death—exultant dance in dying light; the
moon as symbol of cyclic regeneration; birth as a bestial annuncia-
tion, a rending of flesh, which must be embraced as part of life.
Within the radical juxtapositions, a single mood is built, as it
were, cumulatively. Unity of apprehension is assisted by the continual recourse to rhyme, which always forces the mind back to
previous lines. The effect is a surprising relaxation of the formality
usually associated with rhymed iambic pentameter—this because
the radical shifting of images thrusts against the tight control and

polished form, distorting the ordered lines. In a sense Roethke has redeemed formal rhyme for twentieth century poetry by showing how it can be made to contain the violence that is so much a part of that sensibility.

To chart the development of an artistic sensibility is, as Allan Seager put it, a dangerous task. If it can be done at all, it is always with the assumption that the glance is retrospective. From the outside, a body of work may seem to move in a smooth progression, but this is only because the artist has wisely supressed his false starts and stumblings on the way. If we seek a retrospective order in Roethke's work, I think it must be acknowledged that "The Dying Man" is a very important poem because of the attitude he expresses in it toward his father. In one of his earliest poems, Roethke had complained: "Exhausted fathers thinned the blood," and insisted that "The spirit starves/Until the dead have been subdued" (*C.P.*, p. 4). Here he realizes his error, and learns that the dead father can be of aid to the son in his quest for identity: "I found my father when I did my work." What begins as the familiar fear and guilt before the father ends with one of the first sympathetic portraits Roethke has drawn of him. He sees him as a vulnerable, yet courageous, human being facing death, and in that vision finds his own assurances against mortality:

> I saw my father shrinking in his skin;
> He turned his face: there was another man,
> Walking the edge, loquacious, unafraid.
> [*C.P.*, p. 155]

Finally able to write about his father's death, Roethke could begin to stave off his own impulse to dissolution which was the paradoxical consequence of his fear of mortality. It was no longer so imperative to struggle for affirmation, and a new equanimity now enters his poetry. Death itself could be confronted, not with the frenzy that characterizes the earlier poems, but meditatively pondered, thought through.

The next poem Roethke was to write is called "Meditations of an Old Woman." It is deeply dependent upon conventions from mystical literature. He had always been interested in mysticism as it accorded with his own personal experience. Yet he was not above mocking it, as in the poem "The Pure Fury," where Plato, Parmenides, and Boehme are the learned men who can set no one straight. In his new poems, he begins to explore mysticism as a solution to the poet's dilemma. These explorations are the subject of the next chapter.

⚹ VI ⚹

Wet with Another Life
MEDITATIONS OF AN OLD WOMAN

> I recover my tenderness by long looking.
> By midnight I love everything alive.
> Who took the darkness from the air?
> I'm wet with another life.
>
> [*C.P.*, p. 173]

It is always the case with the true poet that after the opening mis-
cellany of a first book, his work seems, even if in retrospect,
programmatic and consecutive. There is a continuity to his
thought through all its transformations as he moves toward a uni-
fication of his vision. Many critics would like to deny Roethke this
order, insisting that after the sequence of love poems, he fell into
self-repetition, and that his poetry achieved no new insights. If it
is true that he had one central preoccupation, few could have been
larger and more encompassing. This was his desire to trace the
evolution of spirit—as he said, "to see the self so completely that
it might become the soul." He wrote: "To know what is happen-
ing within us, this is the most difficult awareness. To be loyal to
what happens to me" (Notebooks, Reel 13, no. 185). He pursued
this awareness systematically so that his poetry took on the consecutive order of his life, a finding and piecing together of his knowledge of an inner self.

He began his interior excavations with the *Lost Son* sequence, attempting to penetrate the terrors and vicissitudes of his own
mind. Like Rimbaud, he at least partly induced his first experience of mental disorder, deliberately seeking out preternatural experience in an effort to break down the domination of the con-

scious ego. The process was disintegrative, a breaking up of the
established modes of consciousness in order to break back into intuitive vision. In those early poems, the poet was a kind of nocturnal fisher, penetrating to the racial unconscious in an attempt to
relive his selfhood back to its mindless source. But the process
brings with it the threat of madness. Roethke insisted on this. He
wrote in his notebook begun November 1955:

> I can't go flying apart just for those who want the benefit of a few verbal
> kicks. My God, do you know what poems like that cost? They're not written
> vicariously: they come out of actual suffering; real madness."
> "I've got to go beyond. That's all there is to it."
> "Beyond what?"
> "The human, you fool. Don't you see what I've done: I've come this far and I
> can't stop. It's too late . . ." [1]

If, through the experience of psychological disorder, Roethke
came to fear madness, he nevertheless discovered what he felt to be
a natural propensity for mystical insight. The discovery was inherent in the experience itself. Periodic bouts of manic depressive
psychosis subjected him to violent oscillations between extreme
psychic states of expansion and contraction; poles which can be ar-
tificially reproduced, as in Rimbaud's famous experiments with
drugs. In certain cases, the affective intensity of the experience of
mania has been compared to natural mystical experience, defined
as an intense "enthusiasm" stimulating a sense of numinous energy, as though the self had penetrated to a center of feeling little
in keeping with the conscious mind. [2] This "natural" experience is
examined by William James in *The Varieties of Religious Experience.*
In John Custance's *Adventure into the Unconscious* and *The Diary of
Vaslav Nijinski,* both of which Roethke read, the experience of ex-

---

1. Quoted by Allan Seager, *Glass House,* p. 224, these lines are from a play Roethke
worked on continually but never finished.
2. R. C. Zaehner, *Mysticism Sacred and Profane: An Inquiry into Some Varieties of Praeternatural Experience,* a good study of the various kinds of mysticism, from natural mysticism as stimulated by affective intensity, drugs, mental disorder etc., to orthodox
Catholic, Sufi, and Buddhistic mysticism. Zaehner refers to mysticism in its broadest
sense as simply "numinous" experience, as the term is used in this study.

pansion and release is a direct consequence of mental aberration.[3] Roethke's private psychic experiences were thus the source of his interest in mysticism. As was apparent from the *Praise to the End!* sequence, he subjected these to rigorous analysis, rejecting the delusions of elation as well as the temptations of depression. But he remained convinced of the mind's inherent capacity to extend beyond the self, as have all who have had such experiences. After his experiments with drugs, William James wrote: "I feel that the experience must mean something, if only one could lay hold of it. I cannot escape from its authority." [4]

It must be said that Roethke's interest in mysticism was not orthodox. He never submitted to the discipline of the senses which has as its end the apprehension of Absolute Being. In the last year of his life he admitted: "I can 't claim that the soul, my soul, was absorbed in God. No, God for me still remains someone to be confronted, to be dueled with" (*S.P.*, p. 26). Yet his interest in mysticism was not a literary affectation. He turned to it as a means to unify and order a life disordered and deracinated to the extreme. Allan Seager indicates that, at this period of his life, a profound impulse toward wholeness and unity was movingly apparent, perhaps as a reaction to the fatuity of extreme responses characterizing his earlier experience. Seager diagnoses this new equanimity and search for harmony as the consequence of a final, total acceptance of his periodic disorders, hitherto dismissed as unpleasant incidents. Acceptance was an initial step toward resolution. Seager insists that Roethke's tremendous dignity as a human being, which everyone felt who met him, came from his heroic determination to resolve the discords of private life into an affirmative poetic order (*Glass House*, p. 224).

Mysticism was a subject which always interested him. He had been reading Saint Theresa, John of the Cross, and Meister Eckhart as early as 1942, but only in "Meditations of an Old Woman"

3. John Custance, *Adventure into the Unconscious; The Diary of Vaslav Nijinski*, ed. Romola Nijinsky.
4. William James, *Varieties of Religious Experience*, pp. 388–89.

are the fruits of this reading strongly apparent in his poetry. Two books, in particular, helped him to formulate his attitude toward mysticism, and are therefore seminal to an understanding of this new sequence: Paul Tillich's *The Courage to Be,* a study of the existential anxiety he was trying to identify and transcend; and Evelyn Underhill's *Mysticism,* an exploration of the inward transmutation of consciousness in mystical experience. But until as late as the "Sequence Sometimes Metaphysical," he was apprehensive of the exclusive other-worldliness of orthodox mysticism, defined as the encounter with Absolute Being. He wanted, instead, a "rampant, triumphant, fleshly mysticism, the full spasm of the human, not simply beauty and darkness" (Notebooks, Reel 14, no. 197). One is reminded of Yeats, who insisted that his mystical concept "unity of being," far from being "distant and therefore intellectually understandable [would be] immanent . . . , taking upon itself pain and ugliness, 'eye of newt, and toe of frog.' " [5] This notion of a secular mysticism, that is, a mystical apprehension of a spiritual reality which is immanent and not transcendent, embracing the vicissitudes of natural experience, is important in assessing Roethke's understanding of the works of both Tillich and Underhill.

In the case of the former, he was deeply affected by Paul Tillich's analysis of existential anxiety as the desperate awareness of the threat of nonbeing which is inherent in existence itself. He borrowed this definition of anxiety for his own poem "The Pure Fury," and also mentions the idea in his commentary on the poem "In a Dark Time." In *The Courage to Be* Tillich formulates an ontology of anxiety, dividing the concept into three categories: the anxiety of fate and death, of guilt and condemnation, of emptiness and meaninglessness; and traces the historical predominance of each. His essential point is that contemporary consciousness is threatened by spiritual nonbeing: the anxiety, potentially present in every individual, which has become a general conviction—that the spiritual center is lost, that the determining causes of existence

5. W. B. Yeats, *Selected Criticism,* ed. A. Norman Jeffares, p. 263.

have no ultimate necessity. Roethke took this problem of self-affirmation as the subject of "Meditations of an Old Woman." He identified the emotional poles of the poem in a phrase in his notebooks: "Horror, which is unbelief, is the opposite of ecstasy" (Notebooks, Reel 14, no. 200). The poem moves from horror, the threat of spiritual nonbeing, to joy, "the entirely unique experience of the courage to say yes to one's own being." [6] After Tillich, this courage is an existential act—the affirmation of one's essential being in a courageous leap of faith which incorporates the anxiety of nonbeing into itself.

Critics have complained that the specific causes of anxiety in Roethke's later poetry are often difficult to locate. The implication is that he failed to define the source of what are presumed to be his neurotic preoccupations.[7] But his darker poems are rarely concerned with private neurosis; their theme is Tillich's existential anxiety—the vague, yet overpowering presentiment that the self can be totally, utterly annihilated. It is this presentiment which lies behind the brooding fear and undirected exasperation of so many of the poems. Transcendence could only be achieved by a deeper penetration into the numinous experiences of expansion and release which have played such a large part in his poetry. Consequently, he turned to Underhill's *Mysticism,* a book which, as his notebooks indicate, he considered seminal to his work.

In *Mysticism* Evelyn Underhill defines mystical experience as a psychological process, an alchemical transmutation of consciousness from the egoistic center to a deeper center of meaning.[8] She traces this spiritual metamorphosis through various stages: from the moment of initiation when the mystic sense is awakened and suprasensible reality breaks in upon the soul, through a purgative cleansing of vision, to illumination, the indwelling conviction of a

6. Tillich, *The Courage to Be,* p. 14. The notebooks corroborate Malkoff's assumption of Roethke's indebtedness to both Tillich and Underhill. See Malkoff, *Theodore Roethke,* p. 124.
7. See particularly Martin Seymour-Smith, "Where is Mr. Roethke?" *Black Mountain Review,* 1 (Spring 1954): 44.
8. Evelyn Underhill, *Mysticism: A Study in the Nature and Development of Man's Spiritual Consciousness.*

divine presence—all preliminary stages to the more drastic spiritual encounter, union with the Absolute. Through Underhill, Roethke found both a descriptive order and imagery which made sense out of what were obviously personal experiences of inward transmutation, charged with the highest and deepest numinous significance. So many of his poems, especially "Meditations of an Old Woman" and "The Abyss," follow the psychological progression as she describes it. They begin with the painful apprehension of personal insufficiency, aggravated by the awareness of the possibility of a deeper reality. This is followed by a desire for purification through self-castigation and mortification, which Underhill calls the painful descent into the "cell of self-knowledge." This leads to illumination, a sudden breakthrough to a heightened visionary joy in the awakening of transcendental consciousness. These are only the first three, as it were, secular stages of mystical insight; he never laid claim to the last stages which lead to union with Absolute Being.

Roethke accepted Underhill's analysis of mystical vision while rejecting the doctrines of Christianity itself; for he was never interested in formal religion and only toward the end of his life did he use the term God freely and with conviction. He wrote, "In crawling out of the swamp, I don't need a system" (Notebooks, Reel 14, no. 194). Instead, he acknowledged her basic premise— that nihilism, which is a despair of meaning to existence, can only be countered by trust in man's "innate but strictly irrational instinct for the Real" and by a belief in that ground of personality, inarticulate but inextinguishable, by which one is aware of a greater energy transcending the self. From this perspective, mystical experience is essentially a psychological process, a reintegration with the numinous substratum of being achieved through a purgative cleansing of vision, a stripping away and casting off of the old self until a new core is reached where, as Eliot would say, humility is endless.

Roethke once wrote that the subject of his poetry was the quest for identity. In his terms, this meant a "hunger for a reality more than the immediate: a desire not only for a finality, for a consciousness beyond the mundane, but a desire for quietude, a desire for joy." He called the state he was seeking (taking the phrase from Stephen Spender), "a final innocence" (*S.P.*, p. 19). He insisted that contemplation instills a method of being, and defined meditation as one simple state, the contemplative merged like a bird in air, in fullness, clearness. Obviously he thought of contemplation as a process of integration, an act of self-perception. The self, he insisted, once perceived, becomes the soul. "I am not speaking of the empirical self, the flesh-bound ego; it's a single word: *myself,* the aggregate of the several selves, if you will" (*S.P.*, p. 21). He came to believe in the individual soul as other than the ego, something of which this "other self" is the imperishable center, and to which death has no meaning. As in all notions of mystical apprehension, he saw the ego as the limitation that opposes itself to the infinite. The state of consciousness, freed from the ego, lost in a vaster consciousness, can initiate the deeper self into modes of infinite being. He was seeking the inexhaustible power of simple things, the purity of elemental being; and he wanted to re-establish an original relation to the universe. In this he aligned himself with the American transcendentalists, particularly with Emerson. The way back into divine nature was through the innocent eye. The old woman in his sequence can say: "I recover my tenderness by long looking/By midnight I love everything alive" (*C.P.*, p. 173). The innocent child becomes her perfect image of the buried soul; the child as a symbol of the primitive state of being, relieved of the active will and conscious thought and reabsorbed into the flowing continuum of unselfconscious nature. Consciousness is the curse—fractured, rational consciousness, straining after metaphysical assurances and alienating the self from the source of its sustenance in nature. To consciousness, Roethke opposes the order of "not-knowing, bearing being itself" (*C.P.*, p. 221). It is clear from his notebooks that he came to this notion through his readings of mystical literature, particularly the fourteenth-century anonymous tract, *The Cloud of Unknowing.*[9] The

9. *The Cloud of Unknowing,* trans. Clifton Wolters.

underlying idea of this treatise is that Reality can never be apprehended through intelligence. Roethke wrote in his notebook: "In
the very real sense, don't know anything." [10] In this assertion he
aligns himself with the mystical tradition of anti-rationalism. As
Henri Bergson put it most succinctly: "Intelligence enables us to
conceive possibilities, it does not attain any Reality." [11]

Many critics, the most eloquent among them W. D. Snodgrass,
have seen in Roethke's anti-rationalism and his consequent idealization of primitive life an impulse toward regression for its own
sake and a retreat from the complexities of human relationships.
His interest in mysticism appears to them as a desire to lose all
awareness of otherness in an ecstasy of withdrawal into the illusion
of eternity. [12] Such complaints have been raised against mysticism
in general. Jung, for example, in the early stages of his career,
identified the mystic impulse with the drive to recover the undif-
ferentiated bliss of the ouroboros. Later he came to repudiate this
entirely, seeing in mysticism an attempt to explore the transcendental instinct as an elemental part of the human personality. The
difference in attitudes seems to be one of temperament as well as
one of emphasis. One attitude sees in mysticism only the withdrawal from reasoned order and moral discrimination. The other
sees it as an attempt to trace the evolution of spiritual consciousness. From the perspective of the poet, the most serious accusations against mysticism are those of exclusive other-worldliness and
of rejection of this life for the illusion of eternity. Most apologists
of mysticism, Evelyn Underhill, R. C. Zaehner, Henri Bergson,
insist that, on the contrary, mysticism which ends in the solipsism
of Buddhism is an aberration. True mysticism leads to action; the
mystic is the exploratory consciousness of his race. Whether this is
generally acceptable is not important here. What is important is
that Roethke always saw the allurements of withdrawal into ecstasy as entirely negative and life-denying. In the "North American Sequence" he wrote: "And I acknowledge my foolishness with

10. Wagoner, ed., *Straw for the Fire*, p. 21.
11. Bergson, *Creative Evolution*, p. 180.
12. See Snodgrass, " 'The Anguish of Concreteness,' " pp. 86–87.

God,/My desire for the peaks, the black ravines, the rolling mists
. . . /The unsinging fields where no lungs breathe" (*C.P.,* p.
196), and many of his poems record his struggle against this impulse. As has been said, he wanted a rampant, triumphant, fleshly
mysticism, the full spasm of the human. One might complain, as
many critics have done, that in Eliot's particular brand of Catholic
mysticism this destructive process is at work. Man is plagued by
hints and guesses of an ideal which can neither be reached nor
brought into the twittering world of peripheral reality, except by
the saint. But like Yeats, Roethke tried to find the realm of the
spiritual within life itself. The pure moments he speaks of continually are moments of unity of being, a primitive variant on
Yeats's theme; moments of calm beyond doubt during which he
seems to discern the deepest rhythms of nature not described but
felt passionately, ubiquitously; moments transcending death because accepting it as an inevitable process of life. Roethke's most
determined conviction was the belief that "Eternity is now." Once
the doors of perception are cleansed, the world will appear as it is,
infinite. Like Blake or Yeats in his later life, he sought not withdrawal, but a transfiguration of present life and the present self.

Roethke began "Meditations of an Old Woman" in 1955
shortly after the death of his mother, who is the model for its central figure. Her death seems to have goaded him to a systematic
exploration of his basic beliefs. In *Words for the Wind* he had
turned to love as a sustaining principle of order; but, in the retrospective glance of old age, there comes a time when love is no
longer possible. He sees his mother in this situation: an old
woman forced to meditate on death and to will transcendence of
it. In the sequence he tries to reproduce her final meditations, her
sense of isolation and estrangement, her anxiety over death and
meaninglessness, her desperate gropings for an answer, however
symbolic and indirect, to the question of meaning to existence. In
effect, she tries to piece together, from the minor moments of
spiritual ecstasy of her lifetime, a coherent impression of the soul.

In writing his poem Roethke confronted a problem central to
the poet who would make spiritual consciousness the subject of his

poetry. Because the modern poet has at hand no universally held conscious formulation of belief, he can take nothing for granted. He has not only to find his own language for experiences which Donne, Herbert, Vaughan, or Traherne could convey through traditional metaphors, but he must also identify those intuitive experiences within an order that genuinely interprets, makes sense of spiritual experience.[13] If, like Eliot, he believes in Anglo-Catholicism, he must still make his belief emotionally understandable to the sensibility unprepared to accept that tradition. Or if, like Yeats, he erects his own elaborate scaffolding to accommodate his spiritual vision, he must begin with experiences like unity of being which the reader can identify as his own. In other words his position is defensive; he must begin at the beginning, tracing the evolution of his own spiritual consciousness starting with vague suggestions which are explored until the mind reaches an intuition. The modern poem attempting to relate spiritual experience to contemporary consciousness must be a private exploration of religious instinct, eschewing all conventional pieties which might be acceptable in a less heterogeneous age.

Without the systematic imagination of a Yeats, Roethke was forced to withdraw into the interior world of psychological experience to examine the phenomenon of consciousness itself. He discovered assurances of spiritual reality in the pure moment of intuitive being—those minor moments of spiritual blessedness which come to the self as a kind of reprieve. It is for this reason that the old woman begins her anatomy of the spirit by examining her own alternate modes of consciousness: moments of ecstasy, reverie, dream, memory, hallucination, tracing those powers in the self that are inconsistent with its limitation to quotidian reality and may form the basis of a new conception of the self.

The withdrawal into the world of inner experience brings with it its own kind of imagery: an imagery deriving from dreams, not from observation, and retaining the inconsequence, the half-understood but deeply felt significance of dreams, their symbolic truth.

13. Helen Gardner explored this problem in her study, *The Art of T. S. Eliot*, pp. 61–68, which I am indebted to for the following analysis.

The development of the poem is not the development of narrative but is rather a deeper and deeper exploration of an original theme. There is less a progression of thought than a circling round a state of mind, a final innocence, which is aspired to, yet continually despaired of. The overall movement of the sequence is successfully climaxed in the experience of rebirth, the movement from the stasis of the entirely quiescent self to the freedom of new life.

The first poem opens with the old woman's description of the landscape, but in Roethke's traditional manner, all natural objects are assimilated until they become symbols of the mind's emotional tone: trees tilt, stones loosen, the wind "eats at the weak plateau" (*C.P.*, p. 157). The spirit's journey is objectified in metaphors of frenzied aimless mobility: a cross-country bus ride, dreams of abortive journeys, and marine images, of the lobster's backward motion, of the salmon's movement against the current; all images of constricted, partial vision as the spirit searches for "another life,/Another way and place in which to continue" (*C.P.*, p. 159). What the old woman seeks and cannot find in her searches among the "waste lonely places/Behind the eye" is the moment of revelation. Inevitably she is disappointed; there can be "no riven tree, or lamb dropped by an eagle." There are only moments of heightened consciousness in nature, in which we recognize what Eliot has called the "hints and guesses," moments impossible to define except as a kind of stillness in which there is expectancy:

> A fume reminds me, drifting across wet gravel;
> A cold wind comes over stones;
> A flame, intense, visible,
> Plays over the dry pods,
> Runs fitfully along the stubble,
> Moves over the field,
> Without burning.
>
> [*C.P.*, p. 160]

This image of light playing over dry stubble in winter which appeared for the first time in "The Lost Son" holds for Roethke the persistent fascination that "light on a broken column," the image associated with the rose garden, held for Eliot. The word "reminds" is implied in both experiences. It seems that the moment wakens in the mind a sense of loss, a memory half guessed or hint half understood. If only the memory can be awakened and probed for its meaning, a spiritual equilibrium might finally be achieved. It is as though Roethke were insisting that the psychic disposition for mystical experience is there potentially, awaiting only a signal to express itself in action.

In the second meditation, the intimations of the autonomy of the spirit begin to be explored. "Why," Eliot has asked in *The Use of Poetry and the Use of Criticism,* "for all of us, out of all that we have heard, seen, felt, in a lifetime, do certain images recur, charged with emotion, rather than others? The song of one bird, the leap of one fish, at a particular place and time, the scent of one flower . . . such memories may have symbolic value, but of what we cannot tell, for they come to represent the depths of feeling into which we cannot peer." [14] In Section 3 of the meditation the old woman reverts to such moments: the overwhelming memory of perfume from half-opened buds when a dress caught on a rose-brier; fleeting images on the sill of the eye in the slow coming out of sleep; palpable hallucinations of tree-shrews from a remembered illness. Such moments forbid a premature closing of accounts with reality because they bring a conviction of definite types of mentality inconsistent with ordinary consciousness. In such moments consciousness seems to come in contact with the deeper unnamed feelings which form the substratum of our being and to which we rarely penetrate. These moments, charged with numinous energy, bring the joyful sensation of release: "The body, delighting in thresholds,/Rocks in and out of itself" (*C.P.,* p. 163). The conviction comes of the mobility of consciousness which has been arbitrarily limited to the rational. The problem becomes one of vision: "The eye altering, alters all." The limitations placed on reality are subjective, and inward transmutation is the clue to preternatural experience.

Louis Martz has called the subject of the meditative poem "the

14. Eliot, *The Use of Poetry and the Use of Criticism,* p. 148.

creation of the self." [15] In her third meditation, the old woman touches, if only momentarily, this deep-buried self, the ghost within her own breast:

> A voice keeps rising in my early sleep,
> A muffled voice, a low sweet watery noise.
> Dare I embrace a ghost from my own breast?
> A spirit plays before me like a child,
> A child at play, a wind-excited bird.
>   [*C.P.*, p. 165]

Roethke describes the interior revelation as a "low sweet watery noise," a voice from the unconscious. Explained in psychological terms, the long process of inward contemplation has activated one of the traditional archetypes from the unconscious—that of the divine child, always a symbol of nascent spiritual life and of immanent rebirth.[16] In mystical terms the self has experienced the initiatory moment of spiritual awakening. From his notebooks, it is clear that Roethke was familiar with the Jungian concept of individuation through the activation of the archetypal symbol—a process of transmutation of personality from a state of dissociation to a higher unity through integration with the unconscious mind. Yet is hardly seems necessary to invoke elaborate psychological justification for what is an ordinary conception—the soul perceived as innocent child, unless the inference of M. L. Rosenthal is accepted as general: that Roethke has resuscitated the rustic memorial of a belief in the soul.[17] The perception is so delicate and evanescent that no strong claims are made as to its authenticity. The experience brings nothing that can be known in the sense of a sustaining dogma, but simply a sense of union with a presence, momentarily exhilarating, but for that very reason dangerously tenuous. In fact, the old woman comes to dismiss it herself as a possible illusion.

15. Louis Martz, *The Poetry of Meditation: A Study in English Religious Literature of the Seventeenth Century*, p. 322.
16. Jung and Kerenyi, *A Science of Mythology*, pp. 83–84.
17. M. L. Rosenthal, *The New Poets: American and British Poetry since World War II*, p. 113.

In search of assurances she turns in Section 3 to a sustaining memory from youth when, for one mystical moment, "reality" came closer and the mind exceeded its finite bounds. The one conviction Roethke held to tenaciously was that there is a wholeness of what we are that can rarely be known, a wholeness which for some inexplicable reason we have been denied. As has been said, mystical experience was for him not so much a search for God as an evanescent intuition of this wholeness when momentarily the confusion of the separate divided selves is transcended. Roethke is very precise in his delineation of the stages of the experience. It begins as a familiar moment of stasis: what he referred to as moments "fixed under the eye of eternity" (Notebooks, Reel 13, no. 186). As in the later poem "In a Dark Time," it is a moment when the correspondences, analogies reminding the self of the invisible world, become apparent. The images of "Islamic moon" and "daemon" seem to be borrowed from Yeats's *A Vision* to define the experience as one of integration, a movement from the pure subjectivity of the empirical self to the higher objectivity that is the ideal of eastern mysticism. This at least would appear to be the only explanation for the curious line: "Out, out you secret beasts,/You birds, you western birds" (*C.P.*, p. 167). In Yeats's symbology, the bird is the natural emblem for the spiritual introspection that is lacking to western sensibility. The daimon, again in Yeats's system, is man's antithetical image, or ultimate self; sometimes it would seem a separate spiritual entity which imposes its remembered life on its mortal counterpart, thus creating the human being's body of fate. Roethke seems to temper Yeats's concept with the more familiar daemon of neo-Platonism, so that the line: "I shed my clothes to slow my daemon down" implies simply a quest for union with the higher spiritual self. It might be felt that Roethke is here too dependent on extraneous symbolism. His terminology is familiar: "Islamic moon," "daemon," "holy line," "western birds," "fire," but it intrudes into the atmosphere of the poem. One minds this invasion from the East because it has not been assimilated to the general emotional tone. Yet it is a momentary invasion, since the frenzied appeal to the primitive realm carries the reader back to a familiar world: "I said farewell to sighs,/Once to the toad,/Once to the frog,/And once to my flowing thighs." The traditional hierarchical progression from animal through man to spirit is never forthcoming in Roethke's work. Instead his spiritual quest is always in some sense a return, a regression to the subliminal world of toad and frog. He sought a primitive kind of innocence, an escape from self to the condition of the bird: "A rapt thing with a name." There is always something fragile and delicate in the purity of being he advocated. Even the purgatorial fire, the cleansing ecstasy of the mystical moment, is to be found in "a small place." The ideal, as the old woman says in the fourth meditation, is to "flame into being!" "to blaze like a tree" (*C.P.*, p. 169). Only primitive life can know this concentration continuously. In Roethke's evolutionary scheme of things, man never looms very large. Little is accorded to the achievements of human intelligence. For him there is no significant difference between what he calls the "coarse short-hand of the subliminal depths" and the "grave philosophical language" (*C.P.*, p. 170)—both are enunciations of the same terror and dismay. Like D. H. Lawrence, he values the natural self.

The sequence ends with the last poem, "What Can I Tell My Bones?" It is a moving elegy to the spirit's hunger and desolation. In it, Roethke achieves exactly what he is after: a personal, intuitive exploration of the meaning of preternatural experience based on the traditional principles of the mystic quest, which are yet so deeply buried as in no way to obtrude upon the delicate surface of the poem.

In the first part of the poem, Roethke identifies the old woman's state of mind in terms borrowed from the traditional mystical description of the purgative state, a state of pain and effort in which the self is only aware of its finitude and isolation while longing "for absolutes that never come." Such desolation is not an obsolescent state. It is part of the contemporary problem of spiritual anxiety, the terror of immanent nonbeing: "The self says, I am;/The heart says, I am less;/The spirit says, you are nothing" (*C.P.*, p. 172). Nothing could be more explicit than the old woman's cry: "The cause of God in me—has it gone?" To speak of the fear of death is to oversimplify; it is more precisely the fear of meaninglessness, of a lack of ultimate purpose to existence. The essential predicate of the religious personality is the desire for a principle of Love to which the belief and power of the individual life may be united. Lacking this principle, the self is without center. The old woman says: "My desire's a wind trapped in a cave. . . ./Love is my wound." She thinks of the essential tenet of mysticism—that God seeks union with the living soul.[18] To her, longing for rebirth, this has a precise and desperate irony: "I rock in my own dark,/Thinking, God has need of me./The dead love the unborn" (*C.P.*, p. 172).

It is difficult to determine exactly what Roethke means when he speaks of God. No doubt it seems easier to accept Yeats's Thirteenth Circle, or Eliot's Word intersecting time, because each is so well accommodated within a system. The closest one can come to Roethke's meaning is to speak of an energetic principle of love directing all of life. Perhaps it is almost impossible to be a lyric poet without some such notion of a deistic principle. Roethke often quoted Meister Eckhart with approbation: "God must be brought to birth in the soul again, and again" (Notebooks, Reel 13, no. 187). The implication is that God's existence is predicated upon the self's bringing God to birth in the soul. This would seem to be confirmed in his commentary on the poem "In a Dark Time" where he writes that the self in the mystical moment "becomes the Godhead itself, not only the veritable creator of the universe but the creator of the revealed God." He adds that God "in his most supreme manifestation, risks being maimed, if not destroyed." It is clear that his conception of God is far from orthodox. He confessed that his vision was very incomplete. Yet he continually professed a hope that "some other form or aspect of God will endure with man again, will save him from himself." [19] His attitude will be defined more thoroughly in Chapter 9, but as it

18. See Underhill, *Mysticism*, p. 38.
19. Roethke, "On 'In a Dark Time,' " p. 53.

is, his refusal to accept preconceived notions of divinity, implying as it does a rejection of dogmatism and an abhorrence of self-delusion—"that pelludious Jesus-shimmer" (*C.P.,* p. 98)—is eminently appealing to modern sensibility.

In Section 3 the movement of the entire sequence toward rebirth finally reaches its climax. If one is not familiar with Roethke's severe economy, the climax will appear abrupt and terse, for it is conveyed entirely through impressionistic images. The central image, familiar from "The Lost Son," is of weeds which "turn toward the wind weed-skeletons" (*C.P.,* p. 173). The verb is active. In the moment of extremity the dead life submits to the natural forces assimilating it to cyclic processes. It is an image of abasement and acceptance. Such is the condition of the self in the moment of reversal which Roethke insisted must come quickly or not at all: "Simply by the leap of the heart do we begin again." "We cry and we are heard" (Notebooks, Reel 13, no. 176). In the moment of extremity the will, with its fear of death which militates against existence, must give way; a new innocence is discovered in submission:

> To what more vast permission have I come? . . .
> I no longer cry for green in the midst of cinders,
> Or dream of the dead, and their holes.
> Mercy has many arms.
>
> [*C.P.,* p. 173]

This new permission hardly involves the notion of God. It is something simpler, more personal; a primitive variant of the purgative cleansing of vision:

> My spirit rises with the rising wind;
> I'm thick with leaves and tender as a dove,
> I take the liberties a short life permits—
> I seek my own meekness;
> I recover my tenderness by long looking.
> By midnight I love everything alive.
> Who took the darkness from the air?
> I'm wet with another life.
> Yea, I have gone and stayed.

Long-looking, the act of meditation by which the self recovers its meekness: "Be still! Be still and know." [20] In submission, the old woman achieves an almost mystical calm of rapport with elemental nature. M. L. Rosenthal compared the stillness of such moments to the light-spirited seriousness which we are told the early Christians possessed, a sweetness of nature derived from the literal rendering of the minutae of nature, and from accepting their meaning without quarreling about ultimates.[21] It is this reverent attitude to nature's particulars that frees the self. "Renunciation does not take away," Roethke wrote. "It gives. It gives the inexhaustible power of simple things" (Notebooks, Reel 13, no. 189). Humility, a capacity for reverence, a new unthought-of nonchalance with the best of nature, is the core of Roethke's aesthetic. John Crowe Ransom wrote that Roethke's old woman makes the best kind of saint it is advisable to try for.[22]

It would be a mistake to seek a rigid intellectual formulation for this "permission" which the old woman achieves. As John Crowe Ransom added: "She has not had to pray for this revelation, and does not bother as to where it came from, being scarcely conscious of her metaphysics." But it can be taken a step further if appeal is made to Paul Tillich, whose influence on Roethke has already been mentioned. The old woman has broken through to that state of absolute faith which Tillich has called "the courage to be." Able finally to abandon the need for certainties, she can say "Yes" to being. No concrete assurances have been discovered that might stem the realities of fate and death; as she knows, Providence and immortality remain fictions. But they no longer concern her because her faith is declared in being itself, and in the transpersonal presence of divinity which is its source. This is what Tillich means by the courage to be which can incorporate nonbeing into itself. It is the leap of faith made without final assurances because faith is all. Roethke's character achieves her personal variant of this

20. Underhill, *Mysticism,* p. 38.
21. Rosenthal, *The New Poets,* pp. 113–14.
22. John Crowe Ransom, "On Theodore Roethke's 'In a Dark Time,' " *The Contemporary Poet as Artist and Critic,* ed. A. Ostroff, p. 32.

courage, although her "permission" is at once more delicate and more energetic than its philosophical counterpart:

> What came to me vaguely is now clear,
> As if released by a spirit,
> Or agency outside me.
> Unprayed-for,
> And final.
>
> [*C.P.*, p. 173]

In the original *Words for the Wind* published in 1958, "Meditations of an Old Woman" concluded the volume. After the strict formality of the love poems, it seemed a radical stylistic experiment, signaling a new departure in Roethke's work. Obviously he had turned to the powerful influence of T. S. Eliot's *Four Quartets* to liberate himself from the formality of his earlier writing. He explained the reason for this in an interview reported by Cleanth Brooks and Robert Penn Warren in *Conversations on the Craft of Poetry:*

There are areas of experience in modern life that simply cannot be rendered by either the formal lyric or straight prose. We need the catalogue in our time. We need the eye close to the object, the poem about the single incident—the animal, the child. We must permit poetry to extend consciousness as far, as deeply, as particularly as it can, to recapture, in Stanley Kunitz's phrase, what it has lost to some extent to prose.[23]

To appreciate this statement it is necessary to remember the atmosphere of the time. The general ambition of poetry of the fifties, stimulated no doubt by the publication of William Carlos Williams' *Paterson* I and II in 1947 and 1948, was to discover larger comprehensive forms of expression to accommodate the intractable nature of contemporary experience. This central stimulus led to the creation of projective verse. Speaking on behalf of the poets of his generation, Charles Olson had written in 1950:

I would hazard the guess that, if projective verse is practiced long enough . . . verse again can carry much larger material than it has carried in our language

23. *Conversations on the Craft of Poetry,* ed. Cleanth Brooks and Robert Penn Warren, p. 61.

since the Elizabethans . . . if I think that the *Cantos* make more "dramatic" sense . . . it is not because I think they have solved the problem but because the methodology of the verse in them points a way by which, one day, the problem of larger content and of larger forms may be solved.[24]

The proliferation of the sequence or series of poems was the obvious result: Allen Ginsberg's *Howl*, Robert Lowell's *Life Studies*, and Olson's own *Maximus Poems*. Yet to some poets, this kind of comprehensiveness was at best ambiguous, the order of a sequence being based, more often than not, on the simple assertion that all of a poet's activities constitute a unity. Eliot's *Four Quartets* seemed, at least to Roethke, to offer a more fruitful example of how the sequence could be made to satisfy demands for larger, comprehensive forms without sacrificing exacting standards of unity and coherence.

It must be admitted that he could hardly have chosen a more difficult poet to emulate. In the *Four Quartets* Eliot found an idiom and a metric that were entirely idiosyncratic, making imitation admittedly dangerous. However, Roethke learned three valuable lessons of poetic technique. First, he learned how to adapt meter to mood, and to incorporate radical shifts of metrical style within the contemplative poem. This was something he had already discovered in the frenetic, rhythmic juxtapositions of the *Praise to the End!* sequence, so that Eliot's example served mainly to reinforce a personal technique. He also learned how to manipulate symbolism as a means to unify the long sequence. It is clear that the thematic material of *The Quartets* is less an idea or myth than certain common symbols, in particular, the four elements: earth, air, fire, water, each a thematic center of images in the separate quartets. Roethke uses symbolism in a similar fashion, if less dogmatically, so that the symbols of wind, fire, water, light, recur within his sequence with constant modification.

Finally Roethke learned from metrical and syntactical innovations in *The Quartets*. In his essay "Vers Libre," Eliot insisted that any good verse he had read either took a simple form like iambic

24. *Selected Writings of Charles Olson*, ed. Robert Creeley, pp. 25–26.

pentameter and constantly withdrew from it, or took no form at all, and constantly approximated a simple one.[25] Helen Gardener seems to have correctly identified the metrical pattern to which *The Quartets* approximate as a four stress line with a strong medial pause.[26] Eliot's syntactical patterns are equally simple. Allen Tate has called his style a form of deliberate peregrination, of statement followed by constant modification, supported by an intentionally fractured syntax.[27] The common pattern is of noun followed by adjectives: "the River/Is a strong brown god—sullen, untamed and intractable." This very resistance to a fluid vocabulary joined to a deliberate metrical uncertainty defines his personal voice.

In parts of his sequence, Roethke comes close to Eliot's metric and syntax. Eliot writes:

> Now the light falls
> Across the open field, leaving the deep lane
> Shuttered with branches, dark in the afternoon,
> Where you lean against a bank while a van passes,
> And the deep lane insists on the direction
> Into the village . . .[28]

Roethke writes:

> Often I think of myself as riding—
> Alone, on a bus through western country,
> I sit above the back wheels, where the jolts are hardest . . .
>
> And we ride, we ride, taking the curves
> Somewhat closer, the trucks coming
> Down from behind the last ranges,
> Their black shapes breaking past . . .
> [*C.P.*, p. 158]

Roethke has borrowed not only the four stress line with strong medial pause, but more importantly, Eliot's prosaic mannerisms: the proliferation of adverbs, prepositional and adverbial phrases,

25. T. S. Eliot, *To Criticize the Critic and Other Writings*, p. 185.
26. W. H. Gardner, *The Art of T. S. Eliot*, p. 29.
27. Allen Tate, *Essays of Four Decades*, pp. 468–71.
28. *The Complete Poems and Plays of T. S. Eliot*, p. 177.

and the fractured syntax of the declarative sentence with its string
of clausal modifiers. These echoes jar against the integrity of his
own voice. Though not numerous in terms of the whole sequence,
they do disturb:

> And we bounce and sway along toward midnight,
> The lights tilting up, skyward, as we come over a little
> rise,
> Then down, as we roll like a boat from a wave-crest.
>
> All journeys, I think, are the same:
> The movement is forward, after a few wavers,
> And for a while we are all alone,
> Busy, obvious with ourselves,
> The drunken soldier, the old lady with her peppermints . . .
> [*C.P.*, p. 158]

Eliot writes:

> When the train starts, and the passengers are settled
> To fruit, periodicals and business letters . . .
> Their faces relax from grief into relief,
> To the sleepy rhythm of a hundred hours . . .
>
> Or
>
> Or as, when an underground train, in the tube, stops
> too long between stations
> And the conversation rises and slowly fades into silence . . .[29]

The effectiveness of Eliot's journey images as metaphors for interior journeys are an obvious temptation to any poet, but Roethke's
syntax and rhythm are again so similar to Eliot's that the echoes
can seem detrimental. Yet it must be added that the imagination
of Roethke's persona, at once more sensuous and affectionate than
Eliot's, lays claim to a very different emotional response.

Sometimes it is the echo of a single line obviously alien to
Roethke's own endemic manner that drives the reader back to the
Eliot source: "It is difficult to say all things are well,/When
the worst is about to arrive" (*C.P.*, p. 172); or "We start from the
dark. Pain teaches us little" (*C.P.*, p. 166). The easy philosophical

---

29. Ibid., pp. 188, 180.

gravity of the lines is a tone Eliot has worked too well. As he himself said, a great poet can exhaust a particular pose for all those who come after him.

Even so, the delicate line between allusion and imitation is frustratingly ambiguous. We can allow Roethke the line "Do these bones live? Can I live with these bones?" (*C.P.,* p. 172), though the memory of Eliot's "Shall these bones live? Shall these/Bones live?" is clearly in mind, because the echo is functional. In both cases, the image sums up a tradition and depends on that tradition for its full implications. Furthermore, the phrase is assimilated to Roethke's characteristic style by its context. The line which follows, "Mother, mother of us all, tell me where I am!" reproduces the desperate, agonized plea that is so much a part of his tone.

One must question the pressures that lead to poetic flaws like unintentional echoes and extraneous or esoteric symbolism. Any poet obviously works under the current pressures of contemporary poetic modes. Roethke was acutely sensitive to the criticism that his poetry was exclusive, self-involved, as opposed to socially relevant, and was aware that the current trend was toward inclusiveness, toward a more philosophical poetry. He wished to extend the capacity of his poetry to explore meditative themes. Inevitably, he felt that an assault on the Eliot cult was in order. But to dismiss "Meditations of an Old Woman" as mere pastiche is narrow and destructive.[30] The poem contains some of the finest passages Roethke wrote, and some of his deepest insights into the introspective workings of sensibility. The pressure of his own imagination, the effortless and inescapable presence of his own individuality, is so palpably pervasive throughout the sequence that such a gesture is patently ridiculous.

When *Words for the Wind* was published in New York in the fall of 1958 it was widely reviewed as the work of a major poet. F. Cudworth Flint in the *Virginia Quarterly Review* wrote that, "of his chosen terrain, Mr. Roethke is master." Richard Eberhart, in the *New York Times,* called the book a major achievement in the Ro-

30. See particularly Clive James, "Tough Assignments" (review of *Selected Letters*), *The Review,* no. 23 (September–November 1970), pp. 47–53.

mantic tradition of American poetry. Delmore Schwartz in *Poetry* remarked that "It is sufficiently clear by now that Roethke is a very important poet"; and W. D. Snodgrass, in the *Hudson Review*, insisted that the new work was an accomplishment in language and form about which many of Roethke's contemporaries had only been dreaming. The book received many of the prominent literary awards of that year, among them the Bollingen Award and the National Book Award, firmly establishing Roethke's reputation and prestige as a poet. It probably convinced him as well that he was ready to begin the poem he had long contemplated, the "North American Sequence."

❧ VII ❧

The Long Waters
NORTH AMERICAN SEQUENCE

> I lose and find myself in the long water;
> I am gathered together once more;
> I embrace the world.
> [C.P., p. 198]

Roethke's last book *The Far Field* was published posthumously in 1964. It was completed, the division and arrangement of poems largely determined, when he died from a heart attack suffered in a swimming accident.[1] These last years had been prolific. Between 1959 and 1963 he had published sixty-one poems, among them the poems of the "Sequence, Sometimes Metaphysical" and the long "North American Sequence." According to Allan Seager, these were years of exhilaration and a new sense of freedom, discernible in the poetry's impulsive drive for harmony and resolution. Roethke seems to have written with a new ease and unwonted confidence, clearly feeling behind him the impact of his prestige as a poet. Yet these were also times of deep depression with periodic bouts of illness, the pressures of which are felt in the poems: "I have left the body of the whale, but the mouth of the night is still wide" (C.P., p. 188). An ambition to find order through poetry is movingly apparent. The poems read like last poems, attempts to integrate his themes and bring his vision to

1. Beatrice Roethke, together with Stanley Kunitz, assumed responsibility for the final editing of *The Far Field*. The order of the poems in "North American Sequence" and "Sequence, Sometimes Metaphysical" was clear from Roethke's manuscript; it was, however, unclear whether he intended poems like "The Manifestation" to be included in the final sequence, and they were relegated to the "Mixed Sequence." See Malkoff, *Theodore Roethke*, p. 172.

final statement. They find their common theme in a fear of death and the threat it poses to the validity and endurance of the self. Roethke's interest in mysticism was directly proportionate to this fear. The act of writing "Meditations of an Old Woman" had probably made him aware of what threatened to be a persistent dilemma—that his drive toward mystical ecstasy could prove to be a drive away from life. The "North American Sequence" is a penitential act of reintegration with nature. A poem of age and parting, its theme is the need to find a way to accommodate the fact of death within an acceptable view of life. It is also the fulfillment of a long-standing ambition to come to terms with the American landscape, interior and exterior.

Throughout his poetry Roethke had written of the desire to encounter the exterior world without threat, without separation, and of the impossibility of doing so while the values of the conceptual mind persist, since the mind cannot enter wholly into nature without fearing that implicit in change is the spectre of its own death. There were two alternatives: either withdrawal into abstract isolation in an attempt to move beyond body, time, and thought, or a deeper penetration into process and change until a vision of order and plenitude in nature was recovered. "North American Sequence" is the celebration of this second alternative; it is a search for the "imperishable quiet at the heart of form" (C.P., p. 188). The expression is uncharacteristically abstract but the idea is not new to Roethke's poetry. He uses the word "form" most often to imply interior synthesis, a clear sense of "serenity radiating from a center of knowledge," [2] or better, of revelation. Reality is "ordered" into form exactly to the degree to which it satisfies thought. Order, in that sense, is the mind finding itself again in things.[3] For Roethke, the perception of order in nature comes, not through rational investigation, but suddenly in moments of stillness, at-one-ment. He can discover the "imperishable quiet" only through what William Meredith has called a "wise

2. Arnold Stein, "Roethke's Memory: Actions, Visions, and Revisions," *Northwest Review,* 11 (no. 3): 22.
3. Bergson, *Creative Evolution,* p. 235.

and attentive passiveness" before nature until order is revealed within it, not imposed, but discovered intuitively in embrace.[4] Any attempt to impose order on nature, and that includes the mechanical order of cause and effect (the terrifying vision of the industrial landscape), as well as abstract idealistic systems of thought (the exclusiveness of ascetic orthodoxy), is anathema to Roethke's sensibility.

The paradox of his attitude toward form is clear in his use of water, the symbol of process and formlessness, to integrate his sequence in its quest for form. Each poem contains a progressive attempt to engage the self with the element of water, the generative principle of life seen as cycle and change, proliferation of being. But water poses a threat to the self which it may not be able to sustain. Even as it offers metamorphosis and change, it threatens dissolution of self, extinction of identity. The metaphorical burden of the sequence is to reconcile the poet with the element of life as water, with its advance and retreat, its havoc, until finally he can experience these fluctuating orders without threat. But to accept the fluidity of experience, he needs a still center, a "point outside the glittering current" (*C.P.*, p. 201) of experience. This need is the theme of the first poem "The Longing."

> I long for the imperishable quiet at the heart of
> form;
> I would be a stream, winding between great
> striated rocks in late summer;
> A leaf, I would love the leaves, delighting in the
> redolent disorder of this mortal life,
> This ambush, this silence,
>
> [*C.P.*, p. 188]

He would celebrate life as redolent disorder, even as ambush and silence (accepting the potentialities of life and death in its manifold activities) if he could begin to discover a principle of order within contingency. The words "quiet," "stillness," are always used in his work to signify an intuition of meaning and coherence:

4. Meredith, "A Steady Storm of Correspondences," p. 41.

"Near the stem, whiter at root,/A luminous stillness. . . . Adore and draw near" (*C.P.*, p. 221).

The need to identify with the generative reality of the here and now moves Roethke to reject any fixed and final order. In the sequence, T. S. Eliot becomes a kind of *doppelgänger,* haunting him with the allurement of release from nature by positing a separate and settled supernatural order beyond life. In clear echoes, Roethke rejects what is obviously a powerful appeal: "There are those to whom place is unimportant" (*C.P.*, p. 202); "I have come to a still, but not a deep center" (*C.P.*, p. 201); "Old men should be explorers?" (*C.P.*, p. 189). The "North American Sequence" is, as it were, an attempt to recover attachment to place by immersion, almost a kind of baptism, in primal waters. The process will be one of unlearning: "I would unlearn the lingo of exasperation, all the distortions of malice and hatred" (*C.P.*, p. 188). His solution is to reject civilized mentality with its egocentric emphasis— "O pride, thou art a plume upon whose head?" (*C.P.*, p. 188) and its alienation from nature, and to begin to feel his way backward toward a more primitive mode of consciousness which might enter wholly and finally into nature. The solution is one of self-effacement before reality. In a later poem he will ask to be "a simple thing/Time cannot overwhelm" (*C.P.*, p. 240). Here, as James McMichael writes so well, he seeks intuitive communion with those mindless things, at once more transient and more permanent than the concepts through which we understand them since they are representative of the natural process that subsumes us all.[5]

Symbolic topography is crucial to this theme. The sequence begins at the Pacific, yet Roethke often reminisces back through the interior continent to the Saginaw, Michigan, landscape of youth and childhood, a movement which reproduces the interior journey into the deeper reaches of the self. It is through this regression and subsequent integration of past and present that the

5. James McMichael, "The Poetry of Theodore Roethke," *Southern Review,* 5, no. 1 (Winter 1969): 21—one of the best essays on the sequence, which McMichael sees as a quest for God through the medium of nature.

poet recovers the attitude of mind which will allow him finally to merge with the dark and oncoming waters. This process is one of decreation. The mind trapped by its memories roves backward in search of purification until a new category of memory—almost a racial memory—is discovered in the child's celebration of nature: "Once I was something like this, mindless,/Or perhaps with another mind, less peculiar" (*C.P.*, p. 200). It is a radical metaphor of belief which asks for commitment to the natural world, trusting that it can accommodate the soul even as it annihilates the accepted categories of the self.

The sequence thus follows a loose but meaningful progression which, in Roethke's typical fashion, is also a regression. "The Longing" describes the poet isolated in a predatory world of death which offers no accommodation to the spirit. Yet toward the end of the poem he begins to sense an essential continuity with an earlier, primitive mentality which may afford the hoped-for release from egocentric isolation. In "Meditation at Oyster River," the long process of mergence with elemental waters through a lapsing of rational consciousness begins. Release from constriction is objectified in the image of the break-up of an ice-locked river in spring. "Journey to the Interior" and "The Long Waters" begin the return back, along detours and dangerous raw places, to the interior continent. It is symbolically a journey through the interior psychic landscape to the still center of the self. In "The Far Field," evocative as that image is of the greenhouse world of "The Lost Son," the poet recovers the world of childhood, its reverence before nature, its instinctive acceptance of death. This is a climactic poem offering a vision of man as a "sea-shape" returning to the sea of origins; the spirit, a wind that "gentles on a sunny blue plateau" (*C.P.*, p. 201), a phrase that celebrates the mystery of incarnate carnal being. "The Rose" returns to the Pacific where the present is reinvigorated by a childhood memory from the greenhouse world, a vivid recollection of one of those moments "beckoning out of the self" that Roethke puzzled over and rehearsed all of his life. The memory brings interior reconciliation that is repeated in a symbolic fashion in the final vision of the sea-rose found at the junction of river and sea, land and water, rooted in stone, yet free in the sea-wind.

These themes are elaborated almost entirely through the accumulation of certain basic images that are repeated with constant variation almost in the manner of musical phrases.[6] The poems, despite their seeming casualness, derive their meaning from an underlying code in which these images and their qualities are endowed with stable significations. In keeping with a personal habit of perception, Roethke aligns the images into elemental oppositions: earth and water (land and sea), rock and wind, shadow and light, salt and fresh water. They work largely in terms of a tension between notions of openness, vitality, motion, and of closure, sterility, stasis. Earth, even as it offers the assurance of stability, implies false, restrictive order. Associated to it are ideas of spiritual dryness and aridity, of failure of desire. Journeys into the nightmare interiors of the self find their objective correlative in a car ride through a landscape of dust and rubble, littered with the bodies of dead and dying animals. In contrast, water implies fluidity, even flux, life seen as cycle, proliferation of being; value invested in growth, spontaneity, metamorphosis. In his notebook, Roethke speaks of water as the signature of fruitfulness of body and desire. It holds out the magic, healing power of movement and release through the break-up of constriction. Identifying himself with the natural man in his metaphysical explorations, he chooses the Iroquois of the lakes over the Ogalala of the plains. Wind, the awakening of desire, is a complementary image to water in its freedom and movement. In one instance, he describes the spirit as a monumental wind that "gentles on a sunny blue plateau" (*C.P.*, p. 201). Rock implies stasis but also security. In

6. Hugh Staples, "The Rose in the Sea-Wind: A Reading of Theodore Roethke's 'North American Sequence,' " *American Literature*, 36 (May 1964): 189–203. Staples was the first to notice an alinement of elemental images, although the patterns and significations he describes are somewhat different. McMichael sees rather a hierarchy of images. In his notebook (Reel 14, no. 194), Roethke makes a list of elemental images and their qualities: wind, sea, water, salt, etc., implying that he did intend each image to have some kind of stable signification, though his notes at this time seem only chance jottings.

"Meditation at Oyster River" the poet retreats to the safety of the rock out of the water's reach. The development of the poem will be a process whereby he will learn to risk the return to the element of water. The shimmer and glitter of light and fire are affirmative signals, denoting interior revelation, while shadow implies retreat, withdrawal, diminution of being. A distinction between salt and fresh water, river and sea, implies an opposition between individual life and the encompassing cycle into which it is subsumed, between temporality and the eternal flux which underlies it. Salt was always one of Roethke's eternity symbols (*S.L.*, p. 121). Verbs, as well, carry symbolic import, those of motion and change implying positive ideas of release and liberation: "melting," "shimmering," "widening," "growing," "stretching," "dancing." Negative verbs are those of constriction and diminution: "shrinking," "freezing," "waning," "narrowing," "darkening," "receding."

These verbs and images imply a series of conceptual oppositions in the sequence which involves a debate of values: primarily between ideas of stasis and motion, order and flux, form and formlessness. The poet would work through to resolution rather than choice in a reconciliation of images, wherein neither possibility need be sacrificed, a demand embodied in the vision of the sea-rose. The sea-rose is that point of stasis outside the glittering current, the "imperishable quiet at the heart of form" found at the point of conjunction of fresh and salt water, rooted in stone, yet free in the sea-wind. It is so magically potent because it satisfies his appeal, mirroring a subjective synthesis, for rootedness within fluidity, movement with coherence, stability with spontaneity.

In his desire to abandon all fabricated form, Roethke goes as far as poetry will allow him in the direction of formlessness, fully embracing the organic style idealized by Emerson and practiced by Whitman: a style "emanating from the self as a leaf from a tree." [7] The basic idea is that art can emulate nature, flow with it, grow like it. The consequence to poetry is a willingness to allow a poem to find its own form, expanding naturally, through association and

7. See Richard Poirier, *A World Elsewhere*, p. 6 et seq. for a commentary on Emerson's attitude toward style.

catalogue, the catalogue presupposing only the most embracing connections. Thus a complete unity of theme and style is achieved by embracing the Whitmanesque cadence. Denis Donoghue has called Whitman's technique "a grammar of contact," of catalogue as a way of stringing particulars together as if to embrace the whole.[8] Whitman wrote: "I will not make poems with reference to parts/But I will make poems, songs, thoughts, with reference to ensemble," [9] and he created a style mimetic of this response: a ceremonial style of reverence for the corporeality and plenitude of the natural world. Roethke's central problem in "North American Sequence" is to recover his primal allegiance to the material and incarnate, and he does this through what he earlier called his strategy of long-looking: "I recover my tenderness by long looking./By midnight I love everything alive" (*C.P.*, p. 173). Through Whitman's technique—the cumulative structure, the long, free, cadenced line, and the vocabulary of cosmic passion and sense impression—he had precisely the ceremonial style he needed to re-enact this process—long catalogues celebrating in Whitman's phrase "the primitive sanities of nature," by which the poet is almost hypnotically brought back under its spell.

The "North American Sequence" begins, as have so many American works before it, with the search for the right relation to nature, partly in flight from the mechanized world of human construction; partly in search of an endemic pattern of order which is felt to be discernible in nature. The city is dismissed in a surrealistic catalogue of its horrors in the opening stanza. It is a product of that lust for objects which "fatigues the soul." The dilemma as Roethke defines it is "How to transcend this sensual emptiness?" Relief is identified in the idiom of Yeats: "How comprehensive that felicity! . . . /A body with the motion of a soul" (*C.P.*, p. 188). To desire a body with the motion of a soul is to seek the body as beatitude, to make one's final commitment to embodied form, an aspiration objectified in the long list of symbols of primi-

8. Denis Donoghue, *Connoisseurs of Chaos: Ideas of Order in American Poetry*, p. 41.
9. "Starting from Paumanok," *Leaves of Grass: Reader's Edition*, p. 23.

tive life that concludes the poem: "flower," "fish," "bird," "child," and "Indian." Roethke writes:

> I would believe my pain: . . .
> I long for the imperishable quiet at the heart of form;
> I would be a stream, winding between great striated rocks
> in late summer;
> A leaf, I would love the leaves, delighting in the
> redolent disorder of this mortal life,
> This ambush, this silence,
> Where shadow can change into flame,
> And the dark be forgotten.
>
> [*C.P.,* p. 188]

In beautifully caressing tones Roethke delights in life as incipient growth and proliferation of being, in a dancing child, an opening flower, a winding stream. The isolated element is movement, nature felt as an organic continuum of pure becoming. But the tense of the verbs is conditional. What is cutting the poet off from such a celebration is his own human separateness, his fear that such redolence can in no way accommodate the self. The poem ends with an echo of Eliot: "Old men should be explorers?" (*C.P.,* p. 189). Roethke accepts the challenge but not in Eliot's terms. Beginning to sense the lines of continuity with an earlier, primitive past, he attempts to identify himself with the Indian, the American natural man, seeking his ideal order in a predatory world of death and decay.

The second poem, "Meditation at Oyster River," opens with an image which seems peculiarly tempting to the poetic sensibility: the imagination confronting reality in the guise of the poet gazing at water. For Roethke, Oyster River, in its inexorable yet imperceptible movement, its blue black waves creeping closer without sound, without violence, is a symbol of life as ambush. The marvelous paradox is that he chooses to merge with the obliterating waters, to be with the shy beasts where "Death's face rises afresh" (*C.P.,* p. 190). For some critics this is a withdrawal in acquiescence to the death longing to which he was so fatally attracted.

The impulse to merge is really a deprivation and reduction of life, a mindless and regressive sensuality which has broken down the integrity of self.[10] These divisive interpretations are based on antagonist definitions of what constitutes the self. For Roethke the self is a unity of being rather than a unity of will. He always distinguishes between the ego, which he associates exclusively with false will, and the mystic spontaneous self: mystic in the sense that it transcends the power of the imagination ever to know the self completely. In Roethke's terms the egoistic self, in its disgust and fear of life, withdraws into a spurious integrity which he always describes in solipsistic images: the withdrawal of the snail into its shell or the persistence of a "dying star" (*C.P.*, p. 190), an image of abstract isolate being. This alienation of the will with its frightened apprehensive self-insistence must be broken. Merging with the flux of the waves is, in the poem, an act of self-effacement before reality, the self plunging into the density of an exterior world that exceeds it. One of the most effective moments in the sequence is the description in Section 3 of this poem of the icebound river breaking its boundaries in spring, expressing the ecstasy of release from constriction that is experienced in the escape from self. [11]

The question is whether this is simply escapism; as W. D. Snodgrass remarked, "less a regression to capture something and recreate it, than a regression for its own sake, to lose something and uncreate it." [12] It is true that Roethke was often plagued by a desire to escape the divisiveness of consciousness. But to insist that this was always a negative impulse is to underestimate the positive import of his symbols of pure being, of which the most central is water itself (Notebooks, Reel 14, no. 194). One of the fundamental desires expressed in his poetry is the desire to live blindly with the insouciance and singleness of the simpler forms of subrational

10. See particularly Snodgrass, " 'That Anguish of Concreteness,' " pp. 78–79; and Rosenthal, *The New Poets,* pp. 113–18.

11. Jung explains that the release of the ice-bound river in spring is an archetypal image in the process of individuation. See *Psychological Types or the Psychology of Individuation,* trans. H. Godwin Baynes, pp. 259, 324.

12. Snodgrass, " 'That Anguish of Concreteness,' " p. 85.

life. Obviously the human being can only approximate the primitive unity of instinct when, in rare moments, self-consciousness is transcended. Yet these moments are immensely precious to the romantic sensibility because to inhabit them is to move in the pure gesture of creation unselfconsciously from the deepest self. The aim of the primitive poet is not to sustain endlessly an artificial and morbid ecstasy in nature, as though nature were an exotic intoxicant. More seriously he believes that, through the medium of nature, and the ecstasies it affords, a coincidence with the creative principle of life may be discovered.

That the long journey out of the self is paradoxically a journey to the interior, rather than a counter-impulse toward disembodied transcendence, is made explicit in the third poem. Imagery is entirely symbolic, the exterior landscape a portent of psychological states. There are two journeys: one familiar in Roethke's work—the ascending journey up the narrowing incline along the swollen riverbank toward the dark swampland, the still center of the psychic landscape; the other more problematical, a symbolic journey westward through an American landscape of desiccation and death which seems to telescope the meager heritage of the Midwest with its uniform, concrete houses, its red weather-beaten courthouses, and its desolate graveyards, all representative of the failure of the culture to provide spiritual sustenance. Apparently the very act of repossession of the past constitutes a ritual catharsis, a redemption through acceptance. Stanley Kunitz spoke of this as a "symbolic dying into America, so to speak." [13] It is precisely this—the journey ends with an oneiric vision of the Pacific evoked in the symbol of the mystic rose, the soul at a "still-stand": "I rehearse myself for this:/The stand at the stretch in the face of death,/Delighting in surface change." Roethke's death ritual is paradoxically a ceremony of accommodation to life. D. H. Lawrence once called Walt Whitman a post mortem poet, a poet of the transitions of the soul on the confines of death. In Whitman he found the true rhythm of the American continent speaking out—the soul living her life

13. Kunitz, "Poet of Transformations," p. 26.

along the incarnate mystery of the open road.[14] In his use of the
symbol of the road, Roethke too becomes a post mortem poet,
through an acceptance of death celebrating the natural verities of
life.

In "The Long Waters" the poet turns decisively toward the
world of fluidity and change. With self-mockery, he rejects the
appeal of a fixed and final order and the desire for absolutes as spiritual self-indulgence:

> And I acknowledge my foolishness with God,
> My desire for the peaks, the black ravines, the rolling mists
> Changing with every twist of wind,
> The unsinging fields where no lungs breathe,
> Where light is stone.
>
> [C.P., p. 196]

The simplicity with which he invokes the name of God at the
same time as rejecting all traditional notions of absolutes is moving. In an act of humility, he returns to the sensuous world where
fresh and salt water meet. In retrospect the first lines of the poem
become clear. When he says he rejects the world of the dog, he
simply means that he will turn to the empathic song of minimal
life. It is the most extreme act of faith in the natural world that he
can make. No illusions are courted. The poet knows the unreliabil-
ity of the sensuous world, its transience, its havoc, even its subterranean terrors in the nightmare faces of his tentacled sea-
cousins. Momentarily he appeals to Blake's nurse Mnetha, Mother
of Har, in Blake's mythological system, the mother of false sterile
innocence. Yet the lure of retreat from experience is again rejected
as involving exclusion: "But what of her—/Who magnifies the
morning with her eyes"—the exclusion of the fullness of sexual
being. When speaking of love Roethke often resorts to the old
Elizabethan paradox of love as a death or fall. Here, as a man of
feeling, he chooses love: "Feeling, I still delight in my last fall"
(C.P., p. 197). The act of faith is complete. He has chosen the
"rich desolation" of the landlocked bay where the salt water is

14. Lawrence, Studies in Classic American Literature, p. 161.

freshened by small streams. The subtlety and effectiveness of the water symbolism is clear. It is used in an extremely precise fashion to detail a morality of values.

The poem ends with a symbol familiar from "Meditations of an Old Woman" and poems like "The Song" and "The Exorcism."

> I see in the advancing and retreating waters
> The shape that came from my sleep, weeping:
> The eternal one, the child, the swaying vine branch,
> The numinous ring around the opening flower,
> The friend that runs before me on the windy headlands,
> Neither voice nor vision.
>
> [*C.P.,* p. 198]

This is Roethke's image of the deep-buried principle of life; the soul principle, not merely of the interior self, but of all things. Multiple and seemingly contradictory, it is "child," "swaying branch," "numinous ring"; it is all these things because it is being. If one were to seek for a rationale behind the variable symbols, it is to Jung that one should turn, for Roethke obviously intends the symbols as archetypal images, multiple projections of a transcendent postulate at the core of being.[15] He speaks of the principle as a shape from sleep, weeping. In "Meditations of an Old Woman" it was a low sweet watery noise; in "The Song" a voice from a watery hole. Water is the central symbol for the unconscious. Furthermore the principle is always subterranean—beneath the darkness under the leaves, under earth, root, or crevice. In contact with this deep-buried self, a reintegrative impulse toward life emerges. The poem ends with the magnificent stanza:

> I, who came back from the depths laughing too loudly,
> Become another thing;
> My eyes extend beyond the farthest bloom of the waves;
> I lose and find myself in the long water;
> I am gathered together once more;
> I embrace the world.
>
> [*C.P.,* p. 198]

15. Jung's clearest explication of the concept of the archetype is his chapter "Archetypes and the Collective Unconscious," in *Two Essays on Analytical Psychology*. Roethke lists this book in his notebook (Reel 13, no. 185).

The process has been one of losing and finding, not one of regression for its own sake, but in order to recreate the self. It is being that is affirmed unequivocally.

"The Far Field" takes the explicit theme of death and examines its implications. There is no self-delusion, no fanfare. Among the scattered members of cats, birds, rabbits, at the flower dump (Roethke's earliest image of putrefaction) one learns of the eternal: that it does not exist. The loss however is not drastic. The poet insists, "My grief was not excessive" (C.P., p. 199). It sounds at first like an evasion to say simply that one can "forget time and death," as though the response were not violent enough to counteract the impact of death. It is this absence of rage that has led some critics to accuse Roethke of acquiescence. In his notebook he wrote: "I can no longer renew myself by short rasps of exasperation" (Notebooks, Reel 13, no. 188). To replace rage, he sought faith, as the radical metaphor of reincarnation makes clear:

> —Or to lie naked in sand,
> In the silted shallows of a slow river,
> Fingering a shell,
> Thinking:
> Once I was something like this, mindless,
> Or perhaps with another mind, less peculiar;
> Or to sink down to the hips in a mossy quagmire;
> Or, with skinny knees, to sit astride a wet log,
> Believing:
> I'll return again,
> As a snake or a raucous bird,
> Or, with luck, as a lion.
>
> [C.P., p. 200]

Roethke's tone is hard to assess. It is both nostalgic and serious, yet underlying it is the delicate playfulness that is so much a part of his style. We can think of the idea of reincarnation as a metaphor of belief—in life as value—for him, epitomized not in human consciousness at all, but in the principle of being. Or yet again, his meaning might be more literal than this. In his lifetime he is said to have professed a belief in the primitive doctrine of reincarnation in animal form.[16] By it he implies not the survival of human individuality, but of the essential life energy which, as it were, returns to the primal source for re-creation. As with Yeats this is an affirmation of absolute commitment to life; to man "returning life after life like an insect in the roots of the grass." [17] Roethke's inclusion of the transmigration of the soul in animal form in his scheme is characteristic. He once wrote: "I can project myself more easily into a flower than into a person" (Notebooks, Reel 14, no. 194). The animal world was for him, as it was for Rilke and Lawrence, symbolic of the pure existence to which human existence was inexplicably closed. The metaphor brings relief: "I have come to a still, but not a deep center,/A point outside the glittering current" (*C.P.,* p. 201). The echo of Eliot is an unmistakable challenge. If the "imperishable quiet at the heart of form" for which he had longed has not been discovered, at least he has reached acceptance and without courting fictions like that of absolute transcendence. From his notebooks it becomes clear that for him the "still center" is a psychological rather than a theological conception borrowed from Jung to imply a point of stasis within the self,[18] a statis reached through a willing acceptance of the idea of death:

> I am renewed by death, thought of my death,
> The dry scent of a dying garden in September,
> The wind fanning the ash of a low fire,
> What I love is near at hand,
> Always, in earth and air.
>
> [*C.P.,* p. 201]

The poem closes with an image of the final man which owes much to Wallace Stevens' conception of the central man. Roethke writes of the "old man with his feet before the fire,/In robes of green, in garments of adieu." In "Note towards a Supreme Fiction," Stevens had written of the man "in his old coat,/His slouching pantaloons,

16. Interview with Beatrice Roethke, 12 August 1970.
17. Ellman, *The Identity of Yeats,* p. 162.
18. Notebooks, Reel 13, no. 185. Roethke writes: "There is a still center. There is also a deep center—Jung: *Two Essays on Analytical Psychology.*"

beyond the town." Stevens' figure is generic man, the major abstraction who is at the center of the secular myth called the supreme fiction. He is the man of imagination, purely human, purely fallible, even pathetic; yet, by virtue of his imagination, the connoisseur of chaos.[19] Roethke incorporates this figure to his own conception, for the idea is not new to his poetry. The theme appeared in the "Dying Man": "I am that final thing,/A man learning to sing" (*C.P.,* p. 153); in "Meditations of an Old Woman": "I breathe what I am:/The first and last of all things" (*C.P.,* p. 170); and in "The Bird, the Tree": "Thus I endure this last pure stretch of joy,/The dire dimension of a final thing" (*C.P.,* p. 248). For Roethke the final man is man in the act of leave-taking, faced with his own immensity, the mystery of being which he incarnates and to which the mind can gain no access. He is returning to water, the sea of origin, encumbered with age and memory, the cycle of which he is the returning unit, having almost completed its round.[20] The poem concludes with a celebration of the imagination's capacity for analogy: "All finite things reveal infinitude" (*C.P.,* p. 201). He does not use the concept "infinitude" in the sense of perpetual duration in space or time, but as an ever-present quality, or better, capacity of the soul. One thinks of Emerson for comparison: "They ask me whether I know the soul to be immortal. No. But do I not know the Now to be eternal? . . . I believe in this life."

Roethke brings his sequence to resolution through the symbol of the rose, perhaps the most resonant of all literary symbols. He claims it as his own through characteristic images that define its context. His flower is a single wild rose struggling out of a tangle of matted underbrush, in that place of conjunction where fresh and salt water meet. Free in the wind, the sea-rose represents the reconciliation between rootedness and fluidity, between earth and water, stasis and motion that he was seeking. It is not Eliot's

19. Roethke's notebooks quote numerous excerpts from Robert Pack, *Wallace Stevens: An Approach to his Poetry and Thought,* which emphasizes the themes of reality, imagination, and connoisseurship.

20. The description is D. H. Lawrence's in reference to Herman Melville, but it applies equally to Roethke's figure. See *Studies in Classic American Literature,* p. 124.

heavily acculturated symbol, but a single solitary bloom, growing toward clarity out of confusion. For Roethke, the symbol embodies the energetics of the life process itself. In the rose image, the polar tensions of life are brought to balance in a vision of "The imperishable quiet at the heart of form." The vision does not come out of a vacuum. It is the fruit of the long meditative process of the sequence, and can only be understood psychologically. It must be recognized that the rose in the sea-wind is an objective and emotionally satisfying expression of an inner subjective synthesis. In contrast to the superficial divisiveness of life embodied in the motion of the waves, there exists the stasis of the sea-rose. It is magically potent and mysteriously satisfying because it evokes the hybrid roses of the greenhouse, the two conflated in a union of past and present, a subjective synthesis that is symbolically a reconciliation with the father: "What need for heaven, then,/With that man, and those roses?" (*C.P.*, p. 203). In one of those still moments held impressionably in the memory, the father suspends the child over the natural growth as the roses beckon the child out of himself. The experience is one when the firm, rational distinction between the inner world of feeling and the external world of sense breaks down, an experience of primitive atonement with nature. These moments of release are saving moments, shattering the sense of isolation and separateness which has haunted the poet. This is neither a simple nor a predictable recovery, since the early memories had themselves to be stripped of the old hostilities. For one of the few times in Roethke's poetry, the father is recovered in an intimate and personalized memory of reconciliation and love.

The poem ends with an explicit statement of the new change.

Among the half-dead trees, I came upon the true ease of myself,
As if another man appeared out of the depths of my being,
And I stood outside myself,
Beyond becoming and perishing,
A something wholly other,
As if I swayed out on the wildest wave alive,
And yet was still.
And I rejoiced in being what I was:

[*C.P.*, p. 205]

In a still moment of synthesis, a profound readjustment of personality has taken place: what Roethke called, in a phrase often quoted in his notebooks, the abandonment of the egoistic center of personality to another center of being. It is as though spirit is something to be achieved, a goal in an on-going process, the aim of the self in its ascent on the scale of being. This is no withdrawal into pious mysticism. What is celebrated in the poem through the symbol of the rose is the mystery of incarnate, carnal being. D. H. Lawrence's description of the symbol is, in this respect, closest to Roethke's meaning: "We are like a rose, which is a miracle of pure centrality, pure absolved equilibrium. Balanced in perfection in the midst of time and space, the rose is perfect in the realm of perfection, neither temporal nor spatial, but absolved by the quality of perfection, pure immanence of absolution." [21]

Before turning from the "North American Sequence," it is important to mention the criticisms directed against it. Roethke has two formidable critics, W. D. Snodgrass and M. L. Rosenthal, who find that the sequence indicates a falling off in his work. For them, it is a self-intoxicating rehearsal of the escapist desires which he had been unable to resolve, and which were the product of a fear and detestation of life. It represents a failure of discrimination and intelligence. Instead of mastering his subject he dissolves into it, creating random sensational images without any controlling principle of organization. W. D. Snodgrass writes in his essay, "That Anguish of Concreteness," that the sequence suffers from a failure of desire, a longing for death:

What appears dominant in the last book is a desire to escape *all* form and shape, to lose all awareness of otherness, not through entrance to woman as lover, but through re-entrance into eternity conceived as womb, into water as woman, into earth as goddess-mother. . . .

    . . . The desire to lose one's own form has taken on a religious rationale to support itself . . . [a] search for a state of being, a religious stasis, as an escape from this world of form and becoming . . . for pure space as an escape from time.[22]

21. D. H. Lawrence, *Selected Essays*, p. 26.
22. Snodgrass, " 'That Anguish of Concreteness,' " pp. 87–89.

Rosenthal concludes his commentary on the "North American Sequence" with the insistence that behind the "assumption of an achieved, transcendent quietude lies a deeper impression of inability to cope with the old, still unresolved hysteria, which Roethke had unloosed in his earlier work, and of a consequent resort to the stock cosmic pieties of sagedom from Chuang-tzu on down." [23] The problem for these critics seems to be the suspicion that Roethke courted withdrawal for its own sake, that his poetry acquiesced to the terror and disgust he so clearly depicted, and collapsed into formlessness embodied in the religious longing for an abstract condition of stillness beyond the contamination of this life. The object of attack is what is felt to be his mystical desire for a hermetic state of purity beyond body, time, and thought, which only thinly disguises the death-longing toward which he was so fatally impelled. By this standard the "North American Sequence" is a work of unacknowledged malaise and of general tropism toward death.

Roethke's insistence on using images does indeed create problems of interpretation. The disposition of the images, their balance and repetition, are the only basis from which the conceptual structure of the sequence can be inferred. The sequence has, in fact, no clear-cut paraphrasable meaning, but operates with the impact of music, with the persuasiveness of embrace through an imagery that is self-creating and self-perpetuating. But there is certainly a debate of values between what Snodgrass and Rosenthal speak of as religious escapism, the desire for a disembodied transcendence, and the celebration of incarnate, carnal being. It seems to me that Roethke emphatically rejects the former:

> And I acknowledge my foolishness with God,
> My desire for the peaks, the black ravines, the rolling mists
> Changing with every twist of wind,
> The unsinging fields where no lungs breathe,
> Where light is stone.
>
> [*C.P.*, p. 196]

23. Rosenthal, *The New Poets*, p. 113.

He denies the illusion of any fixed and final form of religious stasis beyond the world of becoming, and seeks to identify with nature as a process of change and fluidity. It is the very depth of his insight into this process which makes him fear for the stability and endurance of the self. Paradoxically, a process of immersion in the flux of life rather than withdrawal into an abstract purity beyond life allows him to recover a sense of rootedness and stasis, of subjective synthesis. In one sense he has rediscovered his own past through recovery of a childhood memory. But more profoundly, through an experience of mystical intensity in which the barriers of form dissolve, he comes to discover that the loss of self is not something to be feared; that death can be accepted with equanimity as a reintegration into the natural processes of life. A poem that comes very close to this idea is D. H. Lawrence's "The Ship of Death," where the soul accepts its journey to oblivion with courage and faith in life itself, leaving the survival of personality as a peripheral question and concentrating instead on the ceremony of accommodation to death as part of the cycle of life.

One of the problems involved in criticism of Roethke is a failure to accept his primitivism at its deepest level. He is profoundly antirationalistic. Being and knowing are opposite, antagonistic states. The more you are in being, the less you know. As Lawrence put it: "The goal is to know how not-to-know." [24] Roethke's primitivism moves him to reject any formal religion. At the same time, however, he will not place final faith in human individuality. He is a mystic, not in his withdrawal from body, time, and thought, but in his total submission to nature, and in his pious recognition of the vital mysterious substance of life itself: "What does what it should do needs nothing more" (*C.P.*, p. 235). The problem for critics like Snodgrass is that these poles are not very far apart. In fact, they meet in their recognition of the need to abandon egocentric self-assertion in deference to a power larger than the self be it called "Nature" or the "Word."

M. L. Rosenthal and W. D. Snodgrass are critical of the new

24. Lawrence, *Studies in Classic American Literature*, p. 107.

style of Roethke's "North American Sequence" because it seems to corroborate their suspicion of an appeal to formlessness as an escape from self. The lack of vigorous control and the impressionistic use of language seem to Snodgrass, in particular, to represent a failure of desire, a self-intoxicating rehearsal of random sensational images which become self-imitating and predictable. To speak of the sequence as a collection of random images without any controlling principle of organization is, however, to underestimate the theoretical considerations that moved Roethke to this style, and to reject out of hand the tradition that validates his experiments.

Roy Harvey Pearce has written that all American poetry must be, in some form, a dialogue with Whitman. The "North American Sequence" is Roethke's dialogue—an attempt to "strike again the naked string / old Whitman sang from." [25] Whitman bequeathed to American poetry a new attitude toward form—a desire to take form not as a given, but as something more important, as a process of discovery, of exploration. He sought to create a form of the loosest kind to embrace rather than order the diversities of external nature. Tony Tanner has called it "a sort of deliberately inchoate form which nudges things together rather than autocratically regimenting them to reveal finished form and total lucidity of arrangement." [26] Whitman's most important contribution to American poetry was to reinvigorate the catalogue as a way of stringing particulars together for maximum evocation of the natural scene without the intrusion of the barriers and filters of formal prosody. He called his technique a "going directly to creation" or in William Carlos Williams' later rephrasing: "No ideas but in things." His emphases were fluency, candor, unpremeditated attention and assimilation, inclusiveness.

Roethke had been waiting a long time to write his "American" sequence. As early as 1944, he was writing to William Carlos Williams of his need for a device to organize his ideas about the

25. Robert Duncan, *The Opening of the Field*, p. 64.
26. Tony Tanner, *The Reign of Wonder: Naivety and Reality in American Literature*, p. 82.

American Midwest (*S.L.*, p. 112). His sequence was to be a celebration of the landscape "WRIT LARGE," as Charles Olson
would say. Even the early poem "Night Journey," his first lyric on
this theme, was an attempt to embrace "the land I love" (*C.P.*,
p. 34). Whitman's long, free, cadenced line, his breadth and
inclusiveness, gave Roethke the style he needed, but not without
posing certain problems. Whitman was content with pure description and association, with long catalogues of cumulative images
celebrated for their own sake. Roethke was moved to a more explicit order and control. As Stanley Kunitz remarked, he could not
be content with simply naming the objects that he loved; he was
"driven to convert them into symbols—that painful ritual." [27]
The problem was how to incorporate things on their own terms
and, at the same time, to convey what he conceived to be their
value without resorting to generalized statement. This ambition
differentiates Roethke from Eliot on the one hand, and from
Whitman on the other. He does want meaning and order, but
without philosophical commentary. He wants the illusion of
Whitman's freshness and informal unselfconsciousness, his hospi-
tality to the vagaries of the eye free from analysis and categoriza-
tion, but with hierarchical and moral values implied. His solution
is to align his images, particularly that of water, to stable significations, as has been demonstrated earlier, so that a perfect ac-
curacy of description is able to imply moral perception. With the
closest attention, the hidden currents which manipulate the surface drift of the images are clearly discernible and the ruse of
unpremeditated attention and assimilation breaks down. As is
clear from his earlier work, Roethke was too devoted to form to
acquiesce to collecting random sensational images. He offers the
illusion of artlessness and artistic self-effacement in order to celebrate the American landscape—the thing in itself. But he is too
much of a conscious craftsman not to create a world which attempts, in the words of Tony Tanner, "to explain, evaluate, and
ordain the real world." [28]

27. Kunitz, *Poet of Transformations*, p. 28.
28. Tanner, *Reign of Wonder*, p. 85.

The "North American Sequence" was composed over a long period from 1958 to 1963. During the same period, Roethke was working on the poems of the "Sequence, Sometimes Metaphysical." The two sequences are diametrically opposed: one measuring the new confidence the poet has achieved; the other, the sporadic cries of rage, outbursts of despair, in which the subjective synthesis won with such difficulty in the "North American Sequence" breaks down. The difference between the sequences is that in one, the poet is able to celebrate being without having to quarrel about ultimates; the other is a drive toward God, a search for final revelation. Nor does one response disqualify the other. Through Yeats we have come to accept that, in an age without belief, the poet must be allowed the liberty to test alternative possibilities. And clearly, there is a reconciliation of the sequences at the deepest level. Even when Roethke embarks on his metaphysical searchings after God, it is primitive nature which is his medium of recovery.

❧ VIII ❧

Being, not Doing
LAST POEMS 1958–63

I have merged, like the bird, with the bright air,
And my thought flies to the place by the bo-tree.

Being, not doing, is my first joy.

[*C.P.*, p. 222]

Many readers of Roethke's last book have noted the impression of finality that *The Far Field* conveys. The poems read like last poems. Allan Seager writes:

The last years of Ted's life, as we look back on them knowing they were the last, seem to have a strange air of unconscious preparation. As the fabric of his body begins to give way, the best part of his mind, his poetry—seeming to have forgiven everyone everything, demolished its hatreds, and solved all its discords—strives toward a mystical union with his Father." [*Glass House*, p. 251]

As Seager makes clear, this sense of preparation was unconscious. Roethke wrote *The Far Field* over a period of five years and, if he was ill much of the time, death when it came was unexpected. The explanation for the impression lies elsewhere. His work has that pattern which only major bodies of art can claim: the sense of a continual forward impulsion which is yet dependent on all that has gone before, so that in any reading the mind is driven back through the whole body of the artist's work to those images, ideas, memories, and obsessions that constitute the core of the creative personality. Roethke's is such a body art because of the way he seemed to write instinctively in phases or outbursts of inspiration which always came in stark contrast to what had preceded. His image for the pattern of psychic energy is best applied to his own work: the onward rush of the wave into stillness before a new impulse of energy is released. After the formal breakthrough the *The. Lost Son* his work bears this repetitive pattern—a sudden release of creativity which is in part the discovery of a new form; in a later phase this impulse is exhausted for the last possible inspiration so that a new phase must begin out of necessity. In *The Far Field* Roethke was in such a period. It is a book of summation, of the poet's mind coursing retrospectively for images over the whole body of his work, seeking the final statement which can release him from his themes. After it one can assume that he would have had to search for new sources of inspiration.

The Far Field is then a book of reconciliation and atonement, of final statements on themes that have preoccupied him from the beginning—themes of love, identity, and the threat posed to these by death, and the theme of God. It is composed of four sections, the "North American Sequence," "Love Poems," a "Mixed Sequence," and the "Sequence, Sometimes Metaphysical." For our purposes, the two middle sections represent a return to earlier themes and images, but it is important to note the unity of tone that pervades them since, in their light, we begin to understand the urgency of Roethke's drive toward God. The "Mixed Sequence" are poems of death, of hunter and hunted, of suffering and betrayal. Often they center on a victim or quarry, usually a small animal, with storm and flight for shelter as persistent images. A terrible sense of isolation and loneliness pervades them, and a deep sensitivity to the vulnerability of life:

> I think of the nestling fallen into the deep grass,
> The turtle gasping in the dusty rubble of the highway,
> The paralytic stunned in the tub, and the water rising,—
> All things innocent, hapless, forsaken.
>
> [*C.P.*, p. 227]

The love poems are equally preoccupied with pain and isolation: "Will the heart eat the heart?/What's to come? What's to come?" (*C.P.*, p. 211). The burden, the enormous threat love poses to the integrity of the self is still on the poet's mind. Even in the lyrics spoken in the persona of a young girl, while love is profoundly sensual and exhilarating, it is not unalloyed with dread. In "Her Reticence" the young lover seeks to give fragments of herself, not daring to give the whole. In "Her Longing" passion equates her with "the black hag," "the cormorant," "the condor." In "Her Time," the images are of storm and shelter: "When every-thing—birds, men, dogs—/Runs to cover:/I'm one to follow,/To follow." Yet Roethke's theme is not the failure of love. Some of his deepest affirmations of love are here:

> I, living, still abide
> The incommensurate dread
> Of being, being away
> From one comely head.
> [*C.P.*, p. 215]

The inadequacy is more fundamental. It lies in the fear of death which is stronger than love. These are the poems of the older poet aware that in love so much has been given only to be lost again to death. The last poem of the sequence, "Wishes for a Young Wife," is moving in its simplicity:

> May you live out your life
> Without hate, without grief,
> And your hair ever blaze,
> In the sun, in the sun,
> When I am undone,
> When I am no one.
> [*C.P.*, p. 217]

The central concern that supports and explains these themes is, of course, Roethke's preoccupation with his own mortality. Death is the chaos that constantly threatens to overwhelm his sense of self, so desperately and laboriously created through the pages of his poetry. Here it is the awareness of death that explains the sense of isolation and vulnerability of these last poems. Throughout his poetry he had tried to free himself from death's obsessive hold by a willed transcendence of it. He called "The Lost Son" ". . . a stage in a kind of struggle out of the slime; part of a slow spiritual progress; an effort to be born, and later, to become something more." (*S.P.*, p. 37). All of his poems are part of this spiritual struggle, nowhere more fierce nor more fiercely resolved than in this final book. It is pervaded by premonitions of death which elicit the most radical response—the attempt to evolve a myth of God. In earlier poems the notion of God was something longed for, hinted at, and recognized chiefly by its absence: "Is it you cold father? Father,/For whom the minnows sang?" (*C.P.*, p. 90); "The cause of God in me—has it gone?" (*C.P.*, p. 172). In the "Sequence, Sometimes Metaphysical" Roethke embarks upon an active search for God. He described these poems as "part of a hunt, a drive towards God, in an effort to break through the barrier of rational experience. They begin at the abyss, at the edge of being, and descend into a more human, more realizable condition. They turn away from loneliness to shared love." (Notebooks, Reel 13, no. 191).

To appreciate Roethke's last sequence, it is necessary to understand exactly what he meant by God, and by the experience of psychic disintegration that led him to seek a transcendent unity. This is the subject of the poem called "The Abyss," in which the state of anxiety which gives rise to the search for God is dramatically defined as a dark night of the soul, the hell that is the trap of self-enclosure. In mystical convention, the dark night is the fourth stage of the arduous quest for the beatific vision, a period of psychic fatigue and mental chaos in which the overwhelming impression is of the loss of God and the acute sense of the imperfection of self. It is the last crisis, the final test in the process of self-purification.[1] Such desolation is not an obsolescent state, nor one reserved for the religious. It can be secular and agnostic, an exis-

---

1. W. H. Heyen in "The Divine Abyss: Theodore Roethke's Mysticism," *Texas Studies in Literature and Language,* 11 (1969): 1051–68, offers a detailed analysis of Roethke's dependence in "The Abyss" on Evelyn Underhill's five stages of mystical illumination. While this is very fruitful, and Roethke is undoubtedly indebted to this source, this interpretation eliminates much of the personal terror of the experience, and is often somewhat rigorous. Roethke denied ever having reached Underhill's final stage of illumination. See *S.P.*, p. 26.

tential night, as in Robert Lowell's poem "Skunk Hour," in which the final point of darkness is reached where the one free act is suicide. Roethke uses the motif of the dark night to identify a psychological state of terrifying self-absorption, defined in the familiar image of the night-fishing otter, the mind retreating instinctively into the obscurer regions of consciousness. The "androgynous" act, "a hole disappearing into itself," "crawling into your hole and pulling your hole after you," is his obsessively persistent image for this condition.[2]

The occasion of "The Abyss" is the approach of the crisis of mental disorder. It is the first time that Roethke has dealt so explicitly with this subject from an entirely adult perspective. The wild frenetic rhythms of the first stanzas, with their mordant humor, catch with hallucinatory intensity the loss of control and sense of terror at the approaching crisis, a crisis which, because it is cyclic, is appalling: "Each time ever/There always is/Noon of failure,/Part of a house." Gradually the rhythms break down in a simulation of the disintegration of will and of desire: "The wind's slowing" (rising wind is always Roethke's image for the awakening of desire). Never has he described the prelude to breakdown more explicitly:

> I hear the noise of the wall. . . .
> Be with me, Whitman, maker of catalogues:
> For the world invades me again,
> And once more the tongues begin babbling.
> And the terrible hunger for objects quails me:
> The sill trembles.
>
> [*C.P.*, p.220]

The fear expressed is of madness itself, of being swept away into delirium.

The phrase "the terrible hunger for objects" refers to personal experience. Seager records that Roethke's breakdowns were preceded by frantic sprees of buying objects, perhaps as a desperate appeal to the material as a stay to dissolution. (*Glass House,*

---

2. Roethke, "On 'In a Dark Time,' " p. 52.

p. 219). Whitman, with his loving catalogues, would be an appropriate protector. The wall denotes the barrier of natural vision, the threshold of the preternatural which threatens to dissolve. The image as used here recalls that remarkable line from Hölderlin's "Hälfte des Lebens": "The walls loom speechless and cold," a poem which also anticipates the coming on of psychic disorder.

The poem comes closest to an analysis of its terror in Section 3 when the crisis of disorder, the approach to the abyss, is defined in terms of images. Of course this places a heavy burden on language since the experience can only be conveyed elliptically. For Roethke it is clear that the abyss is an experience not of gaping void or mesmerizing emptiness as it was for Baudelaire in "Le Gouffre," but of surfeit, "a terrible violence of creation": "Too much reality can be a dazzle, a surfeit;/Too close immediacy an exhaustion" (*C.P.*, p. 220). He uses the term "reality" not in the Platonic sense, but to denote the multiplicity and chaos of matter itself. It seems clear that what he wants to convey is the nausea, the fundamental sense of absurdity which bears in upon the self confronted by the superfluity of physical phenomena when no ulterior purpose is apparent. (One thinks of Sartre's *La Nausée*.) Such is the "flash into the burning heart of the abominable," "the terrible violence of creation" (*C.P.*, p. 221). At last comes the switch-over, the moment of release, which is always forthcoming if only the terror of the experience can be withstood. Roethke insisted that the moment of extremity, of supreme disgust, is the worst. When change comes it is either total and instantaneous or not at all.[3]

The rest of the poem seeks to understand this change, this movement into stillness: "Do we move toward God, or merely another condition?" Rational consciousness cannot approach the mystery. Rather the poet seeks understanding through the intuitive sense akin to empathic response: "I envy the tendrils their eyeless seeking" (*C.P.*, p. 221). In this state of not-knowing the poet can, in the mystical phrase, understand without understanding the peace to which he has penetrated.

3. Ibid.

> In this, my half-rest,
> Knowing slows for a moment,
> And not-knowing enters, silent,
> Bearing being itself,
> And the fire dances
> To the stream's
> Flowing.
>
> [*C.P.*, p. 221]

This state of not-knowing is one of the most fundamental conventions of mystical doctrine which insists that the spiritual intuition which inducts man into the intelligible world can only be achieved through a surrender of the self-conscious will to a state beyond thought. In his notebooks Roethke wrote: "What is there to know? Not-knowing. We think by feeling, what is there to know? The answer is unknowing, the unknowing of the cloud of unknowing" (Notebooks, Reel 14, no. 204). Obviously the source of his terminology is the fourteenth-century mystical tract, *The Cloud of Unknowing,* which describes how the state of being can be approached through contemplation: "Contemplation is just this unknowing knowing, this blind seeing, this presence which is unfelt . . . the earnest of the unmentionable, ineffable glory which is to come." [4] This unknowing, "full blind and full dark," is a state of intensified consciousness beyond will and reason and seemingly beyond acceptable notions of time. It is primarily a state of illumination in which a world of being and eternal forms is experienced, but it involves no final apprehension of divinity. For this reason Roethke asks whether the experience is a movement toward God or merely a moment of self-integration, of union with the subconscious mind. His state of uncertainty is described as one of rocking. As Stanley Kunitz noted, the verb "to rock" is one of Roethke's key verbs of motion, implying a meditative moving backward in search of resolution. [5] Here he rocks between dark and dark, between the darkness of doubt and isolation, and the dark-

---

4. Wolters, trans., *The Cloud of Unknowing,* p. 38.
5. Kunitz, "Poet of Transformations," p. 26.

ness of illumination, the "dazzling dark" (*C.P.*, p. 155) of supernatural reality. He is able to escape this rocking only through
acceptance, a sublimation of the will to know:

> Such quiet under the small leaves!—
> Near the stem, whiter at root,
> A luminous stillness.
> The shade speaks slowly:
> 'Adore and draw near.
> Who knows this—
> Knows all.'
>
> [*C.P.*, pp. 221–22]

Characteristically the impulsion of the images is downward and
under, implying that the source of transcendent quiet is subliminal, an invasion from the depths of self. But the disposition of
the images implies something still more important. The stillness
is at root—both at the root of self and of material creation—
implying an involution of interior being and exterior world in a
kind of correspondence which is called worshipful. According to
Evelyn Underhill this sense of ordered correspondence between the
separate levels of existence, material and spiritual, is the profoundest truth that mysticism has to offer.[6]

The immediate sensuous world, formerly only a violent creation, is now seen in its beauty and plenitude, a characteristic
reversal in Roethke's poetry. The poem ends with the assertion:
"Being, not doing, is my first joy." Perhaps he remembered this
from Underhill's *Mysticism* where she writes: "Being, not doing, is
the first aim of the mystic." [7] "Being" of course, is the word the
mystic uses to denote both godhead and his own identification in
the mystical moment with the divine ground of being. In characteristic understatement Roethke makes no such final claims.
Being, as he uses it here, refers to that state of radical innocence
beyond will and desire which Meister Eckhart called a recovery of
primal existence, when I wanted what I was and was what I

6. Evelyn Underhill, *The Essentials of Mysticism and Other Essays*, p. 23.
7. Underhill, *Mysticism*, p. 380.

wanted.[8] It is a spiritual state, a blaze of being, though as Roethke remarked elsewhere, God "still remains someone to be confronted, to be dueled with" (*S.P.*, p. 26).

There is always the hope that some kind of contact has been achieved: "And my thought flies to the place by the bo-tree." In Buddhistic tradition the bo-tree, as Roethke records in an early notebook (Reel 5, no. 66), is the sacred tree of illumination where Buddha received the heavenly light. His tone is one of longing. He insisted that he had known illumination, the initiation which inducts man into an eternal world of essences and in which, according to mystical convention, the apex of the soul already dwells; but he never claimed that "the soul, my soul, was absorbed in God" (*S.P.*, p. 26). This is a radical distinction. It seems hardly necessary to reaffirm that he was a poet and not a mystic, except that the latter role is often claimed for him to his detriment as an artist.

He has always been one of those poets like Hopkins and Emily Dickinson, who convince that personal survival and poetry are interdependent. It is clear from "The Abyss" that he began his "drive toward God" under tremendous pressure and out of necessity. The need either to expose his experiences as delusory or to substantiate them as the mystical intuitions he thought them to be was paramount. And the furious intensity of division within the self was exacting its price. Human limitation expresses itself in his poetry almost as physical pain. Like the dark sonnets of Donne and the desperate sonnets of Hopkins, these last poems are cries of despair. This new spiritual quality is a measure of Roethke's maturity as a poet.

The complexity and desperation of Roethke's conception of God has often been underestimated. The notebooks which correspond to this period of writing indicate that he was reading religious philosophy with some intensity with a view to evolving his own private notion of divinity, a notion which owes much to the medieval mystic Meister Eckhart. Whether this was ever a coherent

8. *Meister Eckhart: A Modern Translation*, trans. Raymond Bernard Blakney, p. 231.

philosophy or whether such a philosophy might even have been possible is questionable. Certainly Roethke's premature death leaves the question unanswered. But as far as his poetry is concerned it is necessary to see the direction of his ideas if one is to appreciate the intensity of these last poems.

"In a Dark Time" is the most clear and moving expression of his aspirations. The poem shows how far he has come in matters of style. Its power derives from the note of tension and strain, of profound personal pressure Roethke gives to the subject of spiritual conflict. This is as much a matter of form as of content, the end-stopped lines creating a rhythmic tightness and force without sacrificing any sense of continuity. In a symposium in *The Poet as Artist and Critic* edited by Anthony Ostroff, fellow poets John Crowe Ransom, Babette Deutsch, and Stanley Kunitz offer lengthy commentaries on "In a Dark Time" which are followed by Roethke's rejoinder. They are an indispensable addition to any study of the poem.

"In a Dark Time" is clearly a religious or philosophical poem that takes as its subject the esoteric experience of spiritual revelation. It was written in July 1958 during a period of illness and intense depression. To be understood it must be recognized that each stanza of the poem is a self-contained unit representing a single stage in a lengthy process: in the first stanza the dark time is introduced, in the second despair is intensified to a frenetic pitch, in the third a bright blaze of consciousness heralds a storm of correspondences, supernatural signs, and in the fourth despair is redoubled as the soul falls back into solipsism, until at the height of self-disgust the switch-over comes and, with it, final revelation. The transitions between the stanzas are abrupt and can be disconcerting unless the reader is prepared to follow the language precisely; for Roethke is very accurate in his delineation of the stages of this psychological experience. The marvel is that he has been able to deal with it at all, taking this normally abstruse subject and investing it with dramatic intensity. He does this by concentrating upon that part most available to common experience, the dark night itself, the soul in its madness.

The poem begins with a series of paradoxes and verbal repetitions:

> In a dark time, the eye begins to see,
> I meet my shadow in the deepening shade;
> I hear my echo in the echoing wood—
> [C.P., p. 239]

This is the dark wood of confusion, a self-created dark: "Which way I fly is hell! My self am hell." Spiritually desolate, the self fragments; identity is eroded. With night eyes, the poet begins to distinguish his shadow, "my double, my Other, usually tied to me, my reminder that I am going to die." [9] The crisis comes from an overpowering sense of mortality from which the self is usually protected by instinctive rejection. Here, defenses are broken down; the self knows it can be totally, utterly annihilated. "How," Roethke asks, "does one get to the 'dark time'?" It is not he insists, something reserved for the technically manic-depressive (Notebooks, Reel 14, no. 200). Rather for the poet it is a self-created dark, a willed risk that he is driven to take by the limitations of human existence. "What's madness but nobility of soul/At odds with circumstance?" Circumstance is clearly what we know as necessity, mortality itself that the poet is under the old compulsion to exceed. In this poem, Roethke views the poet as orphic visionary impelled by forces beyond himself to extend the limits of human consciousness, even though he risks being "maimed, if not destroyed" in the welter of psychic chaos unleashed. As the desperate later poems attest it is a compelling myth of poetic vision in which he could only partially believe; yet a moving tribute to the capacities of the human mind to transcend itself.

The name of Orpheus is not inappropriately invoked, as in the poem Roethke sees the poet as a primitive man, a lord of nature who "would gather the beasts," calling "upon their powers in my spiritual ascent or assault." In explication of the line: "A lord of

---

9. Roethke, "On 'In a Dark Time,' " pp. 49–53; subsequent quotations are from this essay; early drafts of the essay appear in Notebooks, Reel 14, no. 200, and are used to supplement Roethke's comments where helpful.

nature weeping to a tree," Roethke writes: "The speaker is weeping to a *tree,* a growing thing, which, as a primitive man, he can touch and feel and understand." Of the line "I live between the heron and the wren,/Beasts of the hill and serpents of the den," he adds, " 'I live between': I partake of them all. . . . they protect me; they are my nearest and dearest neighbors." In part the animals serve the poet as symbols, the heron of purity, wisdom, and toughness; the wren of courage and audacity. But more, as a natural man he calls upon their primitive potency. In an earlier poem to the snake Roethke had written; "I longed to be that thing,/The pure sensuous form" (*C.P.,* p. 150). Representative of primitive life, the snake is pure essence, being scaled down to its integrity and therefore fit symbol to contrast the poet's own sense of divisiveness. But it must again be added that there is a further dimension of animistic belief to Roethke's use of such images, a conviction that natural forces can be appealed to for assistance. This involved no superstitions but was more an emotional attitude of reverence toward nature which grew out of his acute sensitivity to nature's particulars. No other poet has singled out the fearful small and the subliminal world of cave, bog, and pond with such loving attention. This reverence secured Roethke's poetry from the asceticism that would have been the natural consequence of his mystical aspirations. There is nowhere the steadily intensifying rejection and denial of life that marks most meditational poetry. In fact the climax of most of his poems, as of this one, comes when this very impulse is resisted; when the poet breaks free of the divisive human will which, fearing death, retreats from life.

In the second stanza of the poem the purity of despair is realized in all its finality. The sense of psychic dualism is most acute—the mortal self is tethered while the spirit seeks transcendence. Fear remains paramount. The spiritual assault or ascent must lead either to impasse or to the winding path—the arduous journey from flesh.

In stanza three the assault is already accomplished. It is possible that the abstraction "correspondences" forces the mind back too quickly to theoretical considerations—the Swedenborgian theory

of correspondences. For what is wanted is the sense of a living actual moment of oracular intensity in which nature becomes instinct with meaning, sending out a veritable storm of signs indica-
tive of an invisible, divine dimension to existence. The experience
is one of extreme joy, a "tearless night" in which the natural self
dies in a blaze of the supernatural.

After this momentary vision "which may last a moment or a
whole night," the self is plunged back into its solipsism, and of
course, in contrast to its former beatitude, the prison house of the
senses is intolerable: "My soul, like some heat-maddened summer
fly,/Keeps buzzing at the sill." Self-loathing, not unalloyed with
fear, has reached the moment of supreme intensity. As disgust
rebounds upon the self, fear is projected upon the very object of
love, momentarily uncovered in the blaze of light—the supernatural, or God himself. The moment of crisis comes as a question:
"Which I is *I?*" "Am I this many-eyed, mad, filthy thing, or am I
human?" These swings in extreme response, "acceleration" up or
down, are what the mind has most to fear from this experience.
"The way up and the way down may be the same, but the pace
often varies, sometimes disastrously," as Roethke puts it. The
point is that after the exalted state the downward acceleration into
the "Nothingness" of despair is absolute and, as he suggests, there
is no guarantee that it can be impeded. Herein lies the desperate
risk to the self; "This is no jump for the timid, no flick from the
occult."

Release comes unexpectedly, miraculously. Roethke writes:
"The moment before Nothingness, before near-annihilation, the
moment of supreme disgust is the worst: when change comes it is
either total loss of consciousness—symbolical or literal death—*or* a
quick break into another state, not necessarily serene, but
frequently a bright blaze of consciousness that translates itself into
action." Given the extremity of his situation the source of release
must remain a mystery, an act of grace detailed in an absent line.
This grace, though that word has perhaps too many theological
connotations, translates itself into action: "A fallen man, I climb

out of my fear." It is a human act—man can will his own salvation, a notion unacceptable to the orthodox. With this self-assertion comes the real transition. "The mind enters itself, and God the mind." Roethke writes: "The mind has been outside itself, beyond itself, and now returns home to the domain of love." In a later poem he will write: "I love myself: that's my one constancy" (*C.P.*, p. 244). Ironic of course, yet the underlying inference is that self-love is a basic and necessary premise of being. In the poem this mainstay has been lost until the mind, the alienating principle, enters itself. Furthermore, God enters the mind. In later poems, as in his commentary on "In a Dark Time," Roethke draws a distinction between the separate notions of God and godhead. He seems to have discovered this idea in his readings of Meister Eckhart and later of Paul Tillich. With a pithy wit which obviously appealed to Roethke, Eckhart wrote: "Godhead is beyond thinking; god is what I think he is." [10] Explained simply, godhead is the All, the ground of being: God is the subjective impression of the notion of godhead, a projection of the profoundest human emotions. Eckhart also wrote: "God must be brought to birth in the soul again and again." In terms of modern psychology God is relative, a symbolic expression of an overwhelming psychological experience, an impulse or inspiration that transcends human understanding. This subjective experience has been surpassed in the poem. The final line, "And one is One, free in the tearing wind," is meant to take the mind one further leap for, according to Roethke, we are to understand "One" as "the Godhead theologically placed above God." What he wants to describe is a final union with the transpersonal presence of divinity, neither subjective nor objective, which is beyond all conventional religious and private notions of God. It is a daring assertion of human freedom for the final emphasis is placed on the poet "free in the tearing wind." Roethke once wrote: "The poet is God's metaphor creating a new world from the void." The poet has here wrenched

10. Blakney, ed., *Meister Eckhart*, p. 225. Random quotations from Eckhart appear throughout Roethke's later notebooks.

from the private abyss of his own despair a vision of the mind and imagination as united in the "ground of being" (the phrase is from Eckhart) thereby becoming the veritable creator of the universe.

These abstractions are difficult to respond to until the final half-line, which reaffirms our confidence. Of this Roethke writes: "I feel there is a hope in the ambiguity of 'tearing'—that the ambient air itself, that powers man once deemed merely 'natural,' or is unaware of, are capable of pity; that some other form or aspect of God will endure with man again, will save him from himself." In amplification in his notes he concludes: "We have only begun our researches. But it's the kind of thing which teases some of us out of thought—that there may be other worlds, other states of consciousness." Bergson's *Morality and Religion* lends support to Roethke's tentative hope. Bergson believed that by exploring the implications of mystical experience, itself a totally unique form of human consciousness closest to the intensity and singleness of instinctive apprehension, an impression of coincidence might be discovered with the generative principle of life. He wrote that intuitions must be turned inward and "if, in a first intensification, it makes us realise the continuity of our inner life, . . . a deeper intensification might carry it to the roots of our being and thus to the very principle of life in general"—the *élan vital* or spiritual current that the mystics call divine.[11] As a poet Roethke had no need of systems; he believed in a personal mysticism unalloyed with allegories or theological doctrines. Yet one cannot help but be interested to see how in trusting solely to his own powers of intuition, he came so close to Bergson's own speculations. Of course Bergson would have approved Roethke's methods, since for him all truly creative insights come spontaneously and unpredictably with an enthusiasm that can fire a soul and consume all that is within it. Roethke wrote that "In a Dark Time" was a "dictated poem, something given, scarcely mine at all." He does not mean that he was saved in this instance from the strain of revision, the mundane labors of the poet. Rather the poem's inspiration is dic-

11. Bergson, *Morality and Religion*, p. 214.

tated. One is moved to believe him, for the absolute transcendental conviction of this poem remains a solitary occasion in his work.

Few major twentieth-century poets have been willing to risk the double heresies of God and of salvation. Eliot, Auden, Yeats, and perhaps Rilke are the exceptions. Without Eliot's willingness to submit to traditional theological dogma, nor Yeats's capacity to construct his own elaborate spiritual system, Roethke found himself in Rilke's position. Emotionally and imaginatively he still felt a strong need for the name of God, yet he was unable to commit himself to any final system of belief. The idea of God becomes in his poetry an emotional hypothesis built out of the sheerest force of will, an act of faith which must be constantly renewed. His poems become cries of their occasion, assertions of longing, of desperate faith and also momentary assertions of despair. They are lyric poems. Roethke speaks of them continually as songs: "In purest song one plays the constant fool" (*C.P.*, p. 244). "I'll make a broken music, or I'll die" (*C.P.*, p. 240). One is reminded of an earlier line: "O to be delivered from the rational into the realm of pure song" (*C.P.*, p. 172). The belief is that if only one can get beyond cerebration, one can begin to attend on final things. Though Roethke is not usually a figure to be associated with Kierkegaard, he is with him here: belief is essentially absurd and can only be achieved by the leap of faith.

"In a Dark Time" was the first of the "Sequence, Sometimes Metaphysical" to be written in 1958. The poems which follow might be said to take as their epigram the line: "Was I too glib about eternal things,/An intimate of air and all its songs?" (*C.P.*, p. 241), for they explore more tentatively and more desperately the affirmation of the earlier poem. They are ordered with Roethke's usual attention to thematic movement: "They begin at the abyss, at the edge of being, and descend into a more human, more realizable condition. They turn away from loneliness to shared love" (Notebooks, Reel 14, no. 191). This movement into simple human affirmation is all important. The imagination, stretched to its limit, begins in a dark time, but Roethke's final concern is with life, celebrated in his favorite image of the dance. If the poems begin in terrible tension they end not far from total joy.

The theme of these last poems is quite simply the hunger for salvation. They are death poems written in the cold light of illness and approaching darkness. As the body breaks down the poet gropes for a means to assert the claims of the spirit without frenzy or servility. For a last time the "lost son" asks: "Which is the way?" hoping that the chain of being he has created will finally lead from the minimal to God.

The book is written almost wholly from a stock of simple, repetitive images. Roethke wrote: "The body of imagery possibly thins out or purifies itself or the mind moves into a more abstract mode closer to wisdom in talent of a high order" (Notebooks, Reel 13, no. 185). Such a purification is apparent here, for the poems are constructed from a simple hierarchy of images. The most important are the pairs of opposite images: waking and sleeping, day and night, light and shadow, inner and outer eye, always familiar in Roethke's work, but now distilled and isolated. They are used in the Platonic sense to contrast the poet's awareness of his human limitations and the perfection, the final innocence he seeks. To contrast the distinction between body and spirit another familiar pair of images is used—bird and tree, or alternately, light and tree: "Light takes the Tree; but who can tell us how?" (*C.P.*, p. 108). The bird, the light, is the true, animate self; the tree is the decaying external rind.

These themes all coalesce in the poem "In Evening Air." "Who would be half possessed/By his own nakedness?/Waking's my care—" (*C.P.*, p. 240). The poet's desire is simply to "wake"— from the prison of temporal diminishing being. Once Roethke had written: "I wake to sleep and take my waking slow" (*C.P.*, p. 108). Now the image is reversed. Life is a half-sleep and death the hoped-for awakening. The rose, "a blaze of being on a central stem," is offered as an image of the final simplicity the poet seeks. Assurances that such a purity is attainable come when physical being is seen as illusory—a tree lost upon the night; night a "dear proximity" that will engulf illusory being. The poem ends with allusions to the Platonic image of the play of light in shadow upon a wall with the poet attentively awaiting the final wakening. The word-play—"dark," "night," "death," "light"—so delicate as to be unobtrusive, makes the poem the moving statement it is. Yet it is a partial statement. Assertion comes too easily to convince that it is more than a lovely fiction.

"Infirmity" and "The Marrow" are much darker poems: the struggle to assertion convinces by its extremity. In an earlier poem Roethke had written: "The spirit knows the flesh it must consume" (*C.P.*, p. 131). Here the spirit rages to consume the dying body in a willful suicide: "I'm son and father of my only death" (*C.P.*, p. 244). Perhaps Roethke was familiar with the Kazantzakian notion of the "saint's disease"—for his theme is that the flesh breaks down under the pressure of the soul's longing, hollowed out from within. With this dissolution come intimations of pure being, familiar in the image of the "shimmer on the stone," which justify him in his audacious claim: "My soul is still my soul, and still the Son,/And knowing this, I am not yet undone." In "The Marrow" the theme is the same. The poem exonerates the will to die. In the half-death of waking life, the poet feels his spiritual powers slipping from him: "My body alters, altering the soul/That once could melt the dark with its small breath" (*C.P.*, p. 246). He feels himself moving from God: "From me to Thee's a long and terrible way." The poem closes with a moving cry for death: "I bleed my bones, their marrow to bestow/Upon that God who knows what I would know."

These are poems written in solitary ecstasy and dread, in an extremity of alienation from nature, from man, and from self. Their theme is religious—the voiding of self, restitution, and atonement. As one critic has said, Roethke's drive toward God often threatened to be a drive away from man, and it would have been had the sequence consisted solely of these bleaker poems.[12] But there are poems of a counter-movement downward and outward,

---

12. Roy Harvey Pearce, "The Power of Sympathy," in *Essays on the Poetry*, ed. Stein, p. 197.

praising the world of limited finite things. In "The Motion" the
willed death of the self is balanced by a willful "rising-up" of the
mind in an act of love:

> Who but the loved know love's a faring-forth?
> Who's old enough to live?—a thing of earth
> Knowing how all things alter in the seed
> Until they reach this final certitude,
> This reach beyond this death, this act of love
> In which all creatures share, and thereby live.
>
> [C.P., p. 243]

It is a moving and primitive act of faith in creative love as the
propulsive force, the motion of life. In the greenhouse world,
child and plant responded to the sun-father in a primitive striving
toward the light. In "The Abyss" the tendrils with their eyeless
seeking toward the light were the poet's image for his own longing. What the images have in common is the notion of a generative principle of energy or, as the poet would have it, of love, at-
tractive and propulsive, acting from within and from without,
which orders the whole of life. This is a common form of mystical
belief but one that Roethke has made imaginatively his own by his
inclusion of the fearful small within its schema.

The last three poems of the "Sequence, Sometimes Metaphysical," "The Restored," "The Right Thing," and "Once More, the
Round," are the final note by which Roethke wished to be remembered. He wrote: "In spite of all the muck and welter, the dark,
the *dreck* of these poems, I count myself among the happy poets:
'I proclaim, once more, a condition of joy' " (S.P., p. 40). In
another instance he said: "Poetry comes out of a moral fierceness.
There is nothing more disconcerting than when a rich nature thins
into despair" (Notebooks, Reel 13, no. 186).

For him despair comes with the mind's searchings after assurances; but the mind can gain no access to the mystery of being
which we incarnate, the only theme which ultimately concerned
him. Instead he calls for rage and wailing and the divine madness
of the dance, as the only appropriate response to life lived in final
terms. Celebrating in his figure of the happy man the capacity to

rest in mystery without feeling the need to reach after certainties, he rejects the self-destructive and in so doing purges a deep impulse in himself. Few poets have known so deeply the capacity for self-destructive probing: "The loneliest thing I know/Is my own mind at play" (*C.P.,* p. 215). His last poem is an affirmation of life, a proclamation in the manner of Yeats and Blake, and its power seems to come from its profound assertion of the will to love. For Roethke the greatest power of the poet was the capacity to face up to genuine mystery and celebrate. The book indeed descends, as he put it, into a more human, more realizable condition, moving from loneliness to shared love.

> Now I adore my life
> With the Bird, the abiding Leaf,
> With the Fish, the questing Snail,
> And the Eye altering all;
> And I dance with William Blake
> For love, for Love's sake;
>
> And everything comes to One,
> As we dance on, dance on, dance on.
>   [*C.P.,* p. 251]

❧ IX ❧

Commitment to the Self

If one were to search for the persistent pattern which unifies Roethke's work, making it such a coherent body of work, one would have to settle on the pattern of rebirth. "All my poems seem to be about dying and being reborn again and again," Roethke said.[1] The poems record a perpetual "journey to the interior," most often a regression to the foundations of the psyche and a subsequent re-emergence of the self reconstituted and participant in new forms of unity. A poet's identity is to be found in the habits of feeling and insight which are particularly, almost obsessively, his own and which distinguish his work from all others. The starting point of Roethke's work is this passion for rebirth, to strip away encumbrances in order to get back to first things. This impulse might possibly be connected with the manic-depressive pattern of his own personal experience, with its violent oscillations between extreme states of joy when the sense of being gained greatest access, and unendurable anxiety which threatened the very stability of the self. These oscillations clearly undermined any sense of continuity of self which Roethke might have been able to secure. The self was for him something that had to be perpetually

1. See David Myers, *In a Dark Time,* a visual interview, including the reading of poems, filmed shortly before Roethke's death (1 August 1963). Distributed by Contemporary Films, Incorporated.

recreated. It was an extremely tenuous concept since it had to be based on assurances of spiritual identity, and confidence continually wavered. Roethke called himself a perpetual beginner. Each time in each new poem, it was as if he had to begin over again, no previous gain being sufficient in the arduous process of self-definition. His work is therefore completely autobiographical in the broadest sense—a compulsive and continual reassessment of the nature of identity. "The human problem," Roethke wrote, "is to find out what one really is; whether one exists, whether existence is possible" (*S.P.*, p. 20). For many this self-consciousness is the source of the intensity and depth of his poetry, since it is seen as central and radial to contemporary sensibility. For others, it provokes only charges of narrowness and egocentricity.

Judging from the multiple articles and reviews of Roethke's poetry, the heresy of the egotistical sublime presents a formidable hurdle to appreciation. M. L. Rosenthal writes: "For the most part Roethke had no subject apart from the excitements, illnesses, intensities of sensuous response, and inexplicable shiftings of his own sensibility." [2] Stephen Spender complains of egocentricity: "His genius was too far determined by intense childhood visions for him to be able to transfer (for example) his interest in organic nature into an equal interest in other people." [3] John Wain feels that Roethke's poetry is "not philosophical" in the simple etymological sense of loving wisdom. Unlike the poetry of Yeats, Eliot, and Blake, Roethke's poetry does not give a sense of total participation in life. "Their poetry meditates on inward things, and then walks out into the air. His stays enclosed. His vision, intense as it is, remains monocular." [4] The consensus is that Roethke is not one of the poets in whose work we encounter the whole range of life, primarily because we do not encounter there the whole range of the living.

There are two arguments involved here: first that Roethke is an

---

2. Rosenthal, *The New Poets*, p. 118.
3. Spender, "The Objective Ego," in *Essays on the Poetry*, ed. Stein, p. 11.
4. Wain, "The Monocle of My Sea-Faced Uncle," *Essays on the Poetry*, ed. A. Stein, p. 76.

egocentric poet, his theme remaining entirely and only himself;
and second, that his poetry is unable to enter into the world of
public relationships, that he has little or no feeling for life as a
"dynamic engagement in time, in place, in history." [5] The criticisms are clearly separate if related problems, and it is often due to
a failure to distinguish between them that Roethke's poetry suffers. The first and most important complaint is that he is an
egocentric poet. It is felt that he chose to record the agonies and
frustrations of his personal experience, particularly as derived from
mental illness, and yet failed to give them an imaginative, poetic
order. His musings remain simply private problems, and as such
relatively uninteresting.

M. L. Rosenthal is Roethke's most astute critic. In a review of
The Far Field called "The Couch and Poetic Insight," [6] he insists
that Roethke's poetry has always been the expression of an unresolved hysteria in the face of the demands of actual life. His only
source of energy is his uncontrolled riotous psyche—the heights of
pure manic recklessness, and the depths of painful and disturbing
dejection. Moreover he used himself up after the first wild orgies
of feeling in his early poems. Such criticisms seem to depend on
the idea that Roethke's poems are simply the expression or
regurgitation of unconscious drives. Roethke, as it were, found his
vein in *The Lost Son* and the *Praise to the End!* sequences in his un-
canny sensitivity to the fluctuations of his own psyche. He pro-
ceeded to make of poetry a couch for the rehearsal of his psychological problems which remain largely opaque and impenetrable to
the outsider. This confessional mode, reduced to a kind of psychic
recharging, became redundant and self-repetitious in his poetry.
This is to assume that Roethke's is a poetry of therapy, of raw ego:
"little more than a rehearsal of common paranoia." [7]

The feeling, it would seem, is that he made no attempt to en-
sure that his intensely personal investigations into the unconscious

5. Denis Donoghue, "Aboriginal Poet," p. 15.
6. M. L. Rosenthal, "The Couch and Poetic Insight" (review of *The Far Field*), *The
Reporter*, 32 (25 March 1965): 52–53.
7. Martin Seymour-Smith, "Where is Mr. Roethke?", p. 44.

self would be expressed in terms of universal predicaments. This is to underestimate his deep sense of poetic tradition and the fund of conventional imagery from which he drew in the creation of his poems. From a close reading of the poems, particularly of the *Praise to the End!* sequence, it becomes apparent how continuously he refers the reader to a heritage of poetry—to Blake, to Wordsworth, to Sir John Davies, to Eliot—which at once defines the cultural or emotional ambience in which the work must be understood and moves the poem beyond the opaque and gratuitous to the realm of general concern. The poetic ancestors seemed to have been an immediate aspect of his experience. In fact, it is remarkable how little sense of pastness is involved in his idea of literary tradition. The ancestors were part of a living present tradition which could be called upon for assistance in his attempts to clarify private themes.

Moreover Roethke was deeply sensitive to problems of opacity and suspicious of the personal poem which might depend upon too private, too febrile emotions. But he also knew that the very process of interior probing could constitute an exploration of general experience if the poet remained faithful to what was most universal in himself. He had read Rimbaud, Maud Bodkin's *Archetypal Patterns in Poetry,* and Jung, each of whom confirmed the possibility of a personal poetry concerned with archetypal experience. Rimbaud was particularly important to Roethke with his theory of objective poetry, postulating as it does an unconscious level of experience which the poet might exploit for its archetypal patterns. Stephen Spender called his essay "The Objective Ego" to emphasize Roethke's debt to this tradition. As he wrote: "The paradox of such 'objective' poetry is that while concentrated in the 'I' it is not egotistic." [8] Through a process of profound subjectivity, the poet arrives at what is actually objective experience. In his early sequences Roethke was able to turn his themes, particularly his relationship to his father and the impact this had on his attempts to evolve an independent identity, into fundamental human con-

8. Spender, "The Objective Ego," p. 9.

cerns by confronting them at the archetypal level of meaning where the magical notions of father and authority accrue. His poems were not structured after a specific myth but created their own myth of the "Lost Son," recording a *Prelude* or spiritual autobiography of the quest for identity. His search for the father thus came to involve metaphysical questions such as the search for essential order and authority. In his last years, Roethke turned to a study of mysticism to extend his quest for identity. As has been pointed out, this interest has been much maligned. M. L. Rosenthal and W. D. Snodgrass feel that Roethke resorted to the stock cosmic pieties of sagedom as a way of escaping the still unresolved hysteria of his earlier poetry. It was simply one more ruse by which to avoid confrontation with his true psychological dilemma. As an attempt to remove what is felt to be the problem of egocentricity from his poetry it failed, since it was simply an evasion. The suspicion of Roethke's interest in mysticism has been increased by the attempts of some of his sympathetic critics to tie his poetry rigorously to orthodox mystical processes. Roethke never claimed that he had reached the final stages of mystical illumination. He was interested in mysticism as a psychological process that terminates in an undefinable but somehow potent sense of illumination. Such an analysis offered him a means to objectify his search for spiritual identity within a structure that is universally recognizable, but this structure always had to be justified in personal terms. His mystical poems actually record the desperate struggle for belief, rather than a formularized ritual.

In both his early and late poetry, if Roethke took the problems of the self as his theme, he was neither egocentric nor narcissistic. The self in his poetry becomes a symbol, interesting to him only when it impinges on representative concerns and not otherwise. In fact he is the least confessional of modern poets. His poems are never private complaints, the record of domestic misfortunes which move for their human content but seem never to exceed themselves. Yet he never evaded the personal either. His poems show how the violence of the self—the problems of alienation, discontinuity, and homelessness—can be written about with subtlety and passion.

Roy Harvey Pearce put the matter most eloquently when he said that he took Roethke's life work to have been directed toward "enlarging and deepening the sense of the authentically personal." [9] He added that Roethke's poetry "controlled the wide and deep areas of the personal, the widest and deepest, I am persuaded, in the work of any contemporary American poet."

This does not, however, answer the complaint of the lack of breadth and inclusiveness in Roethke's poetry. If he is not egocentric in the pejorative sense, his obsessive preoccupation with the generic self is remarkable. Criticism has been very precise on this point. Denis Donoghue comments in "Aboriginal Poet" that the definitive areas of Roethke's sensibility are very far apart. "In the scale of being he lives either below the human or far above it; translating human life downward or upward. . . . his feeling for the specifically human dimension is insecure." His poems have more to do with "the order implicit in folklore, myth, and archetype, than with an anarchy implicit in history, fact, and experience." [10]

Pearce writes that Roethke had achieved a marvelous command of the personal. "For him the world was first I, then (from the minimal to God) thou—but not yet, as with Blake, he, she, or they." Rather, "to have revealed the sacredness of the second person, of all persons (and places and things) as they in truth are second—this is Roethke's achievement." [11] Had Roethke had time, Pearce feels he would have moved into a more objective world into which he might have been able to introduce an awareness of the concrete and particular conditions of modern life.

John Wain reluctantly asserts that of the various kinds of illumination a human life needs, Roethke's poetry pursues only one kind. It does not enter the ordinary world where social concerns

9. Pearce, "The Power of Sympathy," pp. 189–90.
10. Donoghue, "Aboriginal Poet," p. 15.
11. Pearce, "The Power of Sympathy," p. 198.

have their effect. The human world, however palpably present in Roethke, is limited to "an old woman with her life running down, a child being weaned, a man making love to a woman or listening to the wind in the trees—these things are memorably and truthfully captured: and, beneath them, the basic subject of the human being as a creature. But there are other areas—of memory, of history, of personal relationships, of opinion, of custom—which we ordinarily inhabit and which Roethke's poetry does not allow us . . . to revisit." [12]

The balance of opinion in these and other essays is that Roethke's commitment is to the intensely private and personal, leaving untouched the intermediate range of sentiments of ordinary life—the social and historical. Roethke was acutely aware of this. Throughout his notebooks one can see him trying to write poems of a more general or public human concern. A few of these appeared in *Open House* and *The Lost Son:* poems like "Dolor," "Last Words," "Highway: Michigan," and "Judge Not." Ralph J. Mills prints some of them in the *Selected Letters.* Others never emerged from the notebooks: poems which try to reproduce a circle of friends, or a social milieu, even political pastiche.

For the most part, such poems are failures. As Denis Donoghue put it, Roethke had no sense of life as a "dynamic engagement in time, in place, in history." For him all problems centered in the self. He was not interested in the possibility of social forces assisting or thwarting individual identity; in his poems, ambush is always interior—self-aggression or despair. The major premise of his work is the conviction that only when the self is fully in control of its inner world can it turn outward. In this the pattern of his "North American Sequence" is epitomal—the wounded self withdrawing from human society in search of renewal.

The whole question of Roethke's instinctive inability to admit the value of social criteria with reference to the self might be seen against the larger perspective of American poetry. Many critics—one thinks in particular of Richard Poirier in *A World Else-*

12. Wain, "My Sea-Faced Uncle," p. 75.

where and Tony Tanner in *The Reign of Wonder*—have remarked the extraordinary visionary tendency in American literature. So often American poets choose to concentrate on the realities of consciousness and the struggle of the self for a congenial environment of the imagination, while rejecting any social definition of the self. There is a persistent conviction that the idealized self can never function in a world of social and economic systems, so that the retreat from any historically formed environment to a primitive timeless world where there is no encumbrance to the expression of the true inner self—denudation as a prelude to discovery—has become one of its most formidable archetypal patterns. Such terms as "the eye," "nakedness," "childhood," for example, carry highest value in American poetry because its goals have almost always been visionary—the omnivorous eye of the poet discovering relationships, integrating the parts of his vision. Society, even the society of others, is an interference, a distraction, in the compulsive drive to discover an original relation to the universe.

Roethke quite clearly accepted this attitude as part of his literary heritage. What we do not find in his work is double consciousness, a commitment to a visionary dream of the self that can simultaneously accommodate the buzz and din of ordinary life. Instead his poetry is a healing process taking place in isolation, apart from society; the self retreating into itself before returning newly constituted and ready to participate in new relationships. Roethke described the archetypal pattern of his poetry when he wrote of his last poems: "They begin at the abyss, at the edge of being, and descend finally into a more human, more realizable condition. They turn away from loneliness to shared love" (Notebooks, Reel 13, no. 191). His sensibility quickens at opposite extremes of the spectrum, either in spontaneous, inchoate, germinal experience—the unconscious world of the fish, the slug, the frog—or in the intuitive intensity of mystical experience, the soul moving beyond itself.

Roethke also knew that a concerted effort to develop a social or public sense might have violated his gift. As Wallace Stevens remarks in *The Necessary Angel:*

What is the poet's subject? It is his sense of the world. For him, it is inevitable and inexhaustible. If he departs from it he becomes artificial and laborious and while his artifice may be skillful and his labor perceptive no one knows better than he that what he is doing, under such circumstances, is not essential to him.[13]

The fundamental point is whether a poet has a sense of identity at all. With Theodore Roethke, the pressure of his own imagination, the inescapable presence of his own individuality, is always recognizable in the depth of his penetration into the interior processes of personality, and in his acute sensitivity to the subliminal, irrational forces of life.

13. Wallace Stevens, *The Necessary Angel: Essays on Reality and Imagination,* p. 121.

Selected Bibliography

WORKS BY THEODORE ROETHKE

POETRY

Open House. New York: Knopf, 1941.

The Lost Son and Other Poems. New York: Doubleday, 1948; London: John Lehmann, 1949.

Praise to the End! New York: Doubleday, 1951.

The Waking: Poems 1933–1953. New York: Doubleday, 1953.

Words for the Wind: The Collected Verse of Theodore Roethke. London: Secker and Warburg, 1957; New York: Doubleday, 1958; Bloomington: Indiana University Press, 1961.

"The Exorcism." *Poems in Folio,* vol. 1, no. 9. San Francisco: Graphorn Press, 1957.

I Am! Says the Lamb. New York: Doubleday, 1961.

Party at the Zoo. New York: Crowell-Collier, 1963.

Sequence, Sometimes Metaphysical. Iowa City: Stonewall Press, 1964.

The Far Field. New York: Doubleday, 1964; London: Faber and Faber, 1965.

The Collected Poems of Theodore Roethke. New York: Doubleday, 1966; London: Faber and Faber, 1968.

Theodore Roethke: Selected Poems. Selected by Beatrice Roethke. London: Faber and Faber, 1969.

Dirty Dinkey and Other Creatures: Poems for Children. Ed. Beatrice Roethke and Stephen Lushington. New York: Doubleday, 1973.

PROSE

The Notebooks. Theodore Roethke Papers, University of Washington, Seattle.

"On 'In a Dark Time.' " Pp. 49–53 in *The Contemporary Poet as Artist and Critic.* Ed. Anthony Ostroff. Boston: Little, Brown, and Co., 1964.

199

On the Poet and his Craft: Selected Prose of Theodore Roethke. Ed. Ralph J. Mills, Jr. Seattle: University of Washington Press, 1965.
Straw for the Fire: From the Notebooks of Theodore Roethke 1943–1963. Ed. David Wagoner. New York: Doubleday, 1972.
The Selected Letters of Theodore Roethke. Ed. Ralph J. Mills, Jr. Seattle: University of Washington Press, 1968; London: Faber and Faber, 1970.

WORKS ABOUT THEODORE ROETHKE

BIBLIOGRAPHY

Lane, Gary, ed. *A Concordance to the Poems of Theodore Roethke.* Programmed by Roland Dedekind. Metuchen, N.J.: Scarecrow Press, 1972.
McLeod, James R. "Bibliographic Notes on the Creative Process and Sources of Roethke's 'Lost Son' Sequence." *The Northwest Review: Theodore Roethke Special Issue,* 11, no. 3 (Summer 1971), 97–111.
———. *Roethke: A Manuscript Checklist.* Kent, Ohio: Kent State University Press, 1971.
———. *Theodore Roethke: A Bibliography.* Kent, Ohio: Kent State University Press, 1973.
Walker, Ursula Genug. *Notes on Theodore Roethke.* Charlottesville: University of North Carolina Press, 1968.

BIOGRAPHY

Seager, Allan. *The Glass House: The Life of Theodore Roethke.* New York: Mc-Graw-Hill, 1968.

FILM

Myers, David. *In a Dark Time.* A visual interview, including the reading of poems. Spring 1963. Distributed by Contemporary Films, Incorporated.

CRITICAL STUDIES OF ROETHKE

Arrowsmith, William. "Five Poets." *Hudson Review,* 4 (Winter 1952): 619–20.
Atlas, James. "Roethke's Boswell." *Poetry,* 114 (August 1969): 294–97.
Auden, W. H. Review of *Open House. Saturday Review,* 23 (5 April 1941): 30.
Belitt, Ben. "Six Poets." *Virginia Quarterly Review,* 17 (Summer 1941): 462–63. (Review of *Open House.*)
Benedikt, Michael. "The Completed Pattern." *Poetry,* 109 (January 1967): 262–66. (Review of *Collected Poems.*)

Berryman, John. "From the Middle and Senior Generations." *American Scholar,* 28 (Summer 1959): 384. (Review of *Words for the Wind.*)

Blessing, Richard A. *Theodore Roethke's Dynamic Vision.* Bloomington: Indiana University Press, 1974.

————. "The Shaking That Steadies: Theodore Roethke's 'The Waking.' " *Ball State University Forum,* 12, no. 4 (1971): 17–19.

————. "Theodore Roethke: A Celebration." *Tulane Studies in English,* 20 (1972): 169–180.

————. "Theodore Roethke's Sometimes Metaphysical Motion." *Texas Studies in Literature and Language,* 14 (1972): 731–49.

Bogan, Louise. Review of *The Lost Son. New Yorker,* 24 (15 May 1948): 118.

————. Review of *Praise to the End! New Yorker,* 27 (16 February 1952): 107–8.

Boyd, John D. "Texture and Form in Theodore Roethke's Greenhouse Poems." *Modern Language Quarterly,* 32 (1971): 409–24.

Boyers, Robert. "A Very Separate Peace." *Kenyon Review,* 27 (November 1966): 683–91. (Review of *Collected Poems.*)

Brown, Dennis E. "Theodore Roethke's 'Self-World' and the Modernist Position." *Journal of Modern Literature,* 3, no. 5 (July 1974): 1239–54.

Bullis, Jerald. "Theodore Roethke." *Massachusetts Review,* 11 (1970): 209–12.

Burke, Kenneth. "The Vegetal Radicalism of Theodore Roethke." *Sewanee Review,* 58 (Winter 1950): 68–108. Reprinted in *Language as Symbolic Action.* Berkeley and Los Angeles: University of California Press, 1968.

————. "Cult of the Breakthrough." *New Republic,* 159 (21 September 1968): 25–26. (Review of *Selected Letters.*)

Carruth, Hayden. "Requiem for God's Gardener." *Nation,* 199 (28 September 1964): 168–69. (Review of *The Far Field.*)

Ciardi, John. "Poets of the Inner Landscape." *Nation,* 177 (14 November 1953): 410. (Review of *The Waking.*)

————. "Theodore Roethke: A Passion and a Maker." *Saturday Review,* 46 (31 August 1963): 13.

————. "Comments on Theodore Roethke." *Cimarron Review,* 7 (1969): 6–8.

Cohen, J. M. Pp. 249–53 in *Poetry of This Age 1908–1958.* London: Hutchinson, 1960.

Conquest, Robert. "The Language of Men." *Spectator,* 200 (14 February 1958): 210. (Review of *Words for the Wind.*)

Davie, Donald. "Two Ways Out of Whitman." *The Review,* no. 14 (December 1964): pp. 14–17. (Review of *The Far Field.*)

Deutsch, Babette. "Three Generations in Poetry." *Decision,* 2 (August 1941): 60–61. (Review of *Open House.*)

————. "Fusing Word with Image." *Herald Tribune Book Review,* 24 (25 July 1948): 4. (Review of *The Lost Son.*)

————. "On Theodore Roethke's 'In a Dark Time.' " Pp. 36–40 in *The Contemporary Poet as Artist and Critic: Eight Symposia*. Ed. Anthony Ostroff. Boston: Little, Brown, and Co., 1964.

Dickey, James. Pp. 147–52 in *Babel to Byzantium: Poets and Poetry Now*. New York: Farrar, Straus, and Giroux, 1968.

————. "The Greatest American Poet." *Atlantic*, 222 (November 1968): 53–58. Reprinted in *Sorties*. New York: Doubleday, 1971.

Donoghue, Denis. "Roethke's Broken Music." Pp. 136–66 in *Theodore Roethke: Essays on the Poetry*. Ed. A. Stein. Seattle: University of Washington Press, 1965. Reprinted from *Connoisseurs of Chaos: Ideas of Order in Modern American Poetry*. London: Faber and Faber, 1965.

————. "Aboriginal Poet." *New York Review of Books*, 22 September 1966, pp. 14–16. (Review of *Collected Poems*.)

Driver, C. J. "Theodore Roethke: The Soul's Immortal Joy." *Tracks*, 5 (August 1968): 43–48. (Review of *Collected Poems*.)

Eberhart, Richard. "On Theodore Roethke's Poetry." *Southern Review*, 1, no. 3 (Summer 1965): 612–20.

————. "Deep Lyrical Feelings." *New York Times Book Review*, 16 December 1951, p. 4. (Review of *Praise to the End!*)

————. "Creative Splendor." *New York Times Book Review*, 9 November 1958, p. 34. (Review of *Words for the Wind*.)

Everette, O. "Theodore Roethke: Poet as Teacher." *West Coast Review*, 3 (Spring 1969): 5–10.

Ferry, David. "Roethke's Poetry." *Virginia Quarterly Review*, 43 (1967): 169–73. (Review of *Collected Poems*.)

Fiedler, Leslie. "A Kind of Solution: The Situation of Poetry Now." *Kenyon Review*, 26 (1964): 63–64.

Fitzgerald, Robert. "Patter, Distraction, and Poetry." *New Republic*, 121 (8 August 1949): 17. (Review of *The Lost Son*.)

Flint, F. Cudworth. "Seeing, Thinking, Saying, Singing." *Virginia Quarterly Review*, 35 (Spring 1959): 313. (Review of *Words for the Wind*.)

Freer, Coburn. "Theodore Roethke's Love Poetry." *Northwest Review: Theodore Roethke Special Issue*, 11, no. 3 (Summer 1971): 42–66.

French, Warren. "Theodore Roethke: 'in a slow up-sway.' " Pp. 199–207 in *The Fifties: Fiction, Poetry, Drama*. Deland, Fl.: Everett Edwards, 1971.

Galvin, Brendan. "Kenneth Burke and Theodore Roethke's 'Lost Son' Poems." *Northwest Review: Theodore Roethke Special Issue*, 11, no. 3 (Summer 1971): 67–96.

————. "Theodore Roethke's Proverbs." *Concerning Poetry*, 5, no. 1 (1972): 35–47.

Goodheart, Eugene. "The Frailty of the I." *Sewanee Review*, 76 (1968): 516–19.

Gunn, Thom. "Poets English and American." *Yale Review*, 48 (June 1959): 623–25. (Review of *Words for the Wind*.)

Gustafson, Richard. "In Roethkeland." *Midwest Quarterly*, 7 (January 1966): 167–74.

Hamilton, Ian. "Theodore Roethke." *Agenda*, 3 (April 1964): 5–10.

Hayden, Mary H. "Open House: Poetry of the Constricted Self." *Northwest Review: Theodore Roethke Special Issue*, 11, no. 3 (Summer 1971): 116–38.

Heaney, Seamus. "Canticles to the Earth." *Listener*, 80 (22 August 1968): 245–46. (Review of *Collected Poems*.)

Heilman, Robert. "Theodore Roethke: Personal Notes." *Shenandoah*, 16 (Autumn 1964): 55–64.

Heringman, Bernard. "Theodore Roethke." *Earlham Review*, 3, no. 1 (Spring 1970): 20–30.

———. " 'How to Write like Somebody Else.' " *Modern Poetry Studies*, 3 (1972): 31–39.

———. "Images of Meaning in the Poetry of Theodore Roethke." *Aegis*, 2 (1973): 45–57.

Heyen, William, ed. *Profile of Theodore Roethke*. Columbus, Ohio: Charles E. Merrill Co., 1971.

———. "Theodore Roethke's Minimals." *Minnesota Review*, 7 (1968): 359–75.

———. "The Divine Abyss: Theodore Roethke's Mysticism." *Texas Studies in Literature and Language*, 11 (1969): 1051–68.

Hobbs, John. "The Poet as His Own Interpreter: Roethke on 'In a Dark Time.' " *College English*, 33 (1971): 55–66.

Hoffman, Frederick. "Theodore Roethke: The Poetic Shape of Death." Pp. 94–114 in *Theodore Roethke: Essays on the Poetry*. Ed. A. Stein. Seattle: University of Washington Press, 1965. Reprinted in *Modern American Poetry: Essays in Criticism*. Ed. Jerome Mazzaro. New York: David McKay Co., 1970.

Humphries, Rolfe. "Inside Story." *New Republic*, 105 (14 July 1941): 62. (Review of *Open House*.)

———. "Verse Chronicle." *Nation*, 174 (22 March 1952): 284. (Review of *Praise to the End!*)

James, Clive. "Tough Assignments." *The Review*, no. 33 (September–November 1970): pp. 47–53. (Review of *Selected Letters*.)

Kennedy, X. J. "Joys, Griefs and 'All Things Innocent, Hapless, Forsaken.' " *New York Times Book Review*, 5 August 1964, p. 5. (Review of *The Far Field*.)

Kizer, Carolyn. "Poetry: School of the Pacific Northwest." *New Republic*, 135 (16 July 1956): 18–19.

Kramer, Hilton. "The Poetry of Theodore Roethke." *Western Review,* 18 (Winter 1954): 131–46.

Kunitz, Stanley. "On Theodore Roethke's 'In a Dark Time.' " Pp. 41–48 in *The Contemporary Poet as Artist and Critic: Eight Symposia.* Ed. A. Ostroff. Boston: Little, Brown, and Co., 1964.

———. "Roethke: Poet of Transformations." *New Republic,* 152 (23 January 1965): 23–29.

———. "News of the Root." *Poetry,* 73 (January 1949): 222–25. (Review of *The Lost Son.*)

La Belle, Jenijoy. "Theodore Roethke and Tradition: 'The Pure Serene of Memory in One Man.' " Ph.D. dissertation, University of California, 1969.

———. "Theodore Roethke and Tradition: 'The Pure Serene of Memory in One Man.' " *Northwest Review: Theodore Roethke Special Issue,* 11, no. 3 (Summer 1971): 1–18.

Levi, Peter. "Theodore Roethke." *Agenda* 3 (April 1964): 11–14.

Libby, Anthony. "Roethke, Water Father." *American Literature,* 46 (November 1974): 267–88.

Lit, A. "Notes on Roethke's Poetry." *Topic,* 6 (Fall 1967): 21–29.

Lucas, John. "The Poetry of Theodore Roethke." *Oxford Review,* no. 8 (Trinity 1968), pp. 39–64.

Malkoff, Karl. *Theodore Roethke: An Introduction to the Poetry.* New York: Columbia University Press, 1966.

———. "Boundaries of the Self." *Sewanee Review,* 75 (Summer 1967): 540–49.

Martz, Louis. "A Greenhouse Eden." Pp. 14–35 in *Theodore Roethke: Essays on the Poetry.* Ed. A. Stein. Seattle: University of Washington Press, 1965. Reprinted in *The Poem of the Mind: Essays in Poetry English and American.* New York: Oxford University Press, 1966.

———. "Recent Poetry: The Elegiac Mode." *Yale Review,* 54 (Winter 1965): 294–97. (Review of *The Far Field.*)

———. "Recent Poetry: Roethke, Warren, and Others." *Yale Review,* 56 (Winter 1967): 275–77. (Review of *Collected Poems.*)

Martz, William J. *The Achievement of Theodore Roethke.* Glenview, Ill.: Scott, Foresman, and Co., 1966.

Maxwell, J. C. "Notes on Theodore Roethke." *Notes and Queries,* 16 (July 1969): 265–66.

Mazzaro, Jerome. "Theodore Roethke and the Failures of Language." *Modern Poetry Studies,* 1 (July 1970): 73–96. Reprinted in *Profile of Theodore Roethke.* Ed. William Heyen. Columbus, Ohio: Charles E. Merrill Co., 1971, pp. 47–64.

McClatchy, J. D. "Sweating Light from a Stone: Identifying Theodore Roethke." *Modern Poetry Studies,* 3 (1972): 1–24.

McMichael, James. "The Poetry of Theodore Roethke." *Southern Review*, 5, no. 1 (Winter 1969): 4–25.

———. "Roethke's North America." *Northwest Review: Theodore Roethke Special Issue*, 11, no. 3 (Summer 1971): 149–59.

Meredith, William. "A Steady Storm of Correspondences: Theodore Roethke's Long Journey Out of the Self." Pp. 36–53 in *Theodore Roethke: Essays on the Poetry*. Ed. A. Stein. Seattle: University of Washington Press, 1965.

Mills, Ralph J., Jr. *Theodore Roethke*. Minnesota Pamphlets on American Writers, no. 30. Minneapolis: University of Minnesota Press, 1963.

———. "Theodore Roethke: The Lyric of the Self." Pp. 3–23 in *Poets in Progress: Critical Prefaces to Ten Contemporary Poets*. Ed. Edward Hungerford. Evanston, Ill.: Northwestern University Press, 1962.

———. "In the Way of Becoming: Roethke's Last Poems." Pp. 115–35 in *Theodore Roethke: Essays on the Poetry*. Ed. A. Stein. Seattle: University of Washington Press, 1965.

———. "Keeping the Spirit Spare." *Chicago Review*, 13 (Winter 1959): 114–22. (Review of *Words for the Wind*.)

———. "Roethke's Garden." *Poetry*, 100 (April 1962): 54–59. (Review of *I Am! Says the Lamb*.)

———. "Roethke's Last Poems." *Poetry*, 105 (November 1964): 122–24. (Review of *The Far Field*.)

Muir, Edwin. "New Verse." *New Statesman*, 55 (18 January 1958): 76–77. (Review of *Words for the Wind*.)

Nemerov, Howard. "Three in One." *Kenyon Review*, 15 (Winter 1954): 148–54. Reprinted in *Poetry and Fiction*. New Brunswick, N.J.: Rutgers University Press, 1963. (Review of *The Waking*.)

Nyren, Dorothy, ed. "Roethke, Theodore (1908–63)," in *A Library of Literary Criticism*. New York: Frederick Ungar Co., 1960.

O'Gorman, Ned. "Theodore Roethke and Paddy Flynn." *Columbia Forum*, 12, no. 1 (1969): 34–36.

Parkinson, Thomas. "Some Recent Pacific Coast Poetry." *Pacific Coast Spectator*, 4 (Summer 1950): 290–305.

Paschall, Douglas. "Roethke Remains." *Sewanee Review*, 81, (1973): 859–64.

Pearce, Roy Harvey. "The Power of Sympathy." Pp. 167–99 in *Theodore Roethke: Essays on the Poetry*. Ed. A. Stein. Seattle: University of Washington Press, 1965. Reprinted in *Historicism Once More*. Princeton, N.J.: Princeton University Press, 1969.

Porter, Kenneth. "Roethke at Harvard 1930–1931 and the Decade After." *Northwest Review: Theodore Roethke Special Issue*, 11, no. 3 (Summer 1971): 139–48.

Powell, Grosvenor E. "Robert Lowell and Theodore Roethke: Two Kinds of Knowing." *Southern Review*, 3, no. 1 (January 1967): 180–85.

Ramsey, Jarold. "Roethke in the Greenhouse." *Western Humanities Review*, 26 (1972): 35–47.

Ransom, John Crowe. "On Theodore Roethke's 'In a Dark Time,' " pp. 41–48 in *The Contemporary Poet as Artist and Critic: Eight Symposia*. Ed. A. Ostroff. Boston: Little, Brown, and Co., 1964.

Reichertz, Ronald. "Where Knock Is Open Wide, Part I." *Explicator*, Vol. 26 (December 1967), items no. 34.

Rodman, Selwin. "Intuitive Poet." *New York Herald Tribune Book Review*, 28 (2 December 1951): 32. (Review of *Praise to the End!*)

Rosenthal, M. L. Pp. 112–18 in *The New Poets: American and British Poetry since World War II*. New York: Oxford University Press, 1965.

———. "Closing In on the Self." *Nation*, 188 (21 March 1959): 258–60. (Review of *Words for the Wind*.)

———. "The Couch and Poetic Insight." *The Reporter*, 32 (25 March 1965): 52–53. (Review of *The Far Field*.)

Scott, Nathan A., Jr. *The Wild Prayer of Longing: Poetry and the Sacred*. New Haven, Conn.: Yale University Press, 1971.

Schumacher, Paul J. "The Unity of Being: A Study of Theodore Roethke's Poetry." *Ohio University Review*, 12 (1970): 20–40.

Schwartz, Delmore. "Cunning and Craft of the Unconscious and Preconscious." *Poetry*, 94 (June 1959): 203–5. (Review of *Words for the Wind*.)

Seager, Allan, Stanley Kunitz, and John Ciardi. "An Evening with Ted Roethke." *Michigan Quarterly Review*, 6 (Fall 1967): 227–45.

Seymour-Smith, Martin. "Where Is Mr. Roethke?" *Black Mountain Review*, 1 (Spring 1954): 40–47. (Review of *The Waking*.)

Shapiro, Harvey. *Furioso*, 7 (Fall 1952): 56–58. (Review of *Praise to the End!*)

Skelton, Robin. "The Poetry of Theodore Roethke." *Malahat Review*, 1 (1967): 141–44.

Slaughter, W. R. "Roethke's Song." *Minnesota Review*, 8 (1968): 32–44.

Smith, William J. "Two Posthumous Volumes." *Harpers*, 229 (October 1964): 133–34. (Review of *The Far Field*.)

Snodgrass, W. D. " 'That Anguish of Concreteness': Theodore Roethke's Career." Pp. 78–93 in *Theodore Roethke: Essays on the Poetry*. Ed. A. Stein. Seattle: University of Washington Press, 1965.

———. "Spring Verse Chronicle." *Hudson Review*, 12 (Spring 1959): 114–17. (Review of *Words for the Wind*.)

———. "The Last Poems of Theodore Roethke." *New York Review of Books*, 3 (8 October 1964): 5–6. (Review of *The Far Field*.)

Southworth, James G. "The Poetry of Theodore Roethke." *College English*, 21 (March 1960): 326–38.

————. "Theodore Roethke: The Far Field." *College English*, 27 (February 1966): 413–18.

Spender, Stephen. "The Objective Ego." Pp. 3–13 in *Theodore Roethke: Essays on the Poetry*. Ed. A. Stein. Seattle: University of Washington Press, 1965.

————. Review of *Words for the Wind*. *New Republic*, 141 (10 August 1959): 21–22.

————. "Roethke: 'The Lost Son.' " *New Republic*, 155 (27 August 1966): 23–25. (Review of *Collected Poems*.)

Staples, Hugh. "The Rose in the Sea-Wind: A Reading of Theodore Roethke's 'North American Sequence.' " *American Literature*, 36 (1964): 189–203.

Stein, Arnold, ed. *Theodore Roethke: Essays on the Poetry*. Seattle: University of Washington Press, 1965.

————. "Roethke's Memory: Actions, Visions, and Revisions." *Northwest Review: Theodore Roethke Special Issue*, 11, no. 3 (Summer 1971): 19–31.

Swann, B. "Theodore Roethke and the Shift of Things." *Literary Review*, 17 (Winter 1973): 269–88.

Tate, Allen. "In Memoriam: Theodore Roethke 1908–1963." *Encounter*, 21 (October 1963): 68.

Tillinghast, Richard. "Worlds of Their Own." *Southern Review*, 5, no. 2 (Spring 1969): 582–96. (Review of *Collected Poems*.)

Trusdale, C. "Theodore Roethke and the Landscape of American Poetry." *Minnesota Review*, 8 (1968): 345–58.

Vernon, John. *The Garden and the Map: Schizophrenia in Twentieth Century Literature and Culture*. Chicago: University of Illinois Press, 1973.

Waggoner, Hyatt. Pp. 564–77 in *American Poets: From the Puritans to the Present*. Boston: Houghton Mifflin Co., 1968.

Wain, John. "The Monocle of My Sea-Faced Uncle." Pp. 54–77 in *Theodore Roethke: Essays on the Poetry*. Ed. A. Stein. Seattle: University of Washington Press, 1965.

————. "Half-way to Greatness." *Encounter*, 10 (April 1958): 82–84. (Review of *Words for the Wind*.)

Warfel, Harry R. "Language Patterns and Literature: A Note on Roethke's Poetry. *Topic*, 6 (Fall 1966): 21–29.

Wesling, Donald. "The Inevitable Ear: Freedom and Necessity in Lyric Form, Wordsworth and After. *English Literary History*, 36 (1969): 544–61.

Winters, Yvor. "The Poems of Theodore Roethke." *Kenyon Review*, 3 (Autumn 1941): 514–16. (Review of *Open House*.)

Wolff, George. "Roethke's 'Root Cellar.' " *Explicator*, vol. 29 (1971), item 47.

————. "Syntactical and Imagistic Distortions in Roethke's Greenhouse Poems." *Language and Style*, 6 (1973): 281–88.

OTHER WORKS CONSULTED

Alvarez, A. *The Savage God: A Study of Suicide.* London: Weidenfeld and Nicolson, 1971.

Auden, W. H. "On 'A Change of Air.' " *The Contemporary Poet as Artist and Critic.* Ed. Anthony Ostroff. Boston: Little, Brown and Co., 1964.

Baring-Gould, W. S. and C. Baring-Gould, eds. *The Annotated Mother Goose.* New York: Clarkson N. Potter, 1962.

Bergson, Henri. *Creative Evolution.* Trans. Arthur Mitchell. London: Macmillan, 1911.

———. *An Introduction to Metaphysics.* Trans. T. E. Hulme. London: Macmillan, 1913.

———. *The Two Sources of Morality and Religion.* Trans. R. A. Audra and Cloudsley Brereton. London: Macmillan, 1935.

Blackmur, R. P. *Language as Gesture: Essays in Poetry.* New York: Harcourt, Brace and Co., 1952.

Blake, William. *The Poetry and Prose of William Blake.* Ed. David V. Erdman. New York: Doubleday, 1965.

Bodkin, Maud. *Archetypal Patterns in Poetry: Psychological Studies of Imagination.* London: Oxford University Press, 1934.

Bogan, Louise. *Collected Poems.* New York: Noonday Press, 1959.

Brooks, Cleanth, and Robert Penn Warren, eds. *Conversations on the Craft of Poetry.* New York: Holt, Rinehart and Winston, 1961.

Burke, Kenneth. "Freud and the Analysis of Poetry." Pp. 114–41 in *Psychoanalysis and Literature.* Ed. Hendrik M. Ruitenbeek. New York: E. P. Dutton and Co., 1964.

Coleridge, Samuel Taylor. *The Complete Poetical Works of Samuel Taylor Coleridge.* Ed. Ernest Hartley Coleridge. Vol. 1. 1912; rpt. Oxford: Clarendon Press, 1957.

Custance, John. *Adventure into the Unconscious.* London: Christopher Johnson, 1954.

Davies, Sir John. "Orchestra." *Silver Poets of the Sixteenth Century.* Ed. Gerald Bullett. London: J. M. Dent, 1947.

Dickinson, Emily. *The Complete Poems of Emily Dickinson.* 3 vols. Ed. Thomas H. Johnson. Cambridge, Mass.: The Belknap Press of Harvard University Press, 1955.

Duncan, Robert. *The Opening of the Field.* New York: Grove Press, 1960.

Eckhart, Meister. *Meister Eckhart: A Modern Translation.* Ed. Raymond Bernard Blakney. New York: Harper and Brothers, 1957.

Eliot, T. S. *The Complete Poems and Plays of T. S. Eliot.* London: Faber and Faber, 1969.

————. *The Use of Poetry and the Use of Criticism: Studies in the Relation of Criticism to Poetry in England.* London: Faber and Faber, 1933.

————. *To Criticize the Critic and Other Writings.* London: Faber and Faber, 1965.

Ellmann, Richard. *The Identity of Yeats.* 2d ed. London: Faber and Faber, 1964.

Emerson, Ralph Waldo. *The Complete Essays and Other Writings of Ralph Waldo Emerson.* Ed. Brooks Atkinson. New York: Random House, 1940.

Faulkner, William. *As I Lay Dying.* New York: Modern Library, 1946.

Freud, Sigmund. "Beyond the Pleasure Principle." *Complete Psychological Works.* Ed. and trans. James Strachey et al. Vol. 18. London: Hogarth Press, 1955.

————. "Mourning and Melancholia." *Complete Psychological Works.* Trans. James Strachey et al. Vol. 14. London: Hogarth Press, 1957.

————. "Notes upon a Case of Obsessional Neurosis: The Father Complex." *Collected Papers.* Trans. Alix and James Strachey. Vol. 3. London: Hogarth Press, 1925.

Frye, Northrop. *Romanticism Reconsidered: Selected Papers from the English Institute.* 3d ed. New York: Columbia University Press, 1963.

————. *Fearful Symmetry: A Study of William Blake.* Princeton, N.J.: Princeton University Press, 1947.

Gardner, W. H. *Gerard Manley Hopkins: A Study of Poetic Idiosyncrasy in Relation to Poetic Tradition.* Vol. 1. New York and London: Oxford University Press, 1958.

————. *The Art of T. S. Eliot.* London: Cresset Press, 1949.

Gascoyne, David. *A Short Survey of Surrealism.* London: Franc Cass and Co., 1935.

Grinker, Roy, et al. *The Phenomena of Depression.* New York: Harper and Row, 1961.

Hamblem, Emily. *On the Minor Prophesies of William Blake.* London: J. M. Dent, 1930.

Herrick, Robert. *The Poetical Works of Robert Herrick.* Ed. L. C. Martin. 1956; rpt. Oxford: Clarendon Press, 1963.

Hoggart, Richard. *Auden: An Introductory Essay.* London: Chatto and Windus, 1961.

Hopkins, Gerard Manley. *The Poems of Gerard Manley Hopkins.* 4th Ed. Ed. W. H. Gardner and N. H. Mackenzie. New York and London: Oxford University Press, 1967.

Horney, Karen. *Self-Analysis.* London: Routledge and Kegan Paul, 1942.

James, William. *The Varieties of Religious Experience: A Study in Human Nature.* London: Longmans, Green and Co., 1902.

Joyce, James. *The Portable James Joyce.* Ed. Harry Levin. New York: Viking, 1955.

Jung, C. G. *The Integration of Personality.* Trans. Stanley Dell. London: Kegan Paul, Trench, Trubner, and Co., 1940.

———. *Modern Man in Search of a Soul.* Trans. W. S. Dell and Cary F. Baynes. London: Routledge and Kegan Paul, 1933.

———. *Psychology and Religion.* 1938; rpt. New Haven, Conn.: Yale University Press Paperbound, 1960.

———. *Psychological Types of the Psychology of Individuation.* Trans. H. Godwin Baynes. London: Kegan Paul, Trench, Trubner and Co., 1946.

Two Essays on Analytical Psychology. Collected Works. Vol. 7. Trans. R. F. C. Hull. London: Routledge and Kegan Paul, 1953.

———, and C. Kerenyi. *Essays on a Science of Mythology: The Myth of the Divine Child and the Divine Maiden.* Trans. R. F. C. Hull. 1949; rpt. New York: Harper Torchbooks, 1963.

Laing, R. D. *The Divided Self: An Existential Study of Sanity and Madness.* Harmondsworth: Penguin Books, 1970.

Lawrence, D. H. *Studies in Classic American Literature.* 2d ed. 1924; rpt. London: Heinemann, 1971.

———. *Selected Essays.* Harmondsworth: Penguin Books, 1950.

Levy-Bruhl, Lucien. *The "Soul" of the Primitive.* Trans. Lilian A. Clare. 2d ed. 1928; rpt. London: George Allen and Unwin, 1965.

Martz, Louis. *The Poetry of Meditation: A Study in English Religious Literature of the Seventeenth Century.* New Haven, Conn.: Yale University Press, 1954.

Matthiessen, F. O. *American Renaissance: Art and Expression in the Age of Emerson and Whitman.* 1941; New York and London: Oxford University Press paperback, 1968.

Miller, J. Hillis. *Poets of Reality: Six Twentieth Century Writers.* Cambridge, Mass.: The Belknap Press of Harvard University Press, 1966.

Murray, Alexander S. *Manual of Mythology.* New York: Tudor Publishing Co., 1935.

Nijinski, Vaslav. *The Diary of Vaslav Nijinski.* Ed. Romola Nijinski. London: Jonathan Cape, 1937.

Olson, Charles. *Selected Writings.* Ed. Robert Creeley. New York: New Directions, 1966.

Pack, Robert. *Wallace Stevens: An Approach to His Poetry and Thought.* New Brunswick, N.J.: Rutgers University Press, 1958.

Poirier, Richard. *A World Elsewhere.* London: Chatto and Windus, 1967.

Rimbaud, Arthur. *Collected Poems.* Ed. and trans. Oliver Bernard. Harmondsworth: Penguin Books, 1962.

Rougement, Denis de. *The Myth of Love.* London: Faber and Faber, 1963.

Sanders, N. K., ed. *The Epic of Gilgamesh.* Harmondsworth: Penguin Books, 1960.

Smart, Christopher. *A Song to David with Other Poems.* Ed. Edmund Blunden. London: Richard Cobden Sanderson, 1924.

Spender, Stephen. *The Making of a Poem.* London: Hamish Hamilton, 1955.

———. *Struggle of the Modern.* London: Hamish Hamilton, 1963.

Steiner, Nancy Hunter. *A Closer Look at Ariel: A Memory of Sylvia Plath.* New York: Harper's Magazine Press, 1973.

Stephen, Karen. *The Wish to Fall Ill: A Study of Psychoanalysis and Medicine.* Cambridge: Cambridge University Press, 1933.

Stevens, Wallace. *The Collected Poems.* London: Faber and Faber, 1955.

———. *The Necessary Angel: Essays on Reality and the Imagination.* London: Faber and Faber, 1960.

Strode, William. *The Poetical Works of William Strode.* Ed. B. Dobell. London: The Editor, Charing Cross Road, 1907.

Tanner, Tony. *The Reign of Wonder: Naivety and Reality in American Literature.* Cambridge: Cambridge University Press, 1965.

Tate, Allen. *Essays of Four Decades.* London: Oxford University Press, 1970.

Thompson, Stith, ed. *Motif-Index of Folk-Literature: A Classification of Narrative Elements.* Bloomington: Indiana University Press, 1945.

Tillich, Paul. *The Courage to Be.* London: Nisbet and Co., 1952.

Tillyard, E. M. *The Elizabethan World Picture.* London: Chatto and Windus, 1943.

Traherne, Thomas. *Thomas Traherne: Centuries, Poems and Thanksgivings.* Ed. H. M. Margoliouth. Vol. 1. 1958; rpt. Oxford: Clarendon Press, 1965.

Underhill, Evelyn. *The Essentials of Mysticism and Other Essays.* London: J. M. Dent, 1920.

———. *Mysticism: A Study in the Nature and Development of Man's Spiritual Consciousness.* 12th ed. 1911; rpt. London: Methuen, 1960.

Vaughan, Henry. *The Complete Poetry of Henry Vaughan.* Ed. French Fogle. New York: Doubleday, 1964.

Whitman, Walt. *Leaves of Grass: Reader's Edition.* Ed. Harold W. Blodgett and Sculley Bradley. University of London Press, 1965.

Wolters, Clifton, trans. *The Cloud of Unknowing.* Harmondsworth: Penguin Books, 1970.

Wordsworth, William. *The Poetical Works of William Wordsworth.* Ed. Ernest de Selincourt and Helen Darbishire. Vol. 5. Oxford: Clarendon Press, 1958.

———. *The Prelude or Growth of a Poet's Mind.* 2d ed. Ed. Ernest de Selincourt; revised by Helen Darbishire. Oxford: Clarendon Press, 1959.

Yeats, W. B. *The Collected Poems.* 2d ed. 1933; rpt. London: Macmillan, 1950.

———. *Selected Criticism.* Ed. Norman Jeffares. London: Macmillan, 1964.

———. *A Vision.* 1st ed. London: T. Werner Laurie, 1925.

Zaehner, R. C. *Mysticism Sacred and Profane: An Inquiry into Some Varieties of Praeternatural Experience.* Oxford: Clarendon Press, 1957.

Index

imagery in, 32; language in, 118; creativity and, 171; mentioned, 50, 196
The Lost Son sequence, 37-56; order of, 38*n*, 40; theme of, 38-40; symbolism in, 39-41; psychoanalytic interpretation and, 54-56; composition of, 88; identity and, 92; spiritual search in, 123; Rosenthal and, 192; mentioned, 34, 118
Love: theme of, 52, 158; "I Need, I Need" and, 63-64; "O Lull Me, Lull Me" and 69; *Words for the Wind* and, 99; transcendence and, 103; identity and, 106, 107; guilt and, 107, 109; *The Far Field* and, 172; "The Motion" and, 188; mysticism and, 188; final celebration of, 189
"Love Poems": in *The Far Field*, 171
"Love's Progress," 109
Lowell, Robert: *Life Studies*, 9, 142; "Skunk Hour," 174; mentioned, 21
Lucas, John: on "The Lost Son," 42, 55
"Lull," 14

McMichael, James, 150
Malkoff, Karl: *Theodore Roethke*, 24*n*, 74, 106; on Oedipus complex, 54-55
"The Manifestation," 166
"The Marrow," 187
Martz, Louis, 135-36
"The Meadow Mouse," 171
"Meditation at Oyster River," 155-56; "North American Sequence" and, 151; symbolism, 153
"Meditations of an Old Woman," 131, 132-41; mysticism and, 122, 125-26, 128, 148; anxiety and, 127; Roethke's mother and, 131; criticism of, 145; "The Far Field" and, 162; mentioned, 148, 159
"Memory," 109-10
Meredith, William, 24*n;* on Yeats, 92, 97; mentioned, 148, 149
Mills, Ralph J., 92, 196
"The Minimal," 34
"Mixed Sequence": *The Far Field* and, 171-73
Moore, Marianne, 78
"More Pure than Flight" (unpublished poem), 15
"Moss Gathering," 29
"The Motion," 188

Mysticism, 108-9, 124-31, 176, 177-78, 184; expansion of consciousness and, 10-11, 50, 74-75, 104-5, 113, 187; love and, 101, 106, 188; "Meditations of an Old Woman" and, 122, 136, 137, 138; "North American Sequence" and, 148, 165-67; criticized, 166, 194. *See also* Bergson, Henri; God, concept of; Underhill, Evelyn

Nature: alienation from, 4, 28, 29, 49, 72, 110-11, 148; identification with, 15, 21, 23, 47, 49, 53, 73, 78, 140, 148-51, 157, 165; rhythm of, 25, 29, 30, 32, 53. *See also* Bergson, Henri
"Night Crow," 34
Nijinski, Vaslov: *Diary*, 124
"No Bird," 17-18
"North American Sequence," 148-69; allusion to Eliot in, 94; unity with nature in, 148, 150, 154; journey symbol in, 150-51; order, 154; Walt Whitman and, 154, 167-68; criticism of, 164-65; "Sequence, Sometimes Metaphysical" and, 169; *The Far Field* and, 171; self-withdrawal and, 196; mentioned, 130, 146, 176
Notebooks: references to psychic disorder, 10, 12, 13, 18, 38, 124; references to mysticism, 12, 126, 127, 128, 136, 139, 173, 178, 197; stylistic experimentation in, 83, 87, 93-94; mentioned, 16, 45, 70, 92, 99, 123, 130, 156, 160, 161, 185, 186, 188
Nursery rhyme, 69, 71, 79

Oedipus complex: in *The Lost Son* sequence, 54, 55. *See also* Malkoff, Karl
"The Old Florist's Lament," 7
Olson, Charles: projective verse, 141-42; mentioned, 168
"O Lull Me, Lull Me," 43, 68-69, 86. See also *Praise to the End!* sequence
Onanism: in "Give Way, Ye Gates," 66-77; symbol, 70; in "Praise to the End!," 71-72. *See also* Autoeroticism
"Once More, the Round," 188, 189
"On Identity" (prose essay), 4, 11, 42, 75, 77, 90, 104, 107, 178, 191
"On the Road to Woodlawn," 8